AF607245

"This is a really innovative concept—a brilliant read that reframes seed stage startups as mighty weeds."

—CHRIS WILKES, vice president, HearstLab

"There are few books that I've come across in my life that cause me to drop everything I'm doing. For me, those books include *The Hard Thing about Hard Things*, *Crossing the Chasm*, and now I add Stu's masterpiece—*How to Grow Your Business like a Weed*."

—AMMANUEL SELAMEAB, founder of venture-capital-backed startup Accrue.io

"Weeds teach us that our business roots must take hold in conditions that enable growth and scale. Weeds also show us that while we must remain grounded, agility is the key to sustainability. As we read this practical, must-read guide to growing any business, we couldn't help but notice that Stu Heinecke consistently mentions 'conditions' (culture) and 'grounding' (values) before growth, scale, and agility. In other words, throughout this book, Stu provides leaders with the best possible advice: before building a business that can thrive in even the harshest of environments, we must intentionally create—and consistently maintain—an inspiring foundation."

—S. CHRIS EDMONDS AND MARK S. BABBITT, coauthors of *Good Comes First*

"Stu Heinecke has delivered a fresh and deep-thinking approach to strategic business leaders who need to disrupt, pivot, and adapt for rapid growth."

—MARCIA DASZKO, author of *Pivot, Disrupt, Transform*, speaker, and strategic change consultant

"We've always known what it means to grow like a weed. This book tells us how to *scale* like a weed."

ROBERT MANKOFF, former cartoon editor at the *New Yorker*, cofounder of Cartoon Collections

"Gardeners have been waging war with weeds, but we have neglected to learn from these skirmishes. In *How to Grow Your Business Like a Weed,* Stu Heinecke shows us the many lessons we can learn from these invasive plants. Like weeds, these ideas will creep into your thoughts and inspire you!"

—CHARLES BIRNEY, cofounder of Podville Media

"For millions of years, weeds have perfected their processes to adapt, spread, and grow. Stu brilliantly outlines how weeds are genetically programmed to execute their process and the unique attributes that give them their unfair advantages to dominate. I highly recommend this book as part of your own process to grow and scale your business."

—ERIC BRISTOL, director of Demand Generation at *Salary.com*

"Stu Heinecke's book opened my eyes to how the weed ecosystem and the world of professional sales are so similar. The sales process is replete with positive growth agents such as referral sources, social media influencers, and reference customers, while there are also negative agents such as the competition, objections, and ghosted prospects. I love how he presents this intertwined set of forces as fighting and at the same time, working in tandem."

—FRED DIAMOND, president and cofounder, Institute for Excellence in Sales

"Successful entrepreneurs are a lot like weeds. Both adapt to thrive despite the environment, challenges, and competition they face."

—JEREMY KNAUFF, entrepreneur, columnist, CEO of Spartan Media

"This book brought back to me the Marines who stood up with the Marine Special Operations Command as a part of SOCOM in 2006. We were a weed to the rest of the Marine Corps. Our commander, General Dennis Hejlik, saw how we were going to create our long-term relevancy as the world migrated away from traditional military operations. The establishment wanted us to go away, but we persevered to resist the desire to pull us out of the ground. I have taken this mindset into my practice as a digital marketer. Many scoff at the idea, but like a weed, virtual live-selling has become even more important with the challenges that the pandemic created for brick and mortar companies. Weeds are the out-of-the-box thinkers of our planet and look to thrive no matter what the circumstances."

—JIM FUHS, Lt. Col. USMC (retired), president of Fuhsion Marketing

"Next time you spot a weed, take a closer look. It's a miracle of evolution, mindset, process and growth strategy. As Stu explains in this book, there is a lot to learn from weeds that can transform the scale of any business."

—JIM HUFFMAN, CEO, GrowthHit

"In *How to Grow Your Business Like a Weed,* Stu Heinecke shares his exhaustive research including interviews of everyone from billionaires to scientists regarding the parallel of growing a business or nonprofit or community to the amazing garden weed. Those building a business in today's changing landscape will benefit from the Weed Mindset and the W.E.E.D.S. model for success. Once the right process and mindset are in place, growth can be massive. This book leads the way for that to happen."

—LORI RICHARDSON, author of *She Sells,* CEO, Score More Sales

"The mark of a good book is that it gives you insights and strategies to be successful. The mark of a great book is that it transforms how you think, how you feel, and how you react to challenges and opportunities. Stu Heinecke has written a great book—one that should be read and referenced over and over again. The weed metaphor is a powerful illustration of how to capitalize on the shifts happening in our marketplace, expand our sales organizations and grow our businesses. Just brilliant!"

—MERIDITH ELLIOTT POWELL, author of *THRIVE,* keynote speaker, CEO

"I speak with thousands of small business owners every year, and they always ask the same question—how do I grow my business? From now on, my answer will be, 'Buy this book!'"

—RAMON RAY, Smart Hustle founder, SCORE podcast host, and author of *The Celebrity CEO*

"Today, what every business is looking for is resilience and the ability to scale new ideas in even the toughest environments. Author Stu Heinecke in this new book shares his decades of experience, expert case studies, and a brilliant new perspective on how you can grow your business 'like a weed!' Highly recommended reading you can take practical actions from immediately."

—SCOTT NEWTON, managing partner, Thinking Dimensions

"I've worked really hard throughout my entire career. As a result, I now find myself with a beautiful garden that I am extremely proud of. Stu's book has challenged me to rethink the value of the dandelion. It disrupts a gorgeous green field with almost no effort at all. I want to be that dandelion."

—TED CLOUSER, president/CEO, PCA Technology Solutions

"With *How to Grow Your Business Like a Weed*, Stu continues to open our eyes with his insights into new perspectives, possibilities and ideas to market and grow our businesses. His astute observations regarding the parallels between business growth and sustainability to that of 'weed strategy' will benefit any entrepreneur interested in accelerating their success!"

—TODD A. GOLD, president and managing partner, REOC San Antonio

STU HEINECKE

HOW TO GROW YOUR BUSINESS LIKE A WEED

A Complete Strategy for Unstoppable Growth

Foreword by Nicola Corzine

This edition first published in 2022 by Career Press, an imprint of
Red Wheel/Weiser, LLC
With offices at:
65 Parker Street, Suite 7
Newburyport, MA 01950
www.careerpress.com
www.redwheelweiser.com

ISBN: 978-1-63265-199-0
Library of Congress Cataloging-in-Publication Data available upon request.

Cover design by Kathryn Sky-Peck
Interior by Happenstance Type-O-Rama

Printed in the United States of America
MP

10 9 8 7 6 5 4 3 2 1

To all the weeds out there,
human or otherwise, who have
so much yet to teach us, and
so many more ways to amaze us.

CONTENTS

FOREWORD

THERE'S NOTHING QUITE like the arrival of spring to lift our spirits. The first bloom of roses, those first days of blossoms sprouting, the newly vibrant green hue of the grass. Of course, that's also when we're reminded of the annual invasion of weeds.

But among entrepreneurs, their arrival should be met with wonder, not disdain. For each spring, we are treated to a masterclass of strategy and growth, right at our feet. While polite plants make themselves comfortable in our gardens, the weeds are running their fierce processes, planning their next takeovers and positioning for disruption.

I've been fortunate to have learned and worked beside tens of thousands of entrepreneurs in my career, all of whom were inspiring new visions and perspectives in the world. The ones who thrive do it with entrepreneurial ingredients that we have all come to recognize in great leaders: tenacity, grit, persistence, adaptability. These are creative thinkers who forge ahead despite challenges that come from every angle.

It is in this rarified space in the business world that Stu has masterfully synthesized a new framework—the weed strategy framework—to help entrepreneurs and leaders of organizations drive explosive, sustainable growth.

Throughout this book, you'll discover underutilized elements that can bring forward your greatest business differentiators that facilitate exceptional scale in an efficient and purposeful environment, and that can be embraced by internal and external stakeholders.

With more than fifteen years observing weed-like behavior from remarkable entrepreneurs, it took this moment, and this framework, to bring it all together. As an entrepreneur, investor, and leader of the Nasdaq Entrepreneurial Center, I have seen that true potential lies in a vision for disruptive growth, and a tough, weed-like mindset to make it a reality.

But disruption isn't restricted to a handful of individuals chosen by the universe in some grand way. We all hold the promise of being disruptive leaders in life, our communities, and work. By pausing with the weeds to take measure of what triggers your unique growth in this world, you will gain new confidence and perspectives that were never seen before.

Throughout my journey as an entrepreneur, there are two elements that have always been present: always being curious, and always being open to bridges that are yet to be built. The greatest entrepreneurs have always been the most persistent disruptors. They persevere despite many reasons why they should have failed along the way. It is this radical belief in their vision that drives them forward.

Accessing a framework that can yield such growth and potential is not only a business nice-to-have, but a must-have for all stakeholders. Whether you are just beginning your entrepreneurial journey or looking to invigorate growth in your organization, this is a "must" action book that will drive new perspectives, new ideas, and new outcomes for your company, no matter the industry, stage, or geography.

What's remarkable about the weed framework Stu has described in this book is that it appears to be "the theory of everything" concerning growth. As entrepreneurs and business owners, we're constantly told if we want to succeed, we must be optimistic, persistent, aggressive, urgent, adaptive, and resilient. We're told we must be ready to pivot, that we must disrupt our markets. We're told to cultivate brilliant cultures and movements, to create our own categories, to build for scale, to move with agility and deep emotional intelligence, and so much more. What's surprising is that the weed framework takes all of it into account.

The weeds have it all neatly organized into a process that is millions of years old, yet are able to adapt instantly to any challenge. And why not? The weeds have been at this for a very long time. It is their perfection that shines through in this book, in a very practical way, to help you grow your business like a weed.

My three-year-old son turned around this spring, grasping two big dandelions, and with the biggest smile blew as hard as he could. I saw those seeds lofting far across our garden and across our fence. (Sorry, neighbors!)

In that moment, he was entranced by the magic of that weed, with all its potential and unexpected beauty. As you read this book, I am confident you'll be similarly transformed by the wonder and inspiration of applying Stu's weed strategy framework to accelerate yourself as a leader and growth in your business.

As Stu perfectly reminds us, the weed framework unlocks "a whole new world of strategy, mindset, and scale, of tactics and unfair advantages and force multipliers." It is this methodology that can help us cultivate a whole new way of being in business, based on a time-tested model that obviously works extremely well. Just look in your garden if you need proof.

Historically, growth has been limited by access to resources, lucky timing, and aligning of the stars. It is only when we realize our potential to grow like a weed that we, too, can step into a new paradigm to bring our visions to life. If we listen and learn from weeds, explosive growth is possible and available to us all.

Enjoy each and every chapter of learning that unfolds throughout this book. And if you get a chance, do it outside to appreciate the grand spectacle of weeds all around you. Watch as they use their fierce mindset, perfected processes, and unfair advantages to achieve massive scale. Then imagine doing the same yourself, in your own business.

Nicola Corzine
Executive Director
Nasdaq Entrepreneurial Center

"Give a weed an inch and it will take a yard."

—ANONYMOUS

"I wish my vegetables had the same will as weeds do to thrive in my garden."

—ANTONIO DITOMMASO, Weed Ecologist, Columbia University

"From a military standpoint, weed attributes are essential."

—RETIRED FOUR-STAR GENERAL BARRY MCCAFFREY

"An entrepreneur at heart is a gritty and determined weed."

—BRANDON LEE, Serial Entrepreneur

"If you think along the lines of nature, then you think properly."

—CARL JUNG, Founder of Analytical Psychology

"I like scruffy, natural gardens. Formality leaves no room for creativity."

—CARMEN MEDINA, Former CIA Station Chief, Author of *Rebels at Work*

"Like a weed, our entry into disrupted territory created expansion."

—CHERIE WARE, Cofounder, WE Trust

"You have to stand in amazement at the biology of weeds."

—DR. CLARENCE SWANTON, University of Guelph

"Weeds don't have brains, but they're geniuses at running a process."

—DALE ZWIZINSKI, Entrepreneurial Sales Leader

"If you don't have a Chief Weed Officer, you lose."

—DAN WALDSCHMIDT, Author, Turnaround Specialist

"Having weed-like, sheer determination is a tremendous asset as a leader."

—RETIRED FOUR-STAR GENERAL DAVID PETRAEUS

"Weed strategy is Nature's SWOT analysis."

—DOUGLAS BURDETT, Host, *The Marketing Book Podcast*

"When markets are disrupted it becomes easy for weeds to come in and thrive."

—ESTHER DYSON, Investor/Journalist/Board Member

"Bloom where you are planted."

—FRANCIS DE SALES, Bishop of Geneva

"Like a weed, we popped up in the most unlikely places and owned the territory."

—GAREB SHAMUS, Founder, Comic-Con

"Weeds don't give a shit, this is me, this is who I am."

—GIOVANNI MARSICO, Founder, Archangel

"If a weed gets cut down, you think it's gone, but it's not."

—HENRICK FISKER, Founder, Fisker Automotive

"We have to be like a weed, to branch out to have more than one source of income."

—HERB "FLIGHT TIME" LANG, Harlem Globetrotters

"Everyone's trying to grow flowers, but maybe they should be growing weeds."

—IAN RHYS PALMER, Brand Strategist

"Someday we're going to be gone from this Earth, and it will be covered with weeds."

—JONNA MENDEZ, Former Head of Disguise, CIA

"Weeds know if they spread enough seeds, they're going to find the cracks in the concrete."

—JOSH STEIMLE, Entrepreneur

"It's never one weed, it's many weeds."

—KATE SWEETMAN, Former *Harvard Business Review* Editor

"Weeds scale faster than any business. It's in their DNA."

—KATHY IRELAND, CEO, kathy ireland Worldwide

"I have beautiful weeds now in my garden."

—KEN RUTKOWSKI, Founder, METAL

"Time is soil. It's our job to get as many weeds out of it as possible."

—MICHAEL RODERICK, Broadway Producer, Super-connector

"A weed doesn't know it may fail, therefore it won't."

—MIKE PATEY, Entrepreneur, Aviator, Flying Cowboy

"Hidden thorns are nowhere near as effective as publicly known thorns."

—DR. NATHAN MYRVOLHD, Co-founder, Intellectual Ventures

(world's most notorious "patent troll")

"The challenge is how you create a team of weeds that work together."

—NICK LOWERY, NFL Hall of Famer, Speaker

"Entrepreneurs are curious and confident and disruptive. They are our weeds."

—NICOLA CORZINE, Executive Director, Nasdaq Entrepreneurial Center

"Weeds are a plant whose virtues have yet to be discovered."

—RALPH WALDO EMERSON

"Weeds always find a way."

—ROBERT WISNESKI, Angel Investor

"Weeds and entrepreneurship are natural companions; both are evolutionary forces in their respective fields."

—STU HEINECKE, Author of *How to Grow Your Business like a Weed*

"Weeds get things done with little resources. They have to be aggressive to flourish."

—DR. SUNNIE GILES, Author of *The New Science of Radical Innovation*

"Weeds are a metaphor for life."

—WILLIAM DAVIN, Amateur Master Gardener

INTRODUCTION

Dandelion (*Taraxacum officinale*). Dandelions are a herbaceous weed found in every continent but Antarctica. Although classified as invasive, dandelions are also a much-loved source of nutrition and comfort. The entire plant is edible and useful, yielding salad greens, tea, wine, and dye, and it even serves as an ingredient in root beer. Dandelions are a perennial that produces a relatively tame 15,000 seeds per plant, over a five- to ten-year lifespan. credit: © iStock

YEARS AGO, AS I drove the Santa Monica Freeway in Los Angeles, I spotted something that would change my life: a dandelion growing from a crack in the concrete median.

In that moment, thoughts swirled through my head. I wondered how that tiny plant found the one exception—the one spot that allowed it to take root in the middle of twelve lanes of rushing traffic and a sea of concrete and impossibility. But then, we all know how it got there.

Dandelions spread by releasing masses of seeds that float in the air, probing every possible opportunity to colonize new ground. It's significant that a dandelion inhabited that crack, not a rose bush or a petunia. Those plants are too polite, too reserved, too fragile. They have no unfair advantages. They don't have the necessary mindset. *They could never make it as a weed.*

As I drove by, I wondered if I could live up to the example set by dandelions. Could I adapt their traits and tactics and tools to be as effective in business as they are in nature? Could I be as exceptional and audacious as they are? In that moment, I knew I was witnessing a powerful lesson about resilience, determination, even optimism.

If only this book had existed then.

How to Grow like a Weed

A few years ago, I wrote *How to Get a Meeting with Anyone,* which has been named one of the top sixty-four sales books of all time. It describes a variety of audacious, creative methods people have used to connect with their most important prospects. It all started with the discovery that, if I sent someone a cartoon (I'm also one of *The Wall Street Journal* cartoonists), personalized with their name, I could break through to virtually anyone.

I used the method to reach presidents, a prime minister, celebrities, and countless top decision-makers. And I discovered there was an entirely hidden, shadow form of marketing that had no name. I called it "Contact Marketing" in the book and was recently dubbed the "father of contact marketing" by the American Marketing Association.

The book inspired people all over the world to change the way they approached their most important prospects. Careers skyrocketed and businesses were launched based on the book (one just scored a $48 million series B funding round). I have been thanked constantly by readers, who report a stunning change in their sales results, because I helped them conquer a basic need in business. Nothing happens if you can't get meetings.

How to Get a Meeting with Anyone became one of those books people wish they had when they were younger. To write that book, I interviewed many of the top sales thought leaders and asked how they break through to people who are nearly impossible to reach. Their collective wisdom created an entirely new form of marketing.

The process for this book was the same. I interviewed thought leaders, experts and luminaries, and gardeners, weed scientists, and botanists, asking the same basic question: Do weeds have essential insights to offer on growth strategy in business, and if so, what are they? The wisdom they share in this book is stunning.

The weeds from around the world also shared incredibly valuable insights. They're powerful guides for growth strategy and have a lot to teach us. I believe this will be another of those "*I wish I had this when I was younger*" books.

The Nature of Growth, the Structure of This Book

Throughout my career, I have helped clients grow. For my magazine clients, I helped grow their subscriber bases, enabling higher advertising revenues. The subscriber-acquisition campaigns I created produced response gains at a decreased cost per unit, which helped the magazines grow.

Later, when I created contact marketing campaigns to help clients break through to top prospects, I helped them grow by greatly increasing their meeting rates and resulting sales.

I knew I was helping the clients grow, but it wasn't until writing this book that I understood my contributions within an easy-to-understand framework. By increasing magazines' subscriber bases, I provided fuel for growth through increased revenues. But I also contributed a campaign that became a repeatable part of their process, leading to consistently higher revenues. And helping to grow their subscriber base contributed directly to the worth of the company. All of these are significant enhancements to their growth.

There are a lot of people who have the word *growth* in their titles or in their social media profiles. Many of them talk about revenue generation as growth, but producing more sales is really just fuel, and non-strategic. Whatever growth is, it has to be the result of a repeatable process, not randomly occurring events.

Some of these specialists call themselves "rainmakers." That is an apt description, because rain is a random occurrence, and not part of the mechanism that actually produces a plant. Seeds are living things packed with nutrients, biomaterial, and DNA, pre-loaded with strategy, attributes, and process instructions. Without all that, rain would simply get things wet. It wouldn't produce growth.

So, we need a framework, something that makes sense of every aspect of growth. Fortunately, the weeds have given us a simple model that is easy to understand, because it's already so familiar.

The book addresses Weed Strategy in four sections. The first introduces you to the Nature of Weeds. They're one of nature's great disruptive forces, a constant challenge to gardeners and farmers, but also a powerful source of inspiration and wisdom. If we're to learn from weeds, we must first understand what they are, how they work, and how they disrupt. These are valuable lessons for how we'll direct our companies toward growth.

Weeds don't have brains, but they accomplish great feats of growth due to their fierce mindset. They're optimistic, perseverant, aggressive, urgent, adaptable, and resilient. They're programmed to win. The Weed Mindset section will help you adopt that same programming to win battles in your market.

The framework for weed-like growth comes from the W.E.E.D.S. Model. Covering eight levels of strategy, the system enables us to create overwhelming market awareness and traction, defend our turf, mitigate risk from disruption, create unfair advantages, borrow the infrastructure of others to foster our own growth, steward value and worth in the company, and create positive conditions for our growth. Taken together, the model creates a phalanx of force multipliers that ensure your growth, expansion, and dominance.

And finally, the section that will enable Scaling like a Weed. If weeds could talk, they'd have some surprising lessons about our natural orientations that prevent us from scaling. So we examine three levels of scale, as they apply to solopreneurs, small- and medium-sized businesses (SMBs), startups, publicly traded giants, and franchises.

It Just Works

There is a simple formula to how weeds win, but endless variation of how they take form. Weeds are fascinating studies of ingenuity and determination and expression. One of the great joys of writing this book has been getting to know the personalities of each of the weeds that head each chapter. They follow the same formula but couldn't be more different.

Our familiar dandelion lives 5 to 10 years, producing as much as 15,000 seeds. Water hemp lives fast and wild, as an annual producing up to 4.8 million seeds per plant. Some have seeds so well adapted to travel, the dispersion area of a single plant can be more than a quarter million square miles. Others have root systems that reach under roads, buildings, and walls, and reproduce with shoots that can pop up anywhere.[1] They don't even need seeds.

Weeds are more aggressive than their more polite brethren, germinating earlier, growing faster, and unfairly extending their growth seasons. They never give up, always adapt to challenges, and faithfully execute their processes, like an advancing, unstoppable army. They never do anything without built-in unfair advantages.

Their variety and individual expression are very much like our world of business. We see so many forms, so many ingenious solutions, and so much evolutionary disruption and creative destruction. It's only natural we should take inspiration from weeds. We all want our businesses to grow like a weed, and the weeds are finally here to tell us how it's done.

As I explored weed strategy to write this book, it has already affected my own business. I have more partnerships and more sources of revenue. I have productized my professional services, which reside in channels that spread my revenue sources and penetration throughout my market, like never before. And I'm just getting started.

All I can tell you is, it just works. Of course it does. It's been perfected by weeds over millions of years, enabling them to grow, expand, dominate, and defend their turf. That is what awaits you in this book.

THE NATURE OF WEEDS

1

THE NATURE OF WEEDS

Gympie Gympie (*Dendrocnide moroides*). Also known as "stinging trees," dendrocnide have broad, heart-shaped leaves that are covered with microscopic hairs, which function as venomous hypodermic needles. The mere brush of exposed skin against the leaves produces an intensely painful sting that can last for weeks. The trees, native to Australia and Indonesia, can grow to one hundred feet in height. credit: © The Board of Trustees of the Royal Botanic Gardens, Kew

WEEDS ARE EVERYWHERE. They line our motorways, fill vacant ground, and clog prized lawns and gardens. They grow in minute cracks, vast agricultural fields, and places no plant should ever take root. They can be found sprouting from rain gutters, atop barbed-wire-guarded security walls, in nearly any pile of debris. In essence, weeds grow anywhere they're not wanted.

According to the fossil record, flowering plants first appeared on Earth 145 million years ago. We can assume some of those were weeds. In fact, we should assume the most successful of them *are* the weeds of today.

With such an indomitable spirit and appetite for growth, you have to wonder: Why haven't we recognized weeds as a source of strategy for business?

To answer that question, we need to consider their nature.

Weeds are really just plants we deem inconvenient. Their "weed" identity is merely a man-made distinction. They grow where we don't want them to grow, so they're weeds. Gardeners often say a weed is just a plant out of place, but who determines their place—us or them?

Clearly, they don't recognize our authority. They just run their processes with agility, determination, and fierce persistence, no matter what we do in response.

When we look at any plant, in some sense, it's hard to perceive it as alive. They don't move, they don't think, they don't feel. But research contradicts all of that. In his book *The Hidden Life of Trees,* botanist Peter Wohlleben says plants and trees do indeed communicate. Through their lattice of interconnected roots and chemicals released into the air and ground, trees and plants are in constant conversation.[2]

In one passage in Wohlleben's book, he tells of an odd ring of stones arranged in a five-foot circle. Upon closer inspection, he discovered the stones were actually rounded formations of living wood. They were the last remains of a giant beech tree that once stood tall with a five-foot-wide trunk that had been cut down by loggers. To his surprise, the remnants of the tree were being fed nutrients and water by the surrounding trees. They had formed friendships and were keeping their old comrade alive.

When plants are under attack they emit pheromones to warn others. Some initiate immediate defenses. In the African savanna, scientists noticed a group of giraffes grazing on a grove of umbrella thorn acacia trees. Within minutes, the trees pumped toxin into their leaves, instantly repelling the giraffes. Their defense also included emitting a pheromone into the air to warn nearby trees, which also gorged their leaves with the bitter toxin. Their coordinated defense took mere minutes to deploy, causing the marauding giraffes to move on.

Since weeds have been evolving over 145 million years, we might assume their evolutionary process moves at glacial speed, but again, our notions toward these hearty plants would be misguided. When they need to, they can evolve at lightning speed.

One weed, water hemp, is an utterly fearsome invader in North American farmland. In just four years, it has produced immunity not only to glyphosate, the active ingredient in RoundUp®, but fully 75 percent of all herbicides available to farmers. The worst part is, each plant produces up to 4.8 million seeds that ensure it will become a permanent part of the landscape.

When we consider that, in the business world, nine out of ten startups fail, 75 percent of venture-backed startups never return cash to investors, and only one in a hundred achieve "unicorn" levels of scale, whose growth model would you rather follow?[3]

Weeds clearly have a lot to teach us about how to grow an enterprise, a movement, a project, even our own personal stock. Following their example, it seems we can become far more effective at growing *anything.*

Consider what's underfoot in your own yard. Look closely and you can see evidence of fierce competition playing out all around you. It's a battle for turf, for survival, for dominance. It's no different from our own battles for market share and growth. Everyone in business is looking to achieve scale. And weeds expertly show us how it's done.

Weeds are battle-hardened warriors that use specific strategies, winning attributes, and powerful tools to win their battles. They are the perfected product of natural selection.

Charles Darwin, the famed biologist who first hypothesized natural selection, also noticed the impressive qualities of weeds as examples of evolution on the fast track. In his eye-opening book *Weeds: In Defense of Nature's Most Unloved Plants,*[4] Richard Mabey tells stories of weeds affecting culture, helping us heal, and adorning our gardens, while they live their wild and scruffy lives.

Mabey recounts one of Darwin's experiments in the heart of London, a two-by-three-foot plot of land scraped clean, and left to attract whatever plants might find it. Naturally, weeds found and quickly colonized it. Of the 357 seedlings that emerged, 295 were destroyed by insects and birds. But Darwin's attention was focused on the 62 that survived. In similar experiments, Professor Peter Sikkema's University of Guelph weed biology students counted 8,000 Canada fleabane plants and 40,000 water hemp seeds in single square meter parcels of ground. Weeds are quick to adapt and thoroughly weaponized competitors.

Botanist Edward Salisbury followed in Darwin's footsteps, continuing to study the impressive nature of weeds. In one experiment, he tested the aerial efficiency of various wind-dispersed weed seeds, dropping each from a height of ten feet in a stilled room. Buddleia's (*buddleia davidii*) winged seeds fell to the floor within two seconds. Groundsel's (*senecio vulgaris*) tufted seeds took eight seconds. But Rosebay willowherb (*Chamaenerion angustifolium*) seeds took a full minute, effortlessly floating through the air, to make their descent. With a bit of wind, how far do you suppose they could travel, and where might they land?

It's not hard to imagine how weeds have colonized every continent except Antarctica. Their highly mobile seeds, emitted in unimaginably voluminous amounts, are bound to travel large distances, probing every possible opportunity to take root anywhere. Once planted, their fierce determination, resilience, and brilliant domination strategies ensure unhindered growth.

It's no wonder we find them growing in the most improbable places. Weeds are uniquely suited to conquest. Our businesses should be as well.

Points to Remember

- Weeds are everywhere, and for good reason.
- According to the fossil record, they have been on the planet for 145 million years.

- The designation of "weed" is a strictly man-made construct; they're simply plants we deem to be inconvenient or invasive.
- Many gardeners consider weeds simply to be plants out of place.
- Plants of all types are far more alive, aware of their surroundings, and active than we think they are.
- Plants communicate and defend themselves through pheromones dispatched in the air and ground.
- Charles Darwin revered weeds as examples of evolution on the fast track.
- Weeds are uniquely adapted to survival, competition, and explosive expansion of territory.
- Weeds are also uniquely suited to conquest, and our businesses should be as well.

2

EVERYBODY WANTS TO GROW LIKE A WEED

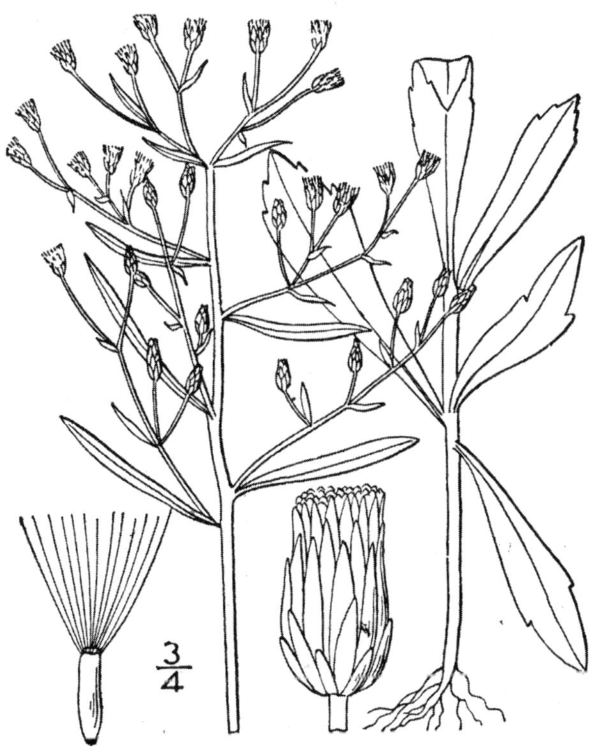

Canada fleabane (*Erigeron canadensis*). Currently the plague of Canadian agriculture, Canada fleabane is considered one of the world's worst weeds. Each plant yields as many as 240,000 seeds, which can travel more than 300 miles. credit: © The Board of Trustees of the Royal Botanic Gardens, Kew

EVERYONE WANTS THEIR business to grow like a weed. We all know what that means.

So why do we attempt to understand their powerful growth strategies with metaphors like flywheels, traction tires, operating systems, scorecards, or stretches of blue water? Why not simply learn from the masters of growth themselves?

We're pretty good at growing things, too. We're wonderfully inventive, fast-learning, and persistent. We create magical contrivances out of thin air. Does that mean we have nothing to learn from weeds?

Let's compare the models.

Canada fleabane is involved in its own sensational burst of growth, in agricultural fields across North America. All plants face serious competition from other plants, but in farmers' cultivated fields, they also face deadly competition from humankind.

Even Charles Darwin, who was fascinated by weeds as examples of evolution on the fast track,[5] would have been impressed by Canada fleabane's recent pivot. Within ten years, it managed to shuck off the effects of glyphosate (again, the active ingredient in RoundUp). And farmers are discovering they can't quite contain its advance.

Add to that the plant's prodigious output of seeds. Each plant can produce as many as 240,000 seeds in a single growing season. Each seed is capable of dispersing across a thousand-kilometer diameter. A single plant's potential seeding area can be seen from space. At a 25 percent germination rate, each single plant can produce 60,000 more plants.

Since the objectives of all weeds are to conquer new territory and create massive scale, these are impressive production numbers. If it were a startup, Canada fleabane would make a fabulous investment.

As we know, the stats for entrepreneurial startups are far less impressive. Nine of ten fail, and only one in a hundred achieves unicorn scale. *Failory.com* notes that in 40 percent of cases, investors lose their entire initial investment in startups. Even worse, 75 percent of venture-backed startups never return cash to investors.[6]

But what would the metrics look like if startups performed like weeds?

If they performed like Canada fleabane, using a 25 percent germination rate, the weed is already 250 percent more successful than the baseline for startups. If each seed were a startup, applying the one-in-100 rate for achieving unicorn status would net 2,400 mega-hits like Uber, Airbnb, and Zoom from a single source.

The seed dispersal of a single Canada fleabane plant can produce as many as 60,000 new plants and cover a 1,000-kilometer diameter—a seeding area visible from space from a single plant. credit: © iStock

But obviously, that's a bit silly. Seeds aren't startups. Germination rates don't translate to startup success rates. But it's clear the scale of weed growth beats our own in the business world. So, what might it look like when someone performs like a weed in business?

T. Boone Pickens, the Ultimate Weed

Thomas Boone Pickens was a historic figure in business. A truly expansive thinker and master strategist, Pickens changed the landscape concerning shareholder rights and value, and the wild and weedy world of hostile takeovers.

From a weeds perspective, Pickens's ultimate gift was his ability to see enormous potential from bold moves. Those allowed him to target companies hundreds of times larger than his own and, eventually, to corner entire markets.

This mindset formed at an early age. When Pickens was twelve, he acquired the smallest paper route in his rural hometown in Oklahoma.

With just twenty-eight papers to deliver, his profit was just a penny per paper per day. But he found a way to thrive with that meager beginning, and when other routes became available, he acquired those, too. It was his first experience in the takeover field.[7] It was also his first experience with thinking like a weed.

In college, he earned a geology degree and went straight to work for Phillips Petroleum. The slow pace, waste, and drudgery of working for a big, bureaucratic company with 20,000 employees soon convinced Pickens his life's ambitions lay elsewhere. So he started his first company, Petroleum Exploration Inc. (PEI), which would later become Mesa Petroleum, the eventual Canada fleabane of the oil business.

At first, he concentrated on what all oil companies did back then: exploring for and building reserves of untapped oil and natural gas. But the clairvoyant Pickens soon had a radically different growth strategy in mind. It came to him one day in the shower: Instead of exploring for new reserves in the ground, why not simply acquire known reserves through the acquisition of other oil companies?

He quickly engineered a process to identify companies whose stocks were undervalued in comparison to the actual value of their reserves. His first target was Hugoton Production Company, twenty-eight times the size of his own. Recalling the words of a friend, "You spend as much time on a big deal as you do a small one," Pickens reached out to Hugoton's CEO to make the deal. And was turned down flat.

Fresh from apparent defeat, he had another shower-time epiphany: If they won't agree to a merger, why not take the company by force?

This was radical thinking at the time. Company mergers were common, but they were done by mutual agreement. Pickens's plan no longer involved asking for permission; he would take on Hugoton, and eventually some of the biggest oil companies in the world, by force.

Each pursuit involved teaming with investors to buy large chunks of stock. The targeted company's executive team would eventually notice and mount a defense, but by then Pickens would have the advantage of surprise. Hugoton was the first to fall, but many of the targeted companies, including Cities Service, Gulf Oil, Unocal, and even his original employer, Phillips Petroleum, would escape his grasp.

Still, a curious thing happened. The premise of Pickens's strategy was that the targeted companies' stocks were grossly undervalued based on assets. Stockholders were being shortchanged. Every time he made a takeover attempt, stock values would soar to new heights, although they were merely correcting to their true value. Shareholders loved it when T. Boone Pickens came riding into town. They all made a fortune.

Even when he failed to take over a company, his own aggressive stock ownership positions, subject to the same meteoric rises in market price, netted enormous profits. He didn't need to acquire new oil reserves or even the companies themselves. The takeover process alone was generating hundreds of millions of dollars.

When Big Oil saw Pickens on the charge, they surely must've thought to themselves, "Man, what a weed this guy is." They would be right. T. Boone Pickens was using many of the strategies, attributes, and tools weeds use to blast through obstacles, crush competitors, and disrupt territory. He was a Total Weed.

Kathy Ireland, a Weed with a Higher Purpose

Supermodel, philanthropist, and multi-millionaire branding entrepreneur Kathy Ireland admits, "I've always felt like a weed."

Ireland grew up in an entrepreneurially spirited household. Her mother always had side gigs to supplement income, and it rubbed off on Kathy at an early age. At four years old, she started her first business, selling painted rocks to neighbors and passersby.

Luck also had a lot to do with her rise, much like the seeds of a weed that go where the wind takes them and thrive wherever they land. As a teen, she was discovered as a model and quickly landed a spot as covergirl for *Sports Illustrated*'s celebrated swimsuit edition. What started as an accidental career soon blossomed into supermodel stardom.

But eventually, she found herself in the position of "an aging, pregnant model," she says, and knew she must reinvent the Kathy Ireland brand. Again, she drew inspiration from weeds. "They can be underestimated, but resilient and strong," she notes. "Weeds scale faster than any business. It's in their DNA."

That day, kathy ireland® Worldwide (KIWW) germinated from her kitchen table, with Kathy surrounded by trusted advisors. Their concept was to lend Kathy's name and likeness to build new brands for clothing and housewares. "It wasn't a grassroots affair," she recalls. "It was weed roots."

Ireland understood what it meant to grow like a weed and to use the metaphor to grow her business. Starting with a modest pair of socks as her first brand launch, she went to work selling into mid-level department stores. The seed had been launched and was growing. More products and partnerships followed, eventually becoming a worldwide network of branded merchandise and high-profile partnerships.

Kathy's growth strategy had been spot-on. She and her team recognized the overwhelming advantage her modeling fame brought to the enterprise. As you'll discover as you read this book, her fame was a Seed Strategy (creating enormous awareness in the marketplace from her name, likeness, and brand), a Rosette Strategy (her fame and highly positive personal brand translated into an unfair advantage in the marketplace), and a Root Strategy (the financial and marketing value of a strong brand that increases the value of the enterprise).

Reinventing herself as a branding powerhouse was a brilliant move. Broadening her platform with an infinitely scalable collection of products sold through an ever-expanding field of retail channels allowed her to depart from the 1:1 Leverage of modeling to achieve massive Collective Scale.

Ireland is a mega-successful entrepreneur and branding maven, but she is equally committed to philanthropy. She understands the vitality of our communities are of critical importance and deserving of positive efforts.

Her work with the U.N. Youth Program to address hunger, disease, human trafficking, and climate issues, along with her support of military families and her direct mentorship to help select small businesses scale up, all combine to create an immensely positive presence in the world. As you read this book, you'll discover this is an important part of Soil Strategy in the W.E.E.D.S. model, to cultivate the best possible conditions for growth for your enterprise, internally and externally.

Kathy is also a total weed. A beautiful, kind, powerful weed with a deep sense of purpose.

The Heart of Entrepreneurship

Growing like a weed is the heart of entrepreneurship. Nicola Corzine, executive director of the Nasdaq Entrepreneurial Center, notes that most venture capital groups are named after trees, but they're really after weed-like growth. "Weeds are scrappy," she says. "They're the ones that surface new solutions that are disruptive."

Corzine figures startups are the evolutionary force in the business world. "Entrepreneurs are curious and confident and disruptive. They are our weeds." She says entrepreneurs need three attributes to succeed: purpose, attraction, and endless curiosity. They must have a compelling vision, but also an unquantifiable ability to attract the impossible to themselves. As angel investor Robert Wisneski explains, "Weeds always find a way."

Weeds are indeed all around us, and I hope you'll begin to see them with new focus, as a constant source of inspiration for your own entrepreneurial aspirations. As Ralph Waldo Emerson once said, "A weed is but a plant whose virtues remain undiscovered." Perhaps we have found their purpose after all, as a simple yet supremely effective model for growth, for growing like a weed.

As you encounter weeds, try to see them differently than you have before. As they unfurl at your feet, watch how they battle for turf, how they compete with other plants, how they dominate with collective scale. They're showing you how to accomplish the same in your own field.

Points to Remember

- To "grow like a weed" is a universally understood and highly desirable outcome for any business.
- The metaphors of popular business growth strategy—flywheels, operating systems, traction tires, blue water, and more—distract from the straightforward lessons weeds have to offer.
- In this book, we will examine the direct factors that allow weeds to grow like weeds.
- Compared with startup success rates and average return on investment, weeds have a far more successful track record than most businesses.

- T. Boone Pickens's story of growth, success, and triumph over much larger rivals serves as a vivid example of weed-like success in business.
- Kathy Ireland's story provides an important example of weed-like success, but also how improving conditions throughout society helps us all achieve greater prosperity.
- Weeds and entrepreneurship are natural companions; both are evolutionary forces in their respective fields.
- Watching the weeds in our surroundings can give us a greater appreciation for what they can teach us about competition, winning, and achieving scale.

3

WHAT WEEDS WANT US TO KNOW

Purple nutsedge (*Cyperus rotundas L.*). Described as "the world's worst weed," purple nutsedge is a grass that quickly spreads a thicket of underground tubers and roots that make it nearly impossible to eradicate.[8] The plant grows quickly but can lay dormant when it senses adverse conditions, allowing it to survive excessive heat, fire, flooding, and drought. credit: © The Board of Trustees of the Royal Botanic Gardens, Kew

IF THEY COULD talk, weeds would tell us the big difference between them and us is how we operate. Weeds don't have brains. Instead, they have processes honed over millions of years infused into their DNA, which they are programmed to execute with brutal aggression and urgency. There is no training involved; there are no decisions to make. They just act, in unison, with great force.

We, on the other hand, have brains and free will. We can do whatever we want. This makes us wonderfully inquisitive and inventive, but requires discipline, which doesn't come naturally. Weeds have the luxury of doing what they do automatically. We have to think about it and work at it.

Weeds don't have brains, but they do have a lot to tell us. And my role is to serve as your translator. Here are the top ten things they want us to know about what it takes to grow like a weed.

1. Deal with What Is.

With free will comes the power to imagine things that don't yet exist. That can lead to innovation, but also to false expectations and entitlements, which then lead to downfall.

The dandelion I spotted all those years ago on the Santa Monica Freeway surely wasn't feeling sorry for itself, living in a crack in the concrete, marooned in the middle of twelve roaring lanes of traffic. It wasn't thinking to itself, "Gee, I really saw myself as living at the beach, not here." It simply set its roots and ran its process. It aligned itself with the reality it found, then adapted and flourished. It dealt with what is.

We must do the same in our businesses. Growing like a weed requires a clear picture of reality, rather than a skewed sense of what we're owed or hoped would be. The weeds are telling us, "Get off it. Face what you don't want to face and directly meet your challenges."

Executive coach Angus Nelson advises clients to develop their own self-coaching mentality. "False expectations lead to disappointment," he says. He counsels business leaders to focus instead on what they can accomplish today, in the present, based on a true assessment of what they're facing.

2. Be the Whole Weed.

Later in the book, you'll be introduced to the weed mindset, the W.E.E.D.S. model, and scaling like a weed. These are the three legs of weed strategy, a stable tripod that only falls if one leg is missing or weak.

Being the whole weed means living the weed mindset, executing the W.E.E.D.S. model, and establishing collective scale. This is not an easy thing to do. The W.E.E.D.S. model, for instance, includes eight levels of strategic focus.

Seed strategy is analogous to anything that creates awareness and intent in others to transact with you. Seed Pod Strategy relates to multipliers of those efforts. Thorn and Segmentation Strategies are defensive ploys to safeguard your enterprise from interlopers and disasters. Rosette strategy cultivates unfair advantages over competitors. Vine Strategy provides dominant access to resources through alliances. Root strategy organizes and reinforces the stewardship of value, wealth, and assets in the enterprise. Soil strategy proactively builds the healthiest, most favorable environment for growth.

Execution of all eight levels is required to achieve explosive growth. We're naturally drawn to the things we're best at. It takes discipline to give equal focus to things we don't naturally understand or do well. The weeds don't care. They're telling us to operate fully on all eight levels, either on your own or within the composition of your team.

3. Process and Evolution Are the Same Thing.

Process is the mechanism through which expertise is generated and shared in an enterprise. It creates alignment and makes the organization a unified and formidable force in its market.

In organizations, process is communicated in document or training form, which gives the impression it is a bureaucratic, dull, and immovable set of rules to follow. It becomes something we naturally resist.

But weeds are saying we need to see process instead as something vital and dynamic, something that keeps things moving at a fast pace, while adapting quickly to opportunities and challenges. Remember

Canada fleabane and water hemp? Even though they've been around for millions of years, in the past ten, they have developed immunity to powerful herbicides. That immunity is now part of their process and evolution.

Weeds want us to know that process is an exciting component of thriving at scale. It allows us to proceed in expert fashion while evolving quickly when needed, as a unified entity. Process becomes a critical asset that adds to the value of the enterprise.

4. Move Ten Times Faster than Your Competitors . . .

When you see a weed rooted in the ground, it appears stationary and inert. It looks like nothing's happening.

But wait a week and you'll suddenly discover weeds all over your lawn. Weeds don't move the same way we do. They don't pick up and go somewhere else. Their movement takes form in their aggressive and urgent execution of process. Dandelions go from flower to fully deployed seeds in a week, and they do that weekly. By doing that, they spread rapidly across the ground. Polite plants might take the entire season to flower and seed.

So weeds are saying, "Run your process ten times more aggressively and faster than any of your competitors. Get there first and keep doing it. Do that, and you win."

Interestingly, weeds are showing us how to move quickly while maintaining an element of stealth. In their playbook, winning is rooted in running your process as urgently and aggressively as possible. You're moving ten times faster than your competitor, but from the outside, it just looks like you're just doing what you normally do. No apparent movement, yet lots of progress.

5. . . . but Take Time to Regroup, Reassess, and Recharge.

Sprinting requires great amounts of energy expended in a quick burst. But it also requires rest. Even though aggressive execution of process is not a sprint. It, too, requires periods of rest and evaluation. Weeds do it every night, but they also take a break throughout fall and winter. Obviously, they prioritize downtime and active time equally.

The question is, do you?

We live a different existence than that of plants. I'm not suggesting taking off six months of every year to recharge. But weeds are definitely telling us to make recharging a higher priority. They're saying taking time off is a force multiplier for our effectiveness on the job.

Archangel founder Giovanni Marsico agrees. "I used to feel if I wasn't working, I wasn't productive," he explains, "but I've discovered self-care and play and time off are just as productive, because my batteries need recharging, too." Psychiatric nurse practitioner Sonya Ruedlinger also agrees: "You enhance your mental health markedly by engaging in a routine that includes eating healthy food, sleeping eight to ten hours a day and exercising. It sounds obvious, but it's surprising what a difference it can make."

Taking a pause also provides an opportunity to examine results and make adjustments. Weeds tell us, if we're always charging ahead, it's unsustainable and we miss the chance to spot valuable new opportunities and correct mistakes.

6. Persevere Overwhelmingly.

In my backyard is a twenty-by-forty-foot patch of Himalayan blackberries. It was planted by previous owners, and by the time we arrived, it was grossly overgrown. We wanted it gone.

Blackberries are an aggressive weed that covers the island where I live in the Pacific Northwest. Their thorny canes can grow as much as two feet in a twenty-four-hour period, forming great loops in the air, and where their arc meets the ground, new root systems appear. Getting rid of them isn't easy.

Our first attempt was with a hired crew and a bulldozer. Every shred of plant material was removed, leaving a bare plot. Within a month, they were already taking over the ground with foot-tall new shoots. We cut each growth and sprayed the stubs with RoundUp. They came back. Next came the pickax. I removed their stone-sized, rock-hard tubers one by one.

We've now been through many rounds of this, and, of course, they always come back. We know perseverance wins battles in business. Sales is often portrayed as a battle of persistence over resistance. Weeds are telling us to step it up by an order of magnitude. They are yelling it like drill sergeants: "Overwhelming perseverance wins battles overwhelmingly!"

7. Win Overwhelmingly.

To persevere is to constantly push back against threats and obstacles, and to remain on course at all costs. It is a way of life, a mode of operation, but usually a response to a struggle. And weeds know it's better to win than struggle.

Sun Tzu wrote in *The Art of War,* "There is no instance of a country having benefited from prolonged warfare. In war, then, let your great object be victory, not lengthy campaigns."[9] He was definitely thinking like a weed.

If persevering is a way to dominate in battle, winning is a way of living in dominance, without further need for battle. It is a far more efficient use of resources. And weeds fully understand that. Once an adversary has been fully defeated, they are easily repelled by just the threat of battle.

Winning overwhelmingly is part of the W.E.E.D.S. model, covered in Chapter 13: thorn strategy. Thorns only have to prick an intruder once to repel them forever after. Both the experience and the sight of a thorn have the same effect, but with far less effort and risk to the plant. Winning means you don't have to expend energy persevering. The weeds are saying do it, and do it overwhelmingly.

8. Root Out and Eliminate All Sources of 1:1 Leverage.

As humans, we're trained to operate on 1:1 scale. Jobs are strictly 1:1 scale. There is no room for rapid expansion because whatever revenue is produced is tied directly to the finite actions of the earner. You can only work so many jobs and so many hours in a day.

Jobs, gigs, freelancing, consulting, anything that requires your constant, direct involvement with an employer or client is strictly 1:1

leverage. Any business activity that cannot be sold to a willing buyer is operating on 1:1 leverage. If you report to a boss, you're 1:1. If you're doing all your own selling, you're 1:1. If you have clients you must constantly tend to personally, you're 1:1. Financial advisors will tell you what you really own is a job. Not a business, and certainly nothing scalable.

Weeds know the secret to scaling is replicable processes executed by a collective group. They work together to multiply their impact. Weeds never appear alone in nature. They're always part of a quickly expanding horde. A single dandelion in your lawn is easy to banish. Thousands of dandelions are an overwhelming, fast-moving, unbeatable force.

It's unnatural for us to break the bonds of 1:1 leverage, because it's counterintuitive, much like the "buy low, sell high" advice we get about investing in stocks. "Buying low" requires us to invest when the market is in trouble, while "selling high" means we must part with stocks that are performing well. Rooting out all forms of 1:1 leverage in your business will require the same level of uncomfortable actions.

Weeds don't waste their time on activities that cannot scale. Neither should you.

9. Build Sources for Multi-Channel Scale Immediately.

To escape 1:1 leverage requires opening new sources of productivity. In the W.E.E.D.S. model, vine strategy replicates the borrowing of infrastructure of others to gain dominant positions for critical resources. Building Multi-Channel Scale requires the establishment of partnerships and alliances.

In the same way dandelions team up to multiply their scale, multichannel leverage directs us to form alliances for referrals with complementary businesses. They provide access to new market segments and more customers, but they do so because your products and services help their clients meet their own needs, too.

If you're doing all your own selling, you're going it alone. If you're teaming with a network of partners to greatly expand sales, you've graduated to multi-channel scale. But don't get too comfortable, because the weeds say this should be a temporary orientation for growth. The real leverage comes from collective scale.

10. Collective Scale Is the Ultimate Goal.

Someone once defined brand as what people say about you when you're not in the room. If that's true, collective scale is how people interact with your company—and each other—when you're not present to influence their actions.

As an author, I see this in action constantly. When posts pop up talking about my book or, better yet, recommending it to others, sales go up. Notice, though, that none of that process involved my participation. I wrote the book, yes, but beyond that, it becomes an instance of collective scale. People in the marketplace are propelling the sales of the book, *not me.*

When you achieve collective scale, you're no longer wasting resources on disruptive clients and their out-of-spec demands, politics, and resistance. Instead, you have large pools of members, students, subscribers, and users. Your sales efforts are spread across networks of affiliates, and your sales happen automatically and at scale through digital portals.

Amazon is an example of collective scale in action. Their global reach is complete. They sell anything and everything we can imagine. A worldwide marketplace of small businesses online is contained within the platform. Their sales pour in from dominant search-result positioning, a massive affiliate network, and simple type-in traffic. We all know who they are and it's easy enough to type "Amazon" in our always-open browsers to find anything we need, on the spot.

Amazon is also an innovator of monstrous scale. They were the first to invent affiliate networks, one-click checkout, and real-time delivery updates. Their Kindle tablet was the first e-reader, capable of containing an entire library of books on a single device. Alexa brought AI, voice recognition, and automation to our homes. Soon they'll be delivering packages within thirty minutes of an order, via drone.

For the moment, no one can compete with Amazon's collective scale and the forces driving it—which makes them very weed-like, indeed.

Points to Remember

- If weeds could talk, they'd tell us to face reality and act with aggressive purpose.
- To grow like a weed requires discipline, applied across all areas of weed strategy and the W.E.E.D.S. model.
- Process is the mechanism through which expertise is recorded and applied throughout an organization.
- Weeds also use process to strengthen their species and act decisively on a collective scale.
- Process should be highly adaptable to challenges and changes of circumstance.
- Winning requires persistence, which requires unrelenting effort, energy, and resources.
- But winning overwhelmingly relieves the need for persistence.
- If you perform all duties in your business, or if your business cannot run without your presence, you are operating at 1:1 leverage.
- The weeds tell us to root out 1:1 leverage and replace it immediately with multi-channel scale.
- The ultimate goal is to achieve collective scale, leading to unlimited growth.

4

HOW WEEDS DISRUPT

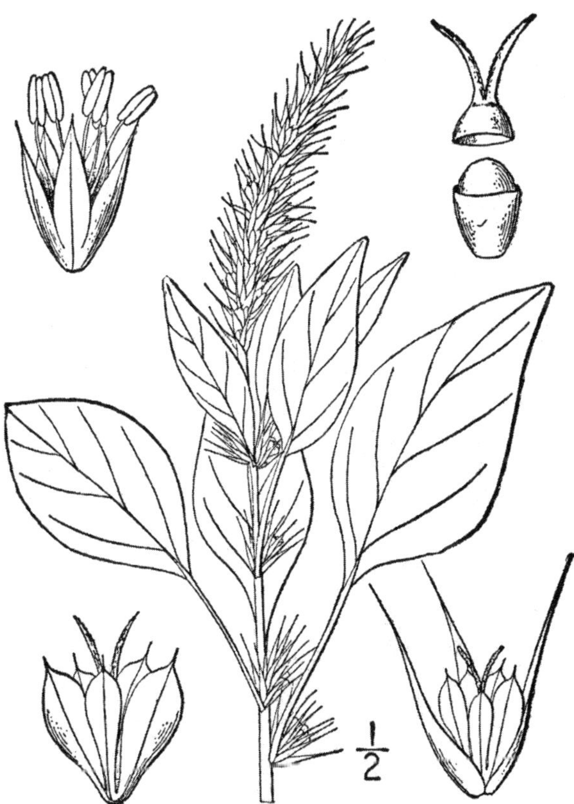

Palmer amaranth (*Amaranthus palmeri*). An aggressive weed currently disrupting agriculture across the U.S. South and Midwest, palmer amaranth can quickly smother crops, while generating 250,000 to 500,000 seeds per plant that germinate throughout the growing season. It is part of a class of weeds that are quickly developing immunity to herbicides used in farming. credit: © The Board of Trustees of the Royal Botanic Gardens, Kew

WEEDS ARE NATURE'S ultimate disruptive force. You could argue volcanoes, hurricanes, tornados, floods, and droughts do more damage. Volcanoes occasionally blast with the force of nuclear bombs. Hurricanes devastate entire coastlines, while tornadoes shred communities like a buzzsaw. Floods and droughts create destruction across large swaths of territory. But none of these employ strategy or process in what they do. Natural disasters are random occurrences. None of them affect nearly every landmass on the planet, or act with persistence, aggression, or deliberation. They have no mission to create scale.

Weeds do all of those things. Their strategies and processes have allowed them to disrupt and conquer six continents, and, despite our best efforts, they're not going away. If anything, they're becoming more formidable as they dismantle our defenses.

Of course, in the business world, disruption is a celebrated commodity. When companies like Uber, Airbnb, and Zoom appear, our lives change. We're shown new ways of doing familiar things, while incumbents suddenly find their markets shifted out of grasp. Such disruptors will soon enough be disrupted themselves by even newer technology and other upstarts, but that's life in the wild and weedy world of business.

Weeds also live a highly volatile life. Disruption is in every fiber of their being. Just like it is for us, disruptiveness is a valued trait in their world, a way of life and a necessary part of their growth, expansion, and domination strategy. The difference is, they seem to have a model for making it happen, while we leave it to chance and discovery.

Our Model versus Theirs

Although the notion of creative destruction—of abandoning older innovations to make room for new ones—is credited to economist Joseph Schumpeter, and even Karl Marx, the modern view of business disruption springs from Clayton Christensen's seminal book, *The Innovator's Dilemma*. In it, he describes companies that were once undisputed leaders in their fields that crashed in the face of disruptive new technologies. Although hard to believe today, for example, Sears was once revered as the world leader in retailing, pioneering such innovations as supply chain management, store brands, catalog marketing, and credit card sales.[10]

The company that once held a 2 percent share of all U.S. retail sales has since been disrupted by discount retailing, e-commerce, and other innovations. And look at who holds that lead now—one-time garage-born upstart, Amazon. There are many more stories of market-leading companies, whose management practices were celebrated as the very latest and best, that were blindsided by disruptive technologies. It happened with Eastman Kodak and digital photography. Blockbuster and video streaming. Yahoo and everything Google. The taxi and car rental industries and ride sharing. The hotel industry and short-term rentals.

Christensen observed that the same celebrated managerial practices that propelled these companies to the top prevented them from capitalizing on the next wave of innovation. Their processes were optimized to support the status quo, not innovate and disrupt. In fact, it's nearly impossible for market leaders to make these leaps, because it requires counterintuitive actions.

When they first emerge, disruptive technologies aren't wanted by current clients, they don't support a sufficient profit margin, and they address a market that is, at first, too small. There just isn't anything compelling in any of it for market leaders. And even if there was, management would demand metrics and projections that don't yet exist before making any moves.

This happened with Eastman Kodak, once the leading producer and processor of camera film. Eventually, film was disrupted by digital photography, and in turn the consumer digital camera market was upended by smartphones with built-in cameras. Ironically, digital photography was invented in 1975—by a junior engineer at Eastman Kodak. The disruptive technology was right under their noses, and they ignored it.

Christensen's solution was for market leaders to spin off new companies to commercialize such new, apparently non-fitting technologies. It's a good approach, but how does it compare to the weeds' model for disruption?

Let's examine three of the most disruptive weeds in the agricultural field: water hemp, Canada fleabane, and palmer amaranth. The three species are threatening to crowd out entire crops of cotton, corn, and soybeans. Their greatest weapons of disruption are enormous flushes of seeds and lightning-fast defensive evolution against herbicidal threats.

Canada fleabane produces roughly 240,000 highly mobile seeds per plant, which can travel more than 300 miles in any direction. Palmer amaranth launches 250,000 to 500,000 seeds, which concentrate in the local area of the parent. Water hemp outdoes both with up to 4.8 million seeds per plant, which also spread to the immediate vicinity. The three species prioritize enormous seed production, but their strategies diverge. Canada fleabane's seeds are made to spread over great distances, emphasizing the colonization of enormous territory. In contrast, water hemp and palmer amaranth's strategy is to strengthen their hold on their immediate surroundings. Dumping millions of seeds per square foot ensures the plants will never leave.

All three species aggressively run their seed-to-germination processes repeatedly, throughout the growing season (unlike the actual crops, which do it once per season). This bold attack allows them to easily outcompete cultivated crops by growing first and closing access to the critical resources of sunlight and water.

When weeds disrupt their fields, they're doing it through the dispersal of millions of seeds. The seeds are identical units that scatter, probe for opportunities, and produce new positions in the battle for turf.

The Christensen model suggests that, in order to disrupt a market, we must first invent something that changes everything. The weeds suggest we're severely overcomplicating the notion of disruption. When they release their motherlode of seeds, they haven't reinvented what a seed is or does. These are not paradigm-shifting versions of what came before. They're just seeds, dispersed widely and in great numbers, that are programmed to aggressively run their process.

Weeds are telling us we don't have to invent the flying car to disrupt a market. Their innovation is simplicity, coupled with overwhelming numbers. Perhaps the work of Christensen and others, and the celebrated "unicorn" examples of success from Silicon Valley, have limited our thinking. The seeds of disruption don't have to be so complicated. Cleverness, audacity, and determination can also compete with mega-funding and world-beating new technologies.

Swearing Parrots and $6 Haircuts

Merriam-Webster defines *disruption* as "a break or interruption in the normal course or continuation of some activity or process."[11] By that definition, almost anything can create a disruption. If not flying cars, what might the simpler version of disruption look like, as suggested by weeds?

The answer may come from a few unlikely sources. The Guerrilla Marketing concepts advanced by Jay Conrad Levinson were based on producing outsized results against bigger, more established, and better funded competitors. The prize was sudden growth accomplished through scrappy, asymmetric marketing warfare. Consider two examples.

During the COVID pandemic, many parrot owners discovered they couldn't stand their pets' incessant racket while confined to working from home. So wild-animal parks experienced a sudden increase in donations of the former pets. One park in particular discovered they got something extra in the bargain.

When the Lincolnshire Wildlife Park, located a hundred or so miles north of London, proudly displayed their new clutch of African grey parrots, they quickly discovered an unexpected talent: swearing. As patrons entered the area, they were showered with obscene insults, while the birds themselves told each other to "fuck off." The managing director complained of especially derogatory remarks every time she walked past.

News of the parrots' behavior quickly spread across the globe, making the wildlife park world famous—and fascinating. Park management reflexively removed the birds from public display, fearing they might turn away visitors. But the weeds would recognize the millions of sudden impressions and newfound fame as a windfall in the park's favor. Let's hope their management figures out what a powerful attraction they've been handed and embraces the disruptive marketing power of their swearing parrots. They could easily eclipse the UK's top tourist destinations and explode their scale.

Meanwhile, once upon a time, there was a particular barbershop that cut everyone's hair in their town. Everything was fine until a franchise shop moved in. Business quickly started draining away, after the franchisee erected a billboard across the street proclaiming, "We give $6 haircuts," greatly undercutting the incumbent. Desperate for a solution, the original shop's owner made a bold move, with a billboard of his own. Placed atop his shop, and directly across from the offending billboard, it read, "We fix $6 haircuts." Guess who won the haircut war?

In my books *How to Get a Meeting with Anyone* and *Get the Meeting,* I describe a method for achieving rapid growth by targeting and connecting with the people who can change the scale of our businesses. The contact marketing methods are audacious and clever, but also carefully plotted to create a highly positive response to requests for meetings. I described the use of swords, pigeons, email, interviews, personalization, gifts, full-page newspaper ads, cartoons, and more to break through. While conventional marketing typically produces low response rates (1 percent or less) and returns on investment (ROI), contact marketing campaigns often generate shocking metrics. The record for response to a contact campaign stands at 300 percent (due to viral pass-along), and the highest ROI is 69,500,000 percent (a $28 contact ad on Facebook produced a $20 million result).

All of these are examples of highly disruptive results, pushing extreme levels of growth. None involved the invention of world-changing technologies. The weeds are right. Disruption can be achieved by anyone in business, not just well-funded Silicon Valley startups.

The Experts Weigh In

Talk disruption in a roomful of business experts and Amazon is sure to come up in the conversation. They all agree that, of all the companies in the world, Amazon is one of the best examples of acting—and growing—like a weed. Amazon is also a prime example of constant disruption and evolution at work, much like what Charles Darwin admired about weeds in his research. As speaker/author Jeff Sheehan points out, "Amazon's R&D expenditures are the highest of any company in the world."

Amazon is constantly looking for new ideas to disrupt competitors. CSO Insights and Sales Mastery co-founder Jim Dickie says they have been particularly aggressive about creating a culture of out-of-the-box thinkers that question everything. "They're constantly looking at their people, process, knowledge and financial angles in different ways, and suddenly, there's new innovation," he says, adding, "They're a company of innovators." We have all witnessed how Amazon uses innovation as a way to disrupt not only competitors, but even itself.

Startup strategist Pierre-R Wolff asks, "Is it possible to disrupt yourself? Of course it is. Amazon does it all the time." Wolff points out when Amazon first started, they just sold books, but they established their signature approach early when they took the concept of "bookstore" well beyond what it was before. Suddenly, it was a worldwide platform that offered every book imaginable.

The brick-and-mortar bookstore model was suddenly obsolete. But Amazon has astutely realized they can be disrupted either by competitors or by their own, self-disruption, which they control. It is a strategy that has paid off with many advancements in Internet commerce that are taken for granted today, including affiliate marketing, one-click shopping, two-day shipping, order tracking updates, e-readers, AI home appliances, and more. As a result, the company is rarely, if ever, disrupted by competitors.

Amazon, along with Elon Musk's Tesla and SpaceX, Uber, and others, will come up often in our discussion of weed strategy and business later in this book. They are examples of what can be done when you have seemingly unlimited budgets to create anything that can be imagined. But most of us live in a different reality, where funds are limited and we're not trying to lead the effort to colonize Mars. We just want to sell our products and services. So how do the rest of us disrupt our way to success?

Christopher Lochhead wrote a deeply insightful book that offers an elegant solution. In *Niche Down: How to Become Legendary by Being Different,* Lochhead argues lasting disruption comes from creating not just your own brand, but your own *category.* He says when you do that, you are the undisputed leader, because you *are* the category. Netflix did this in its reinvention from renter of DVDs to the movie-streaming platform we know today. It became a category of one and quickly made the business of movie rentals on physical media obsolete. Even now, with Amazon, Disney, Hulu, and many others following Netflix's lead, they are still the undisputed category leader.

Building new categories has become so important, Lochhead says the big venture capital firms won't invest in a startup unless it's also the start of a new category. "Jim Goetz, the number one tech venture capitalist at Sequoia Capital," Lochhead points out, "says if the category already exists, they're not interested." They won't invest in a startup if it doesn't also represent a new category opportunity. His main contention: if you can create your own category, you can remain dominant for a long time. Like an invasive weed, once it takes over a patch of ground, it's much harder for others to take root.

The capacity for reinvention shows up throughout the study of weeds as a metaphor for growth strategy. The COVID-19 pandemic forced everyone in business to rethink their models, as a matter of survival, but also as an opportunity to improve and grow. Before the disruption, Zoom was a business-only video-call solution little known in the consumer world, and Peloton was tangled in a flap about a misconstrued commercial gone viral. Both companies were in very lucky positions, as they became integral parts of the work-from-home, exercise-at-home societal shifts. But they still had to disrupt their own models to seize the new growth opportunities.

Less fortunate were businesses whose models relied on customers being physically present. This dynamic killed many restaurants, but others thrived by reinventing the way they catered to the new needs of their customers. Trainers and speakers responded by moving their services online, delivering keynotes from home, and pushing into online courses. Account-based marketing evangelist Sangram Vajre explains, "To disrupt, you have to be an agent of change." He suggests partnering with the community you want to serve and identifying the problems you can help them solve. "Reverse-engineering a solution from a community that cares enough about a problem enables you to build a platform, not just a product."

Disruption can also be a matter of careful observation and then taking bold steps. Venture capitalist Esther Dyson says the bottom 5 percent of performers in any industry are counting on not being disrupted. They become complacent and miss opportunities. And good companies take advantage of that. "When markets are disrupted it becomes easy for weeds to come in and thrive," she says, explaining further, "Weeds don't have a conscience, they go where they're not welcome. They are present without permission, which is basically what a weed is." Clearly, there is an attitude of weedy irreverence that must be part of any plan to disrupt and grow.

Chief Weed Officer

Professor Christensen suggested spinning off new companies to capitalize on disruptive technologies, but turnaround specialist Dan Waldschmidt proposes an interesting alternative. He says, "If you don't have a Chief Weed Officer, you lose." In his area of specialization, working with companies that are being disrupted is Waldschmidt's comfort zone. He says turning around a company in trouble is a simple matter of following two rules: be incredibly easy to do business with, and be so awesome, people ask for more. In other words, be like a weed.

So we now have two versions of disruption to follow. One involves the invention of new technologies, as used in Silicon Valley, and the other, being clever and relentless and weedy.

Brand Intervention author David Brier captures the weed doctrine beautifully: "Disruption is synonymous with resiliency and ingenuity, being alert to opportunities, watching for repeating patterns, similarities and redundancies." He says reinvention and disruption come from asking, "Why not that? What if we try this? That happened over there, could it happen here, too?" The weeds are telling us to connect the dots others miss. That's a pretty useful assessment of what it takes for any of us to disrupt our markets and grow like a weed.

Marketer Rick Bennett touts Oracle founder Larry Ellison's golden rule as the ultimate expression of weed-like disruption. "Ellison's Law states, 'You're not allowed to tout anything your competitors can also say.' Forcing ourselves to go beyond what our competitors do and say allows us to use disruption as a constant, strategic element of our enterprises. Again, like a weed.

Tying It All Together

We're on our way toward understanding how weeds grow at such prolific rates, and how we can absorb their processes into our own. As we examine the strategies and attributes weeds use to win so decisively, we're also building toward the W.E.E.D.S. model we'll use later in the book.

In this discussion of disruption, we can see that weeds disrupt in order to clear new ground for growth and expansion. They do it by dispatching overwhelming amounts of seeds, by cultivating unfair advantages, and through their bulletproof growth processes. These actions fit perfectly within seed, segmentation, and rosette strategies. In the model, seeds are analogous to anything that creates awareness and intent in others to transact with us. Segmentation strategy encompasses damage and risk mitigation, including responding to disruptions with clever new solutions that allow us to serve our clients even better. And rosette strategy pushes us to cultivate unfair advantages no one else can match.

Dan Waldschmidt is right. If you're looking to sow the seeds of disruption and you don't have a chief weed officer, you lose. But you're already on your way to becoming your own chief weed officer—a truly unfair advantage.

Points to Remember

- Weeds are nature's ultimate disruptive force.
- *The Innovator's Dilemma* author Clayton Christensen says market leaders almost never capture the next wave of disruption.
- Christensen says disruption stems from new technologies.
- But the weeds are telling us a much simpler form of disruption exists that is available to us all.
- Water hemp, Canada fleabane, and palmer amaranth are examples of weeds that have placed a high priority on producing massive amounts of seeds.
- They suggest we don't have to produce dramatic inventions, but instead take big, bold, and clever actions to disrupt our markets.

- Guerrilla marketing, contact marketing, and category invention are three ways we can disrupt without the need for the massive budgets to invent new technologies.
- An attitude of weedy irreverence must be part of any plan to disrupt and grow.
- Turnaround specialist Dan Waldschmidt says, "If you don't have a chief weed officer, you lose."
- Disruption, and the other strategic elements that follow, all feed into and are part of the W.E.E.D.S. model.

THE WEED MINDSET

5

IRREPRESSIBLE OPTIMISM

Belladonna nightshade (*Atropa belladonna*). Nightshade is a broad family of plants that include tomatoes, potatoes, and eggplants, but also several weed varieties, all of which are poisonous and invasive to crops, yards, and gardens. Of the weed varieties, Belladonna nightshade is most toxic. Just two of its black berries are enough to kill a child, and twenty will kill an adult human. Several nightshade varieties are troublesome to agriculture, as they harbor pathogens and insects that are harmful to crops. credit:

THE WEED MINDSET is a set of attributes weeds use to run their processes, but it's much more than that. It's a code of conduct, a mode of battle, an accelerator of results. The weed mindset is how weeds get things done—how their process moves with devastating effect.

We'll unpack that process when we examine and apply the W.E.E.D.S. model in the following section. But first, the weeds require a transformation from us. In order to create weed-like growth, we must first assimilate the mindset of a weed. The six short chapters in this section reveal how weeds use irrepressible optimism, ruthless persistence, brutal urgency, fearsome aggression, nimble adaptability, and alien resilience to neutralize threats, defeat adversaries, and dominate new ground.

All weeds act with unfair advantages and deadly effect. The Belladonna nightshade's secret weapon, for example, is its poisonous berries. Just two can kill a child and twenty an adult human. This weed is serious. All weeds are serious. And that's the benefit of assimilating the weed mindset: it will make you just as dominant in your field, as you execute your own weed strategy with commanding effect.

Is It Possible for Weeds to Be Optimists?

When I spotted the dandelion growing from the crack in the freeway median all those years ago, it certainly seemed to exude optimism. Its flowers radiated that signature fluorescent amber hue while its seeds lifted off in the noisy turbulence of freeway traffic, each embarking on its own exciting adventure.

As the weed swayed and bounced in the smoggy turbulence, it looked as though it was actually having fun. It didn't seem to care that its own lot in life, to be anchored to a freeway median, was less than ideal. It surely wasn't thinking to itself, "Well, this sucks."

To understand the mindset of weeds, we need to recalibrate. We're not looking for individual thought, but collective intelligence. As a group, each weed executes their strategy for growth, survival, and dominance. There is no room for interference from stray thoughts or feelings; they're not relevant to the mission, not part of the plant's programming.

Still, we can see strong markers for optimism in their actions. They run their processes for growth, for flowering, for seeding, for defending against threats, for cultivating more dominant positions on the ground with buoyant conviction. Their actions suggest an unfailing belief that it will all work out if they follow the plan. That is classic optimism.

Optimism Fuels Success

Optimism can be defined as the belief that all is good in the world, that everything works out in the end. It is the sunny, energetic faith that we can shape our world, that we have agency over our outcomes in life. But we can also define optimism as a lack of pessimism. It is the opposite of depression.

Pessimism corrodes our belief in positive results, thus our efforts to achieve them. If we don't believe our actions can make a difference, our will to persist disintegrates. Pessimism fuels failure.

Optimism, on the other hand, fuels success. It changes the way we respond to challenges. Optimism lowers production of stress hormones, boosts immune responses, and causes greater and quicker recovery from illness. It is a required trait for entrepreneurs, the ultimate optimists, who must create new visions and push against a resistant world for positive change.

There is an old saying: if you don't try, you're guaranteed to fail. If you never ask, the answer is always no. Optimism is the motivator that makes success possible. As former four-star general and secretary of state Colin Powell said, "Perpetual optimism is a force multiplier."[12] It turns out, it's one of many force multipliers in the W.E.E.D.S. model.

Can Optimism Be Learned?

It's universally accepted that optimism is a valuable trait, and a predictor of success, but can it be learned? Well, yes, but it's not as simple as saying, "Okay, now let's start seeing the glass as half full instead of half empty."

Psychologist and *Learned Optimism* author Martin Seligman says the key to changing from a negative to a positive outlook hinges on changing our self-explanatory style. If we see challenges as permanent and out of our control, we're likely to fall victim to the effects of pessimism. The trick is to see those same obstacles as temporary and the outcomes as within your control.[13]

Not surprisingly, weeds have a radically different take. Lacking our emotions, weeds skip those altogether and go straight to the end result of optimism. When we're depressed, our output and responses are diminished, but when we're optimistic, we're back on track, accomplishing things ahead of schedule and happily pursuing our goals.

Weeds always jump directly to that optimistic state. They're always aggressively running their strategic processes—always going for the win. When they suffer setbacks, they simply pick up again, running the processes that consistently allow them to grow and win.

If weeds were teaching us their form of optimism, they would start by telling us, "Deal with what is." How profoundly simple that is, but difficult to execute. Our emotions are always getting in the way. When we suffer setbacks, we respond with anger, resentment, or resignation, and these all prevent our return to the high productivity state that is the product of optimism.

When we hinder ourselves with emotions, weeds would tell us, "Stop wasting time. Deal with what is. Move on and get back to what makes you win." They might also ask, "What makes you happier and more motivated: *thinking* about winning or *actually* winning?"

Dispatch from the CIA

I can't think of a more extreme, more weed-like source of intel on optimism than the CIA. Think about their reality. Operatives live in the most hostile environments, under threat of execution if caught. Their mission is to gather critically important, top-secret information on threats to the state. If ever there was a mission in need of irrepressible optimism, this is it.

Jonna Mendez has had one of the most fascinating jobs imaginable. As former head of disguise for the CIA, her job was to ensure field operatives and foreign in-country sources remained hidden and safe. "We had to be optimistic," she explains. "The consequences were always on our minds, and they were always worse for foreign assets than us personally. It was an unimaginable responsibility."

Mendez says the key to maintaining optimism was knowing their mission was worth doing, and that they could succeed. "We were always teaming up to provide the safest possible platform for our asset," she says, "and optimism was always part of the operation."

Rebels at Work co-author and former CIA station chief Carmen Medina celebrates the spirit of bucking the system to produce positive change. "Intelligence deals with negatives," she says, "so being optimistic is *de facto* rebellion." She believes irrepressible optimism is a necessity for organizations and people to flourish.

"The intelligence community is steeped in the belief that the world is a terrible, fearful place," Medina explains. "It's an 'If you knew what I know about the world, you'd never leave your home' kind of mentality. Optimism is what allows you to keep going." She also sees optimism as an important element enabling creative people to bloom. "Elon Musk is a great example. Born in South Africa, moved to Canada and the U.S., he has lived a very weedy life," she explains. Optimism and outrageously outsized goals realized are Musk's life story.

And finally, the former director of the CIA himself weighed in. General David Petraeus cautions that optimism must be realistic, rational, and informed. "We should be optimistic," he cautions, "but we must always be realists. Sometimes things are just hard all the time, but hard is not hopeless." His words seem to echo those of the weeds: deal with what is and move on to what makes you win.

Founders and Entrepreneurs

Henrik Fisker is no stranger to hardship and setbacks in his storied entrepreneurial life. Fisker is a celebrated automobile designer, having penned designs for the Aston Martin V8 Vantage, DB9, and BMW Z8 roadster, the latter of which appeared in the James Bond 007 movie series. He then founded Fisker Automotive, which promised elegant electric luxury vehicles but crashed during the difficult financial years of the early 2000s. He's back again, with a new eponymous automotive company and a new digital model for the industry.

Fisker believes optimism fuels all entrepreneurial ventures. "Depression never gets me down," he says, adding, "optimism is always about the glass being half full, but even if it has a few drops in it, there's a chance." Fisker says the trick to being optimistic is always believing what you do has value, and you can do it better than anyone else. "It's just a human being running that billion-dollar company over there, just like me," he explains. "There's no reason I can't be as good or better."

"No matter how tough the circumstances, weeds thrive and survive," adds Outbound Edge founder Chris Ortolano. "We should always be looking for people who thrive" as a way to build optimism into teams. Venture capitalist Esther Dyson agrees: "Weeds don't get scared and stop. We need to be the same way." She says optimists don't sit around waiting for conclusive evidence, they simply assess and act. They follow the weeds' definition of optimism: deal with what is and do what makes you win.

Entrepreneur Josh Steimle sees optimism laced throughout everything weeds do. "Weeds find any opportunity for new growth. If you're creative," he continues, "you will always see there's opportunity to spread seeds and create growth." Steimle explains, "That's how weeds are, they know if they spread enough seeds, they're going to find the cracks in the concrete."

Sales entrepreneur Alice Heiman sums it up this way: "Weeds volunteer in a garden. They just hop right in." Dyson adds, "They're present without permission, that's basically what a weed is." And if that isn't the very definition of irrepressible optimism, what is?

Weed Mindset at a Glance

1. Irrepressible Optimism

I deal with what is and focus on the things that make me win (my process). My actions lead my emotions, not the other way around.

Points to Remember

- Weeds don't have brains, but they have an unmistakably fierce mindset.
- The weed mindset is a set of attributes weeds use to execute their process with devastating effect.

- The mindset of a weed is characterized as irrepressible optimism, ruthless persistence, brutal urgency, fearsome aggression, nimble adaptability, and alien resilience.
- Pessimism corrodes our belief in positive results, thus our efforts to achieve them.
- Optimism changes the way we respond to our environment and challenges.
- Weeds suggest letting our positive actions lead to feelings of optimism and excitement.
- The CIA thrives on weed-like optimism in its cloak-and-dagger missions.
- Optimism keeps intelligence operatives always one step ahead of adversaries—and alive.
- Venture capitalist Esther Dyson says, "Weeds don't get scared and stop. We need to be the same way."

6

RUTHLESS PERSISTENCE

Himalayan blackberry (*Rubus armeniacus*). The Himalayan blackberry is invasive and nearly impossible to eliminate. The plant quickly forms an impenetrable thicket of thorn-covered canes that can grow to a height of twelve to fifteen feet, and to lengths of up to forty feet. Its flowers can produce seeds without fertilization, while every place the canes touch the ground produces even more root systems and instances of the plant.[14] credit: © iStock

WE'RE TOLD THAT to be successful in business, we must be persistent. We're told that so often, the word has nearly lost its meaning. You can only be told "just keep going" so many times. I believe its meaning is diminished because we lack a mental picture of what true persistence looks like. We need an inspiring visual we can see in our mind's eye.

Fortunately, weeds give us an easy example to follow. In my backyard, we have a twenty-by-thirty-foot patch of Himalayan blackberries, planted by the property's previous owner. When originally sited, the blackberry patch was set up in two neat rows the owners could walk through to pick the berries. But they should have known Himalayan blackberries are an offensive visitor that quickly overruns any human-made intentions.

By the time we moved in, the two patches had become a fifteen-foot-tall mass of tangled canes arching skyward, fangs bared. And the twenty-by-thirty-foot plot was nearly doubled as it moved to take over the yard. Something had to be done.

So we hired a crew with a tractor to dig it all out. They removed several loads of debris and restored the patch to bare ground. But not for long. It was soon covered with a shaggy carpet of blackberry shoots already two-to-four-feet tall. Out I went with my pickax, to douse the new growth.

As I swung the tool, I noticed there were many hard spots in the soil—heart-sized root crowns so hard they caused the pickax to bounce out of the ground. After hours of back-breaking work, the site was cleared, but weeks later, new shoots were back, quickly reclaiming the area. This cycle has continued repeatedly, the only respite coming when the weeds hibernate during winter. And then they're back at it again in the spring.

This has become a yearly struggle, and without reinforcements and heavy construction equipment, I'll lose the battle. It doesn't matter what I do, the blackberries have only one mode of operation: charge forward. Relentlessly. *Persistently.*

Weed-Think

If we've lost touch with the meaning of persistence, weeds make it easy to reacquire. The blackberry struggle in my backyard is the same one we all witness, taking place in disrupted ground all over the world. Weeds make it easy for us to visualize ruthless persistence. All we have to do is watch.

If they help us see it differently, it's fair to wonder: How do weeds view persistence?

Weed-think is characterized by two factors. Lacking emotion, feelings are never part of the equation. And they're extreme in their execution of process. If they could speak, the weeds would once again tell us to remove all emotion and act with great force. Like a computer, they're configured to follow their programming without question or hesitation. Meanwhile, we live a more complicated existence.

Our emotions kick in, filling our heads with doubt about desired outcomes. *This probably won't work. They don't want to hear from me again. I should just give up.* Weeds are not impeded by such feelings, so they proceed with the actions defined by persistence (and the other attributes throughout this section). What a luxury to be free of doubt when pushing ahead with your mission.

The weeds are also telling us the core function of persistence is simply to control the velocity of execution. That's it. It's a throttle. Persistence controls the speed of growth. That's why it's a critical part of every success story ever told. You can't go anywhere if you don't step on the gas.

Weeds give us a simplified concept of persistence, as a throttle, but let's return to that greatest of complicating factors, our emotions. It's easy for weeds to tell us to ditch our emotions, because they don't have them. But I don't think that is the intention.

Instead, the weeds are telling us to find a new way to manage our emotions. Generally we experience emotions and decide whether to act upon them. That mistakenly allows our feelings to determine our actions. But we want to direct our actions based upon our mission and goals. Our emotions will catch up and reinforce our motivation.

In the previous chapter, the weeds advised us to act in optimistic ways to produce optimism. By doing the things we would when we're excited about our futures, we become more optimistic. They're saying we've been letting our emotions run our actions, when we should be doing the opposite. Our actions should drive our emotions.

This is not a new concept—actions determining emotions. Psychologists have long noted the correlation between deeds and feelings. Their behavioral approach to depression, for example, has been to reintroduce the behaviors that provide positive reinforcements to their patients, pulling them out of their funk.

Weeds are suggesting the same psychological model here. Act optimistically and you will become optimistic. Act with ruthless persistence and you will become an unbeatable force in your field.

Persistence Shapes Our World

I wrote a chapter on persistence in my earlier book *Get the Meeting,* in which the goal was to get meetings that lead to important sales outcomes. In the sales profession, we're always told persistence is critical to our success, and there are plenty of stories to back that up.

There was the story of the salesperson who sought a meeting with a Fortune 500 executive. After sending seventy-nine emails, she finally broke through on the eightieth try and got the meeting. And there was the grandmother in Korea who finally succeeded in earning her driver's license on her 960th attempt. Thomas Edison, the inventor of the lightbulb, failed ten thousand times before finally alighting upon his momentous discovery.

Real estate guru Brian Buffini tells one of my favorite stories of persistence. Buffini operates training events that are always headlined by someone who'll draw an audience. One year, he set his hopes on Neil Armstrong, the first human to walk on the moon.

There was just one problem: Armstrong was notoriously shy about making public appearances, refusing to take the stage even for NASA events. Buffini knew this, but persevered anyway. His approach was to send handwritten letters, repeatedly, asking Armstrong to appear as his keynote speaker. Week after week, Buffini sent notes and heard nothing.

Finally, one of his letters was returned with Neil's jotted reply. "Are you going to keep sending me notes?" Buffini replied, "Yes," and sent it back. And with that, Armstrong agreed to be Buffini's star speaker that year.

By persevering, Buffini opened the throttle on the growth of his business. Sales thought leader and trainer Alice Heiman says being persistent is not at all about being a pest. "Be consistent, put the right message out, and deliver value," she says, adding, "Persistence is just as important after a sale as it is before."

The Experts Speak

Vibes senior vice president Bill Scott observes that persistence isn't fun, it's hard work: "This is not a happy thing, this is about aggression and battle." Early in his career, Scott pursued a weed-like persistence plan to fuel growth. As a college student, he was offered an opportunity selling books door to door.

After a rousing initial sales training session, he and his fellow sellers were set loose on neighborhoods. It didn't go well. He decided he didn't want to be weeded out, so he redoubled his efforts. "Walking the railroad tracks in town, I was always looking for another house to call on," he recalls, "despite feelings of depression, fatigue, dealing with dogs and police."

His efforts finally paid off, as he kept turning up the throttle on his persistence. After five summers, he became one of the top 10 percent of sellers for the company. He learned to create a crisp, well-jointed story and discovered how to build interest, deliver a compelling demonstration, and then close in a calm, reassuring way. His persistence called for knocking on more doors, while continually honing his process, much the way weeds would if they were selling books.

General David Petraeus recalls the value of persistence during the surge he commanded in Afghanistan. "The first six months were brutal," he recalled, adding, "The belief that 'we'll lick 'em tomorrow' was crucial." General Petraeus says the weeds' sheer will to live, grow, and expand is the same kind of quality that is crucial to companies and leaders.

Entrepreneur Jay Kim says there's no such thing as an overnight success. "All stories about successful people have one common theme," he says, "No one attributes their success to being smart. It's always because they were ruthlessly persistent." He adds part of being persistent is building mastery of your craft. "A lot of these people didn't achieve success until they were in their forties, fifties, or even sixties."

Automotive entrepreneur Henrik Fisker adds, "Confidence is key. I'm always very persistent and confident when selling a design." Entrepreneur and aviator Mike Patey says, "People give up too easily." Patey has achieved cult status as a YouTube personality and airplane builder, producing world-record-holding racers and magazine-cover-grabbing, fantasy bush planes that land anywhere.

"The guy who stops walking is the one who dies," Patey explains. "Building an airplane and building a business are the same. Have a goal and once you start a project, never stop." He advises doing something every day to move a project forward, which as psychologists—and weeds—would remind us, produces the positive feedback we need to continue. The action produces the result, not the emotion.

Comic-Con founder Gareb Shamus recalls the early days of his quest to bring superheroes into the mainstream. "I was laughed out of the room many times," he says, "but I didn't care. I was fearless." He knew the concept of superheroes would eventually prevail: "I knew this stuff was amazing, and didn't understand why the brand marketers couldn't see it. I always had confidence, which made it easy to persevere."

#SalesTruth author Mike Weinberg tells a fascinating story of a construction equipment company that turned persistence into a regimented part of their sales process. They discovered the key to selling was showing up consistently at a job site, creating trust among job foremen. The result was a ten-step plan, requiring ten visits to a job site before business started flowing. By the tenth visit, the job leaders would remark, "Looks like you're serious. Let's take a look at a few needs we have."

Persistence makes us look serious because we are. Acting with persistence is what powers our growth and puts us over the top.

Weed Mindset at a Glance

1. Irrepressible Optimism

I deal with what is and focus on the things that make me win (my process). My actions lead my emotions, not the other way around.

2. Ruthless Persistence

I persevere beyond reason, because I know persistence is what determines the rate of my growth.

Points to Remember

- We're told so often we must be persistent to succeed that the word has lost meaning.
- Himalayan blackberries give us a vivid example of persistence in the weed world.
- Blackberry shoots can grow as much as two feet a day, quickly producing large thickets of thorn-covered canes.
- Weed-think is characterized by a lack of emotion and extreme execution of process.
- Like a computer, weeds are configured to follow their programming without question or hesitation.
- Weeds tell us the function of persistence is to control the velocity of growth, much like a throttle.
- Weeds tell us to bypass feelings of doubt by letting our actions lead our emotions.
- Shaping emotions through actions is also the basis of behavioral activation therapy in psychiatry.
- Persistence can easily be programmed into a repeatable process.

7

BRUTAL URGENCY

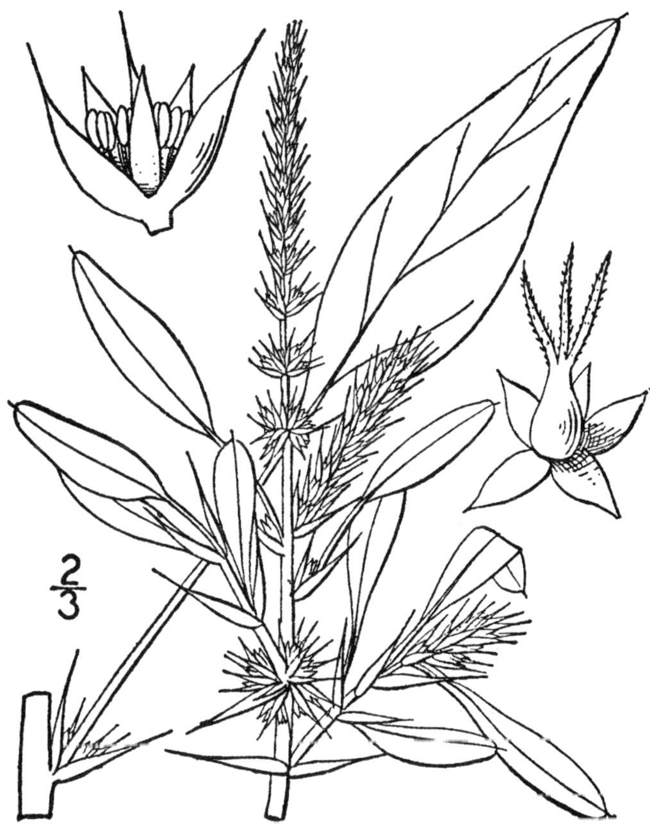

Spiny amaranthus (*Amaranths spinosus*). A bushy, annual invader of farm and ranch land in lower latitudes around the world, spiny amaranthus wields a set of long, needle-sharp spikes at the base of each leaf. Brutal defenders of the plant, the spikes break off in the skin of farm workers, while the leaves are poisonous to livestock. credit: © The Board of Trustees of the Royal Botanic Gardens, Kew

TIME IS NEVER on our side. When we're born, we have a finite number of days, hours, and minutes left in our lives. Delay wastes our most precious resource and diminishes outcomes. It must be minimized at all costs. And yet, it's built into every interaction we have. It's even baked into our own actions. It's often so hard to spot, we don't even notice our time being stolen away.

When someone tells us, "We can definitely get this up and running—in six months," ask, "Why such a long delay? Can it be done sooner? This is *urgent*." When someone asks, "Can you hold?" the answer should always be "*No, this is urgent.*" When you have an appointed call time and the other party asks if you can call back in fifteen minutes, the answer again should always be "***No. This is urgent.***" When a client says they'll engage with you far, far out on the calendar, they're either turning you down or they don't appreciate the importance of the solution on offer.

Delay kills growth and diminishes our relevance. Urgency defines our importance and moves things forward. Each delay is a micro-aggression, eventually amounting to defeat by a thousand cuts. The weeds are telling us to act with brutal urgency in every interaction to ensure our growth and domination in the field.

If this all sounds a bit prickly, consider our friend above, *Amaranthus spinosus*. Clad in razor-sharp spines up to two inches in length, nobody infringes the spiny amaranthus. Its tenacious footing in agricultural fields around the globe—and its importance as a weed—is defined by its barbed iron will. If the prickly amaranthus could speak to us now, it would tell us meekness is no way to respond to any proposed delay.

Behavioral Activation

The weed mindset is based on six attributes that produce an extremely aggressive execution of the strategies to be defined in the W.E.E.D.S. model section to follow. So far, the weeds have told us to lead with our actions, and allow our emotions to follow. That's not an intuitive approach, as we're far more likely to act based on how we feel. The weeds tell us that's a recipe for failure. Psychiatrists also tell us there is a scientific basis for taking the weeds' advice.

Behavioral activation is a widely used mode of therapy, based on the theory that positive actions can produce positive emotions for patients experiencing depression. In the treatment, therapists direct patients to take on new behaviors that mimic those of happy, non-depressed people. They exercise and mingle and act their way out of depression, as the behaviors produce strong feelings of well-being, excitement, and agency. Suddenly, their feelings of hopelessness are replaced with confidence and excitement about their lives. And from those feelings, outcomes and lives change.

The therapy is used to treat depression, but clearly it can be applied wherever new behavioral outcomes are desired. The weeds suggest a different approach, but the outcomes are the same. Weeds don't have emotions, so naturally their approach to winning is strictly action-based. Execute the process and don't allow feelings or doubts to interfere, because for weeds, emotions don't exist.

However we arrive at the conclusion, we have control over our outcomes. That includes generating unlimited measures of optimism, persistence, and urgency (also, aggression, adaptability, and resilience). Behavioral activation can help us instill urgency and importance in ourselves, in our team, and in our markets.

The True Value of Your Time

Have you ever computed the value of your time? You should. When hourly employees are paid, we know the amount is a fraction of the value of their work to the company. Otherwise, it wouldn't be a profitable enterprise. Same for salaried employees. Even highly compensated CEOs are not paid what they're worth to the company. Every employee must be a source of profit or the enterprise collapses.

If you total the potential value you can contribute as a leader, producer, connector, and driver, your annual value should be expressed in the millions of dollars per year. That's not an exaggeration. It doesn't matter whether you currently produce that or not. The fact is, you have the potential to do it always, and I hope this book will help you reach that level.

Weeds seem to know their potential and are always pushing rapidly to reach it. They seem to be saying, "Your potential value and actual value are the same thing. Pick any figure and then reach it. If you say your time is worth $10,000 an hour, then start acting like it."

Again, the weeds suggest allowing our actions to lead our emotions, and choosing actions that increase our sense of worth for our time. If your time is worth $10,000 per hour, how would you respond now if someone asks you to waste precious minutes on hold? Or if a potential partner pushes the start of a new deal out six months?

The focus is what your time is worth to *you.* It's a very different and much higher number than what others might be willing to pay for it. Let this become your internal driver to produce brutal levels of urgency and to eliminate all sources of delay.

The Magic of Deadlines

Assigning a true value for your time is one way to generate urgency. Setting deadlines is another. Both are further examples of behavioral activation in action within the weed mindset, used to help you achieve your goals faster and at greater scale.

There is a certain magic to deadlines. Having worked in the creative field my entire career, I have experienced this firsthand. I'm experiencing it now, as I write this book. There is something about setting a deadline—like setting an alarm in your brain—that keeps us on track and on time. Somehow, our brains recalibrate to the new reality and ensure we complete the action by the due date.

Deadlines can be applied internally or externally. So while they're useful for infusing urgency into your own operation, they also work with clients, suppliers, prospects, and entire markets. Expiration dates, for example, have the effect of pushing people to act according to your time frame, rather than their own. And that's key—if you allow others to dictate your timeline, you lose control over how and when your winning process is executed.

Some are driven by incentives for exceeding a deadline, others by the fear of missing out. Real estate brokers know this well, and constantly stir competition among buyers to move inventory. When touring properties, how many times have we heard, "I have two other buyers bringing offers this afternoon, so you'd better hurry"? It's as automatic as every call to a realtor going to voicemail to capture names and numbers.

Deadlines are a useful behavioral activation tool for gaining control over the urgency of any task—especially when they include early completion incentives or consequences for noncompliance.

The Worst Delays Are Our Own

The most unforgivable, most unnecessary delays are the ones we create for ourselves. The weeds act according to their genetic programming, so their urgency is automatic. Ours can only come from a constant, conscious effort to keep the right things on the fast track.

Most of us don't cause delay in our most important imperatives on purpose. But it's easy to see how those can quickly be hindered by the smallest of details. I see that in my own recent tasks. An important meeting with a large client was pushed back to next week. We agreed on a date and time that indicated an aggressive reschedule, but I hadn't put out the invite yet. It could have easily waited until I finished what I was doing, but dropping everything to get the meeting confirmed on our calendars communicates urgency, and thus importance. Waiting would communicate something else.

Meanwhile, I had an important first meeting with the founder of a company that is becoming an important new strategic partner. I promised to send a signed copy of my earlier book *How to Get a Meeting with Anyone,* but events unfolded and suddenly I find, a few days later, it still hasn't been sent. What does that communicate? *This is not urgent,* even though it is.

The partnership revolves around the book as a marketing engine for the partner's operation, with sponsorship and broad distribution of the online course based on the book, plus co-branded products on their massive platform. The last thing I want to suggest is a lack of interest, and urgency is how we communicate importance.

The weeds might tell us, "Anything worth doing gets done right away, anything that's not gets lost in delay." But if everything is urgent, nothing is urgent. We can't have hundreds of top priorities. If everything must be done right away, it's a recipe for deadlock. The weeds solve this issue with a simple solution—the focus of their urgency is always the execution of their *process,* not a disorganized set of standalone priorities.

The book-send above is a perfect example. If the task is a critical part of my growth process, it gets done right away. If not, it can wait. Since it is central to my effort to create multi-channel scale and it touches one of the founders of the partnering company, it's obvious why it is an urgent task. And at this point, urgent to fix (we're dropping everything to get it out now).

Urgency is also expressed in our style of communication, thus another source for potential delay. When we're insecure, we often over-communicate, adding qualifiers that soften our message. Which of these expresses more urgency and confidence in the importance of the mission?

"Hey, I just wanted to check in with you to see how things are coming along on our partnership deal. I think we were supposed to get this started this quarter, weren't we? Well, I hope things are well, looking forward to hearing from you at your earliest convenience."

Or,

"What's our status? The deadline is Monday."

The latter is shorter, more direct, more important. It says, "We're either moving ahead on time or the opportunity disappears." Which would you be most likely to respond to with your own urgency? The brevity and directness of our communication says more about the importance of our imperatives than our actual words do.

The Experts Weigh In

Retired four-star general and business strategist Barry McCaffrey echoes the need for weed-like urgency. "In combat, it's important to respond with urgency," he asserts. "It's the difference between victory and defeat, in business and on the battlefield." McCaffrey says weed strategy, while useful for the boardroom and C-Suite, is most important at the operational level. "Execution is everything," he says, adding, "Successful businesses are never slow."

General McCaffrey recalls an experience setting up a treasury-direct account with a large financial company. "Their process was Byzantine in complexity," he notes, while setting up the same account with Charles Schwaab was frictionless. "You've got to serve the client's urgency as well as your own," he says.

SaaS CEO coach Dan Martell says urgent, weed-like execution is critical to the startup founders he advises. "Naturally they feel like if they don't get to market quickly enough, someone else will beat them to it," he says. Entrepreneur Josh Steimle agrees. "Gary Vaynerchuck says speed trumps everything," he asserts, adding, "Linda Boff, General Electric's CMO, says speed is the new intellectual property." Hong Kong–based investor Jay Kim echoes, "Speed to execution and speed to market are critical markers for success."

Executive career coach Jonathan Schober tells clients, "Nothing worth getting is going to happen passively," and reminds them to "execute with urgent, deliberate action." In other words, like a weed. Flip My Funnel founder Sangram Vajre says, "Companies have to have insane urgency to succeed," and he says it's especially critical to ignite "urgency in the marketplace," to create weed-like growth.

Nicolás Cerdeira has an interesting view of startups and their causes of failure. As founder of *Failory.com,* he tabulates success/fail rates for startups, while tracking reasons for failures. He observes that nine of ten new startups fail by their fifth year and only one in a hundred achieve runaway success—and weed-like scale. He says, "Compound growth for startups starts slowly and then rapidly scales, based on putting out a lot of seeds to lure investors, money and key employees."

The experts and weeds seem to agree. Urgency starts with you and scales to team members, collaborators, clients, and partners, and eventually to the field. Urgency gives you the leverage to move things forward quickly, which is the only way they'll generate revenues and allow you to reach your goals. As the weeds might remind us, "Anything worth doing gets done right away, anything that's not gets lost in delay."

Weed Mindset at a Glance

1. Irrepressible Optimism

I deal with what is and focus on the things that make me win (my process). My actions lead my emotions, not the other way around.

2. Ruthless Persistence

I persevere beyond reason, because I know persistence is what determines the rate of my growth.

3. Brutal Urgency

Urgency is how I establish the superior importance—internally and externally—of my mission and my time.

Points to Remember

- Time is never on our side. Thus, delays must be minimized at all costs.
- When someone suggests a delayed time frame for a project, ask why there's such a long delay and push for sooner activation.
- Delay kills growth, diminishes our relevance, and devalues our time.
- Urgency is based first on knowing the true value of your time, which is many times larger than whatever you're being paid.
- If you knew every hour of your time was worth $10,000, you would never accept delays of any kind.
- Deadlines are also useful for producing urgency in yourself and others.
- The worst delays are the ones we create for ourselves.
- Urgency can also be produced by reducing the word count in your communications. The wordier it is, the less urgent and thus the less important it is.
- The experts agree weed-like urgency is a key determinant for success.
- General McCaffrey: "Urgency is the difference between victory and defeat, in business and on the battlefield."

8

FEARSOME AGGRESSION

Poison ivy (*Toxicodendron radicans*). A relative of the cashew plant, poison ivy grows in forested portions of the northeastern United States. Residents there are quite familiar with the effects of even the slightest brush of their leaves, which can cause a severely itchy, blistering rash. credit: © The Board of Trustees of the Royal Botanic Gardens, Kew

WEEDS DON'T SNARL or bite. They don't charge at us from behind a rock. When they show up in our lawns, they don't threaten us with death or bodily harm. Still, we know weeds are incredibly aggressive. It's just a quieter, more stealthy form, which makes it even more dangerous.

When an animal is aggressive, it's an overt display; it's a warning that gives you time to respond and defend. When weeds do it, they're ninja-efficient and silent. Because they don't move in ways we recognize, weeds run their process in full view and we never see their aggression coming.

Consider the case of poison ivy. I grew up with the stuff; I know how awful it can be. The plant grows in shady forest floors, and, although it's described as an ivy, it doesn't seem to climb surrounding plants and trees. Thus, it lives at a level roughly equivalent to the exposed area of our legs when wearing summer shorts.

Toxicodendron radicans' nasty weapon is the oily mixture of organic compounds called urushiol, which coats its leaves and creates a deeply allergenic reaction in our skin. Just the briefest contact is enough to unleash a severely itchy rash, which quickly turns to large, liquid-filled blisters. The toxic brew is so reactive, the released fluid from bursting blisters spreads the rash further, until large areas of the skin are affected. The itching sensation is overwhelmingly miserable and lasts for weeks.

The experience motivates us to learn to identify poison ivy and avoid any further contact. The poison ivy plant isn't there to make our lives miserable, it's simply protecting itself. It doesn't want to be disturbed and has developed a highly effective part of its process to prevent disruption.

The extreme and lasting effects of urushiol are also a form of deep aggression. Poison ivy doesn't snarl, but we quickly learn not to mess with it. And that's the form of aggression weeds would like us to take on in our businesses. It's an aggression in the way we run our processes to win, in a manner that never gives our competitors a chance to respond. They'll only notice their defeat after it's already done.

Urgency in Motion

When we look at a weed, there is no sensation of movement, threat, or aggression. But weeds are moving quickly through their process of rapid growth, spreading seed, and creating collective scale. Even as they stand there, nearly motionless. That's the genius of their aggression: we can't see it, but it's fiercely present.

What we're actually seeing is 100 percent efficiency of urgency turned to action. There is no wasted motion, no distractions, no energy or focus lost to emotions. It's the aggressive running of a foolproof process that creates overwhelming success in the field.

In the previous chapter, we examined urgency as an attribute that communicates the importance of your mission and value of your time. Urgency is used as a force to guide our actions, but it also influences others to act aggressively on our behalf. We need their input, help, or cooperation, and we seek to eliminate any source of delay in the transaction.

But aggression is fully self-contained. It is each of us putting our own sense of urgency into action. It's us getting stuff done, within our process, with extreme efficiency, and with weed-like stealth.

The Intertwining of Weed Attributes

In Chapter 6, I described my battle with the patch of Himalayan blackberries in my backyard. No matter what I did, they kept coming back. They were demonstrating perseverance, but also urgency and aggressiveness. As soon as they encountered a setback, they went straight to work, rebuilding damaged infrastructure. It was plain to see this was their top priority. It was urgent to repair the damage, thus they executed their process aggressively.

The attributes of optimism, persistence, urgency, and aggressiveness are tightly intertwined. We know they're related, and we understand we must be optimistic, persistent, urgent, and aggressive to be successful in business. We're told that all the time. But I don't think I've had anyone explain how they all fit together as elegantly as the weeds seem to be doing.

Here's what the weeds are telling us:

Deal with what is. Not what you hoped would be or what you thought you were entitled to. Let your actions lead your emotions to unblock your full potential. Then use persistence, urgency, and aggression to focus on the things that make you win (your process). Be fierce in your execution, while using stealth and surprise so your competitors never know they're losing until it's too late. Be a total weed. That's the intertwined essence of the weed mindset.

There are two more attributes to add to the mix: nimble adaptability, which gives us the flexibility to adjust our process whenever faced with a disruptive challenge, and alien resilience, which gives us the ability to meet any challenge and prevail. But first, let's hear our experts' thoughts on the astonishing utility of aggression and stealth in our actions.

The Experts on Fearsome Aggression

General Barry McCaffrey likens weed-like aggression to the work ethic of the armed forces. "The work ethic of the armed forces in conflict is incredible," he explains. "They're willing to get killed doing their jobs. And they'll do it on three and a half hours of sleep and two meals a day." McCaffrey says truly fearsome aggression comes from an unlimited commitment to the organization and its mission.

Turnaround specialist Dan Waldschmidt believes successful people are those who have nothing to fall back on. "If you give people a chance to back out of greatness," he observes, "they'll never get there." Startup strategist Pierre-R Wolff points to ride-sharing platform Uber as a prime example of fearsome aggression at work in the marketplace. "It's part of their DNA," he explains. "They don't care who they disrupt. They're aggressive to everyone—communities, regulators and especially incumbents."

Nimble founder Jon Ferrara marvels at the stealthy aggressiveness of Microsoft. "Microsoft doesn't innovate, they iterate," he says, adding, "Microsoft executes like no one's business." Nimble enjoys a distinct advantage in that Microsoft is part of the company's seed pod strategy, through a bundling of Ferrara's product with all copies of Office 365. To open a new Nimble account, Office 365 users simply activate it within the program. In that way, Ferrara has exhibited a classic execution of weed-like, stealthy aggression. He secured the partnership with Microsoft, a move his competitors will never be able to match. And they likely never knew what hit them.

Brand growth strategist Ian Rhys Palmer likens aggression to looking for gaps in the concrete. He says many clients describe themselves in terms of their competitors. Palmer counsels a more aggressive approach to brand-building, by focusing on clients instead. "The messaging should talk about pain points," he says. "That's the kind of messaging that spreads like a weed and moves an audience to act." Advertising entrepreneur Rick Bennett adds, "Weeds use a process, not a plan. They fire a lot of seeds into the marketplace, they don't know where they'll land, and they don't care. No matter what, the weeds know their process will be spread with great ferocity."

Startup entrepreneur Jim Pack sees aggression as evolutionary, like wildlife in Africa. "Life is so harsh," he says. "Everything is vicious—the plants, the insects, the animals. Perhaps our environment shapes our evolution and we become much more weed-like and aggressive." *The New Science of Radical Innovation* author Dr. Sunnie Giles likens aggression to scrappiness. "Weeds don't have a lot of nutrition," she says. "They get things done with little resources. They have to be aggressive to flourish."

Environmentalist and philanthropist Marilyn Heiman also takes a weed-like view of aggression as a stealthy way to achieve objectives. "I once spotted a general in a coffee shop," she recalls. "I thanked him for his service and introduced myself," and she told him about her concerns. "Many people simply get angry and demanding, but it's a dead-end. It's honey versus vinegar."

Heiman says her soft approach led to success, and isn't that a lot like what the weeds are telling us about aggression? It is urgency put to action, but always in service of process. And in that way, you win without competitors sensing your aggression—or knowing what hit them.

Weed Mindset at a Glance

1. Irrepressible Optimism

I deal with what is and focus on the things that make me win (my process). My actions lead my emotions, not the other way around.

2. Ruthless Persistence

I persevere beyond reason, because I know persistence is what determines the rate of my growth.

3. Brutal Urgency

Urgency is how I establish the superior importance—internally and externally—of my mission and my time.

4. Fearsome Aggression

Aggression is how I move quickly through my process while maintaining the element of surprise. My adversaries never realize they've lost until it's too late.

Points to Remember

- Weeds don't snarl or bite. Their form of aggression is focused instead on the rapid execution of their process.
- Poison ivy's chemical defense is an example of weed-like aggression; one touch and you'll avoid contact with the plant forevermore.
- The attributes described in the weed mindset intertwine as a whole, based on the aggressive execution of process.
- Weed-like aggression is not overt, it's applied to the execution of process, which makes it a stealthy attack on competitors. They'll never know they lost until it's too late.
- General Barry McCaffrey likens weed-like aggression to the work ethic of the U.S. armed forces in conflict, who are willing to die to do their jobs.
- Turnaround specialist Dan Waldschmidt believes successful people are those who have nothing to fall back on, because they have no choice but to be aggressive and perseverant.
- Nimble founder Jon Ferrara believes Microsoft's ability to brilliantly execute their process is a model of stealthy aggressiveness.
- Advertising entrepreneur Rick Bennett says weeds use a process, not a plan. Plans can be easily disrupted; processes apply in all conditions.

9

NIMBLE ADAPTABILITY

Velvetleaf (*Abutilon theophrasti*). Velvetleaf is considered a noxious, invasive weed, as it invades farmland, orchards, and other disturbed ground and quickly grows tall enough to deprive corn, soybean, and cotton crops of needed sunlight. Each plant produces up to 17,000 seeds, which can remain viable in the soil for up to 60 years. If nutrients are plentiful, it will extend its flowering period and increase seed production.[15] credit: © The Board of Trustees of the Royal Botanic Gardens, Kew

ADAPTABILITY SEEMS TO pop up in two forms. In one, preparations are made for disruptions we might reasonably expect—a plan to mitigate the effects of the next recession, or a berm to protect against the next flood. And then there are the truly unexpected, catastrophic events that show up like a sharpened log in a rambunctious, class-five rapid—a nasty surprise if you're in an inflatable river raft.

The velvetleaf above gives us an example of preparing for the first kind. The plant produces a lot of seeds to ensure continuity, but their activation plan is the ingenious part of the process.

Velvetleaf seeds use an extreme form of strategic timing: they can lurk as much as sixty years before sprouting. The seeds are even capable of sensing conditions in the ground above, choosing the best time to activate.

This allows the plant to adapt to extreme conditions that can last decades in order to survive. It's like setting aside a certain amount of savings for emergencies, although few of us could ever prepare for a disruption lasting as much as sixty years.

Submerged Logs

In Chapter 4, we considered examples from Clayton Christensen's *The Innovator's Dilemma.* In the book, he describes the paradox in which disruptive new technologies are ignored by the big, bureaucratic companies because they're not yet profitable, no data is available for evaluation, or they don't address core needs of their biggest clients.

Christensen suggests setting up separate divisions to bring such innovations to market, thereby hedging the bigger company's market position. That makes sense if you're Eastman Kodak, whose junior engineer happened to invent digital photography, which went unnoticed by the company and destroyed its dominant position in the film market.

Christensen argues they should have paid attention, and should have started a separate division to develop digital photography into what it would eventually become. But, would that have prepared them for the next revolution, when our phones would become superb still and video cameras, ever-present in our pockets?

I don't think so. I also don't see how the taxi companies would have suddenly embraced ride sharing enabled by a phone app. They were so flat-footed, so monopolistic, I don't think they ever saw Uber and Lyft in their rearview mirrors until it was too late. They were the inflatable river raft, and Uber was the submerged log.

Christensen suggests Eastman Kodak and others as sources of insight for dealing with those submerged logs. I suggest studying the weeds' nimble response to RoundUp instead. Agricultural fields around the world are constantly under attack by weeds seeking disturbed ground. The farmers stand ready with an arsenal of tools to defend their plots, but there is concern they may be losing the battle.

If you've ever used RoundUp, you know how deadly the stuff is to plants. A quick spritz and a few minutes' wait is all it takes to turn a weed into a wilted husk. This is serious stuff.

What's fascinating is the rapid adaptation to the pesticide by a growing number of invasive weed species. Canada fleabane, whose seeds can drift hundreds of miles from the parent plant, has become immune to RoundUp in just the past ten years. Water hemp has done it in four, while neutralizing the effects of nearly three-quarters of all herbicides used in agriculture.

Weeds accomplish this feat through their process, which prioritizes responses to threats and challenges. When a threat to their existence arises, their process focuses on urgently adapting to the new situation and creating a solution.

Could Eastman Kodak still be a force in photography if they'd adapted to the submerged log of the smartphone revolution by finding a way to fit in? Perhaps the new opportunity might have been miniaturized camera components, rather than film or even digital photography.

Perhaps taxi companies could have banded together to create their own app platform, but they'd still have to deal with their awful customer service reputation. It would have been a difficult transition, but the alternative is what we see now: an irrelevant, outdated solution to a transportation opportunity served by newcomers instead.

If the weeds were in the taxi or photography businesses, they would have worked it out. They would have quickly adapted and kept on running their growth process.

How Are Weeds Resisting?

Scientists tell us the weed species are adapting to herbicidal threats by randomly mutating, then natural selection favors the useful mutations to create immunity. I would suggest adaptability is already built into their process, that the tinkering of mutations is all part of their plan to bypass threats to their survival.

It seems the weeds, in their collective intelligence, have evolved a nimble stance that always keeps them in balance, always ready to pivot to meet a challenge. Martial artists do this, too. When they move, they practice balance with every move, so they can strike in any direction at any time. I believe there is a ninja-like, ever-vigilant element in the way weeds remain adaptable to any change or threat.

Thus, adaptability becomes a critical part of any process. Adaptability is what gives our processes the ability to evolve as challenges evolve, to meet conditions as they exist, to deal with what is. Adaptability is how we deal with any possible disruption.

We witnessed weed-like adaptability, rapid evolution, and natural selection in action during the COVID-19 crisis, when lockdowns and closures put tremendous pressure on businesses around the world, while others lunged forward. When restaurants faced the total shutdown of their usual way of doing business, seating customers in crowded dining rooms and sidewalk enclosures, many went out of business. But the nimble operators quickly shifted to takeout and delivery service.

The restaurateurs who quickly pivoted were sure-footed and prepared to quickly evolve. They saw the need to connect with customers in new ways and pivoted quickly to using digital marketing to find and influence their markets. They understood the needs and concerns of their patrons and adapted faster than their competitors.

While eateries suffered tremendous disruption, companies like Peloton, Zoom, and Amazon were perfectly positioned to grow during those same lockdowns. As employees suddenly found themselves working from home, core societal shifts caused us to embrace work-from-home/study-from-home, replace gym memberships with home exercise, and shop from home. But explosive growth is also a form of disruption that, without similarly nimble adaptability, can cause businesses to quickly fail.

In 2020, Zoom's earnings shot up more than 33,000 percent, while its market valuation exceeded that of Ford, General Motors, and American and United Airlines combined, at $100 billion.[16] The service includes free and paid accounts, which along with the increased traffic, more than doubled the company's projected revenue for the year, from $910 million to $2.4 billion. But the company quickly discovered there was a downside to all their success.

Zoom suddenly became the target of hackers and suffered outages, forcing quick responses to close security holes and reinforce infrastructure. School districts that initially pulled away from the service due to occasionally salacious interruptions returned once their sessions were protected, and the service has become the world's dominant, go-to videoconferencing service.

In all cases, the companies that thrived responded to their disruptions with weed-like adaptability. No emotions involved—just deal with what is, and do it better and faster than everyone else. And keep an even, balanced stance to be prepared anytime, anywhere for any disruption.

Word from the Field

Eat Their Lunch author and recruiting entrepreneur Anthony Iannarino says, "Resourcefulness is what you want in a team." Iannarino explains that adaptability and innovation should always be instilled in the company culture. He cites the story of a technician's simple suggestion to attach screws at the back of the company's refrigerator units, which made his work much faster. "Not everybody is money-motivated," he says. "A lot of workers just want to know they're valued, trusted and recognized for their contributions."

Venture capitalist Esther Dyson says adaptation and learning are the essence of a living process. "Plants that aren't weeds are cultivated," she says. "They become what humans want them to become. But weeds adapt to their environment rather than human desire." MYOB chief sales and support officer Daniel West adds, "You have a plan, but you have to plan to change as well."

"Is adaptability reactive or proactive?" asks CSO Insights co-founder Jim Dickie. "It's both," he explains, noting that weeds see warning signs of things before they exist. "When confronted with something like RoundUp, their roots counteract the effect," he explains. "Weeds are like Aspen trees, which are all one organism. They act and benefit each other, that's how they adapt."

Dickie says the startup world is the same way, "VCs [venture capitalists] avoid areas where incumbents show a willingness to innovate and protect their turf." He wonders what would have happened if taxi companies had banded together and launched their own app technology. "If you're trying to catch up, you're already behind."

Dr. Sunnie Giles, author of *The New Science of Radical Innovation,* observes that adaptability is so important to weeds, they've evolved the ability to change their DNA. "They change their DNA to become resistant to herbicides," she says, adding, "The more change there is in the environment, the more they evolve."

Nimble founder/CEO Jon Ferrara says initial assumptions about market conditions are often wrong and adaptability is critical to meet actual needs once they're known. "We thought people would live in Nimble," he explains, "but we discovered they were living in their inbox, so we built the platform to adapt to where users work. Optimism, persistence and nimble adaptability allowed us to survive."

Meanwhile, *A Mind for Sales* author Mark Hunter notes some companies follow a contrarian approach to adaptation, opting to respond more deliberately, but with superior operational agility to their competitors. Microsoft takes this approach, often acquiring top performers in new categories and killing competition with superior operational execution. Hunter points out, "McDonald's is slow to respond to many changes, but they catch up." "They were slow on coffee, breakfast all day, health food, an app to eliminate drive-through, but they ultimately deal with what reality is and they continue to dominate."

In whatever form it takes, adaptability is how processes evolve as conditions evolve. Sometimes you're the disruptor and other times it's you being disrupted. Weed processes are tens of millions of years old, containing an unimaginable depth of wisdom, which includes the ability to adapt rapidly to new conditions. A robust process, coupled with a balanced stance and constant vigilance, fosters a critical element of nimble adaptability. It's a critical feature of their process that has allowed weeds to thrive and win for millions of years.

Weed Mindset at a Glance

1. Irrepressible Optimism

I deal with what is and focus on the things that make me win (my process). My actions lead my emotions, not the other way around.

2. Ruthless Persistence

I persevere beyond reason, because I know persistence is what determines the rate of my growth.

3. Brutal Urgency

Urgency is how I establish the superior importance—internally and externally—of my mission and my time.

4. Fearsome Aggression

Aggression is how I move quickly through my process while maintaining the element of surprise. My adversaries never realize they've lost until it's too late.

5. Nimble Adaptability

Adaptability is what enables my process to respond rapidly to emerging challenges and always allows me to win.

Points to Remember

- Adaptability is both proactive and reactive.
- Some disruptions are predictable, like periodic recessions, which can be planned for in advance.
- Other disruptions are entirely unforeseen, and require a nimble stance and constant vigilance to respond to the emerging challenge.
- The velvetleaf uses an extreme form of strategic timing, with seeds that can persist in soil for up to sixty years before germinating, allowing the species to adapt to long periods of potential disruptions.
- Weeds adapt through a process of rapid mutation and natural selection to evolve defenses to new challenges.

- During the COVID shutdowns, restaurants had to quickly pivot from inside dining to takeout and delivery modes of operation.
- Other companies, such as Zoom, Peloton, and Amazon, experienced exploding demand, which required another set of adaptive responses to deal with higher traffic and disruption.
- In all cases, only the companies that exhibited weed-like adaptability thrived.
- Venture capitalist Esther Dyson says adaptation and learning are the essence of a living process.
- *A Mind for Sales* author Mark Hunter notices some companies may respond more slowly but make up ground through superior execution.

10

ALIEN RESILIENCE

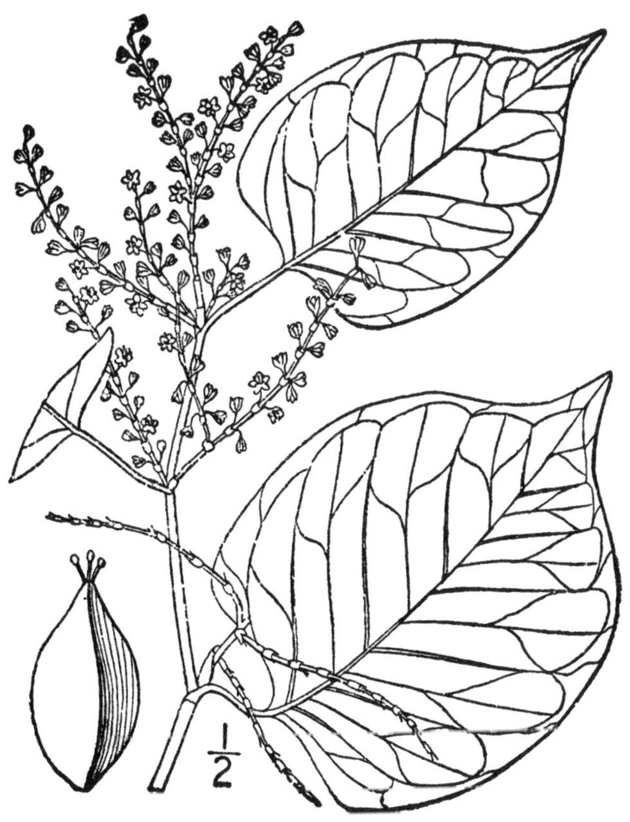

Japanese knotweed (*Reynoutria japonica*). Prized in North America and Europe in the 1890s as an ornamental plant, carefully nestled in fine gardens, Japanese knotweed soon showed its true nature as one of the world's most invasive species. It is nearly impossible to eradicate, as any loose fragment in contact with soil can sprout a new plant.[17,18] credit: © The Board of Trustees of the Royal Botanic Gardens, Kew

BACKBONE, GRIT, DETERMINATION, self-motivation, toughness, fierceness, fortitude, character, spark, tenacity, *joie de vivre.* Resilience is known by many names. In this section, we've examined several key attributes that allow weeds to dominate their space. Optimism keeps us fueled. Persistence is how we hit the gas on our process. Urgency, aggression, and adaptability help us run our process with fierce intensity.

But what makes all of that work?

Resilience is the essence of you, your spark for life, your self-belief system. It's what determines how you act and react to opportunities, setbacks, and essentially every stimulus you will ever encounter. From the moment we're born, we are in competition with every living thing for air, food, and water. And we're in competition with every living person on the planet for every dollar, every opportunity to get ahead, every increment of success in life.

Resilience is what powers our every move. It is what determines whether we prevail in life or not. It's not an action, but ultimately a choice. We choose what kind of person we are, and where we land in the competitive landscape. Ultra-competitive people possessed with enormous amounts of drive and an unswervingly positive expectation of their outcomes are the ones who rise to the top. Everyone else falls somewhere below their level.

One Very Inspiring Weed

All weeds are resilient, but the Japanese knotweed may be the toughest of them all. Originally imported in the late 1800s to North America and Europe as an ornamental addition to well-heeled gardens, the knotweed quickly showed its intentions. *Reynoutria japonica* is no delicate product of polite cultivation, it is a raging bull.

Homeowners soon discovered the knotweed's root system quickly grows out of control, reaching downward and then laterally, reaching past garden barriers, property boundaries, even circumventing roads by reaching underneath. Naturally, gardeners responded by digging up and disposing of the escaping growth, only to discover the knotweed's worst trick.

Once the plant is removed from soil, the only way to discard it is to incinerate it. If simply placed in a heap or even ground to bits, any shred that comes in contact with soil will produce a new plant. Naturally, there is no way to fully remove every root, too, so once it's present, the Japanese knotweed is there to stay.

The knotweed gives us a perfect illustration of resilience in action. The plant is programmed in its DNA to be fiercely resilient, which then defines all other attributes of its execution. It certainly is expansive and optimistic; it likes to wander and explore. It is surely persistent and aggressive. It acts with urgency and adaptability, too. But the weed doesn't decide any of this for itself. It doesn't need to. It's all programmed into its process.

A Few Human Weeds

If *Reynoutria japonica* gives a vivid example of alien resilience in the plant world, Elon Musk, Jeff Bezos, and Steve Jobs are the Japanese knotweeds of our time. Jobs gave us the Mac, iPod, iPad, iPhone, iTunes, and Pixar movies *Toy Story, Finding Nemo, Monsters, Inc.*, and more, but his path was also marked by many failed launches and setbacks. And alien resilience.

Steve Jobs co-founded Apple and was famously sacked nine years later. He then started NeXT, which made significant contributions to the personal computer platform, but never reached the pinnacle—or market—Jobs envisioned. He launched several products that were complete failures for Apple, including the Newton and earlier missteps, the Apple Lisa, Apple III, and Macintosh TV.

But we don't remember him as a failure, because Jobs produced so many well-known, world-changing successes. Jobs always learned from his failures and, as a result, came back stronger and stronger. Resilience is the key ingredient to it all. Without the will to prevail, the vision to elevate humanity with personal computing products, the belief that he was the one to bring it all to us, none of that would have happened. Jobs's resilience is what powered every step, every time he dusted himself off from his latest failure, to go further.

If Elon Musk has his way, we'll soon be a spacefaring, multi-planet-dwelling species. We'll end our dependence on oil for transportation and home energy generation, use, and storage. Already, he has upended the space launch industry, with reusable boosters and crew and cargo capsules that have substantially lowered the cost of reaching orbit. And soon, starships will transport heavy loads and passengers to far-flung cities all over Earth in a matter of minutes, or to Mars and the moon to explore for humankind.

These are big goals, and we have watched as Musk has endured failure after failure. We're all familiar with the spectacular shots of Falcon 9 boosters landing, sometimes even in a syncopated duet. But we forget the many times they didn't stick their landings, instead ending in fiery crashes. For three years, every launch ended with failed landings, but in 2015, Musk's SpaceX finally landed a booster on a terrestrial landing zone, and then a drone ship in 2016.

These represented hundreds of millions of dollars of lost equipment, but they were never viewed as setbacks. They were just a necessary part of Musk's process to get to the good stuff. Images of Falcon 9 boosters setting down with legs extended have become routine, and serve as icons for humankind's technological progress.

They also illustrate the depth of Musk's resilience. Nothing gets him down, every setback is embraced as part of his process. Nothing shakes his belief that his vision is his reality. He wills things into existence, but it's not magic. It's all due to his unshakable belief in his vision and his ability to pull it off. In his mind, Musk can do anything. And as we have seen, he's right.

Jeff Bezos has also been applying deep reserves of resilience and world-changing vision. As founder and CEO of Amazon, he completely changed the retail landscape, along with digital marketing, the worldwide supply chain, and the commercial/retail real estate market. Like Steve Jobs and Apple, Bezos started small, in his garage, with the goal of becoming the biggest bookseller in the world, 100 percent online.

It was an audacious goal, especially operating from a garage, but Bezos saw it as his inevitable reality. At the time, no one was buying anything online. The Internet was considered unsafe for credit card transactions, and the juggernaut of book sales at the time, Barnes & Noble, operated nearly a thousand stores and several sub-brands, including B. Dalton and Bookstop.

But Bezos never flinched in his belief that online sales would greatly surpass physical storefronts. From books, he graduated to virtually anything sold at retail. And from there, Amazon created a number of industry firsts that have become commonplace, including affiliate programs, one-click ordering, an entire storefront ecosystem for small businesses, and more. Amazon has literally spread like a weed, and was perhaps the biggest beneficiary of the sudden disruption to the world economy due to COVID-19.

Where once the world saw the Internet as unsafe for commerce, Amazon transformed it into the channel of choice for virtually any purchase of any retail product. Imagine the energy, stamina, and unfathomably deep belief Bezos had in his vision, his abilities, and his place in the world. He is one of the greatest examples in modern history of the power of resilience. He doesn't care if he fails. It's always an opportunity to learn and grow. If Amazon isn't failing, Bezos knows he and his team aren't trying hard enough. He knows they aren't taking enough risks to stay ahead of the pack.

Isn't it interesting that the presence of great resilience is marked by frequent failures? Resilient people never let failures define them. Instead, they see failures as chances to learn and grow. They see failures as absolutely necessary to make great gains. But always, their pursuit of new breakthroughs is powered by deep levels of commitment to their vision and self-belief.

Resilience Improv

In comedic improv, the overarching rule is you never contradict your partner. They can come up with the silliest things about you, about the moon, about anything, and you're obliged to respond in agreement and then carry the nonsense further. Each participant plays along, and, as the storyline becomes more and more ridiculous, it gets funnier and funnier.

That seems to be the rule for resilience, too, although the focus here is agreement with reality. The weeds keep reminding us to focus on what is, not what we hoped would be or felt entitled to. Whatever that reality is, resilience tells us to immediately accept it—and agree with it. Not only that, but jump immediately to "Okay, that's good. Here's why."

Think of it as "resilience improv." It's an exercise that allows us to go from setback to "That's good. Here's why" to winning at an entirely new level. The weeds would approve of this approach, because they're also reminding us to take our emotions out of any action related to growth, competing, and winning.

They would remind us, "Resilience is part of our programming, it's automatic for us. But for you, all of this is a choice." *Resilience is a choice.* Thriving no matter what happens, triumphing against all odds, embracing the inevitable positives from failures when they happen: all of that is a matter of choice. The weeds would tell us, "This is pretty simple. Choose to be resilient and move on in your process. Move on to what makes you win."

Perspectives on Resilience

Of all the attributes of the weed mindset, resilience struck a nerve, particularly with the most prominent experts, strategists, and personalities interviewed for this book. General Petraeus, General McCaffrey, Kathy Ireland, Olympic coach Terry Steiner, Henrik Fisker, tech angel investor Dan Martell, and others all lit up while examining the nature of resilience. Every one of them recognized its role—of an unnatural, unreasonable belief in their missions and drive to complete them—in their own paths to success.

It's not surprising that the two four-star generals responded immediately to the importance of resilience. As military commanders, toughness in the face of danger or even loss is what wins wars. "Bright people are commonplace, so that's not the discriminator," General McCaffrey observed. "What counts is, when tough things have to be done, can you be counted on?" He also points to a deep level of initiative as a component of resilience. "You want someone who says, 'You don't need to give me instructions, I see a need,'" he says, adding, "A lot of people just won't do that."

"Having weed-like, sheer determination is a tremendous asset as a leader," adds General Petraeus, "but we must always be realists. Things may become hard, but hard is not hopeless." Petraeus sees strategic leaders as different from operational leaders, and says their responsibility is always to get ideas right. "If you're the person where the buck stops," he says, "you've got to rewind the big ideas again and again." And that takes resilience.

Supermodel and branding entrepreneur Kathy Ireland says she's felt like a weed her whole life. "Weeds can be underestimated, resilient and strong," she says. "I relate to being a weed." Business-oriented from a young age, Kathy's sudden discovery as a model opened new possibilities, but none of her success could have happened without deep reserves of resilience.

"At one point, I was reinventing myself as a brand builder," she recalls. "I had to shed my image as an aging model and work really hard to earn the trust of my customers." Again, she drew from her reserves of resilience—and inspiration from weeds. "Weeds don't have limits, they just go," she says. Kathy says being resilient is about getting stronger and stronger, no matter what obstacles stand in the way.

Olympic U.S. women's wrestling coach Terry Steiner says resilience is a key determinant of success at the highest levels of competition. "It's that kid you kick out of the room for acting up, and then you look over and she's standing at the door, and then you look over again and she's closer to the mat. She's not giving up," he explains. "That's the kid who's going to make it." He recalls the weeds on the farm where he grew up. "They would grow in the darnedest spots, under the harshest conditions, and were always the first to pop back up," he says. "Most people aren't like that. They become distracted by obstacles."

Automotive entrepreneur Henrik Fisker has seen his share of failures, but they've always made him stronger. "If a weed gets cut down," he says, "you think it's gone. But it's not." Fisker is the same way, finding new ways to come back to the market with new ways to thrive and disrupt. "We were thinking out of the box by starting a new kind of car company, a digital car company," he says, adding, "It's like the weed finding that one crack in the concrete and being different." Resilience is clearly part of Fisker's strategy.

For tech investor and CEO coach Dan Martell, resilience is the most important factor when evaluating startups and founders. "I'm looking for founders that have had their asses kicked and turned it around," he says. "One founder swam across a great body of water to get free. That's who I'm looking for." He points out that most startups start with one concept and end up with something completely different. Through it all, the winning factor is the resilience of founders and their teams.

Aviation entrepreneur and Flying Cowboy/YouTube personality Mike Patey sees resilience—and success—as a matter of a critical tolerance for failure. "You can't be afraid of everything," he says. "You have to have the confidence to fail enough times, and eventually you'll succeed." Patey says he's constantly approached by wannabe entrepreneurs with ideas and insecurities about their chances for success. "I tell them, just get your first failure out of the way," he says, adding, "It's the ones who stop that fail." Giving up is not an option. Resilience is what keeps us going.

The Extreme Mindset of a Weed

In this section, we've examined the six traits that define the weed mindset. Weeds don't have brains, thus have no capacity for emotion or personalities. They don't have brains, but they have something just as powerful: internal programming based on their well-honed process and a guiding collective intelligence.

Weeds execute their process immediately, without question, in unison, with great ferocity. Whatever they do is done with purpose and for the good of the collective. They are an army and they're out to destroy. They are in competition with every living thing in their environment, and they're there to grow, expand, dominate, and defend their turf.

Theirs is a deadly serious mission, even if they show up in the field with pretty flowers and leafy structures lazily blowing in the breeze. They're running a process we can barely perceive, moving at great speed, to defeat everything around them.

That is the mindset of a weed. If it all sounds extreme, it's by design. The mindset of a weed is extreme by its very nature. And the weeds are imploring us to join them, if we want our businesses to truly grow like a weed. That is their purpose in sharing their code of conduct in this section. Take it seriously and use it to execute your own fierce process.

Weed Mindset at a Glance

1. Irrepressible Optimism

I deal with what is and focus on the things that make me win (my process). My actions lead my emotions, not the other way around.

2. Ruthless Persistence

I persevere beyond reason, because I know persistence is what determines the rate of my growth.

3. Brutal Urgency

Urgency is how I establish the superior importance—internally and externally—of my mission and my time.

4. Fearsome Aggression

Aggression is how I move quickly through my process while maintaining the element of surprise. My adversaries never realize they've lost until it's too late.

5. Nimble Adaptability

Adaptability is what enables my process to respond rapidly to emerging challenges and always allows me to win.

6. Alien Resilience

I am a total weed. I don't go away. I never give up. My failures don't define me, they propel me.

Points to Remember

- Resilience is the capstone of the six attributes of the weed mindset.
- Resilience governs how we react to opportunities and setbacks.
- Of all the other attributes of the weed mindset, resilience is a choice we make about our outcomes in life.
- Steve Jobs embraced failure—and resilience—as a way to learn, grow, and succeed.
- Elon Musk very publicly shows his process of testing and failing, allowing SpaceX to progress to fantastic, never-before-seen realms of space flight, reusable spacecraft, and heights of success.

- "Resilience improv" is an exercise that allows us to meet any setback with the words "That's good. Here's why . . ." to trigger our own resilience.
- General Barry McCaffrey says what counts is, when tough things have to be done, can you be counted on?
- Kathy Ireland says, "Weeds don't have limits. They just go."
- Maverick automotive entrepreneur Henrik Fisker reminds us, "If a weed gets cut down, you think it's gone. But it's not." That's resilience.
- Aviation pioneer/entrepreneur Mike Patey says, "Just get your first failure out of the way." That's resilience.

THE W.E.E.D.S. MODEL

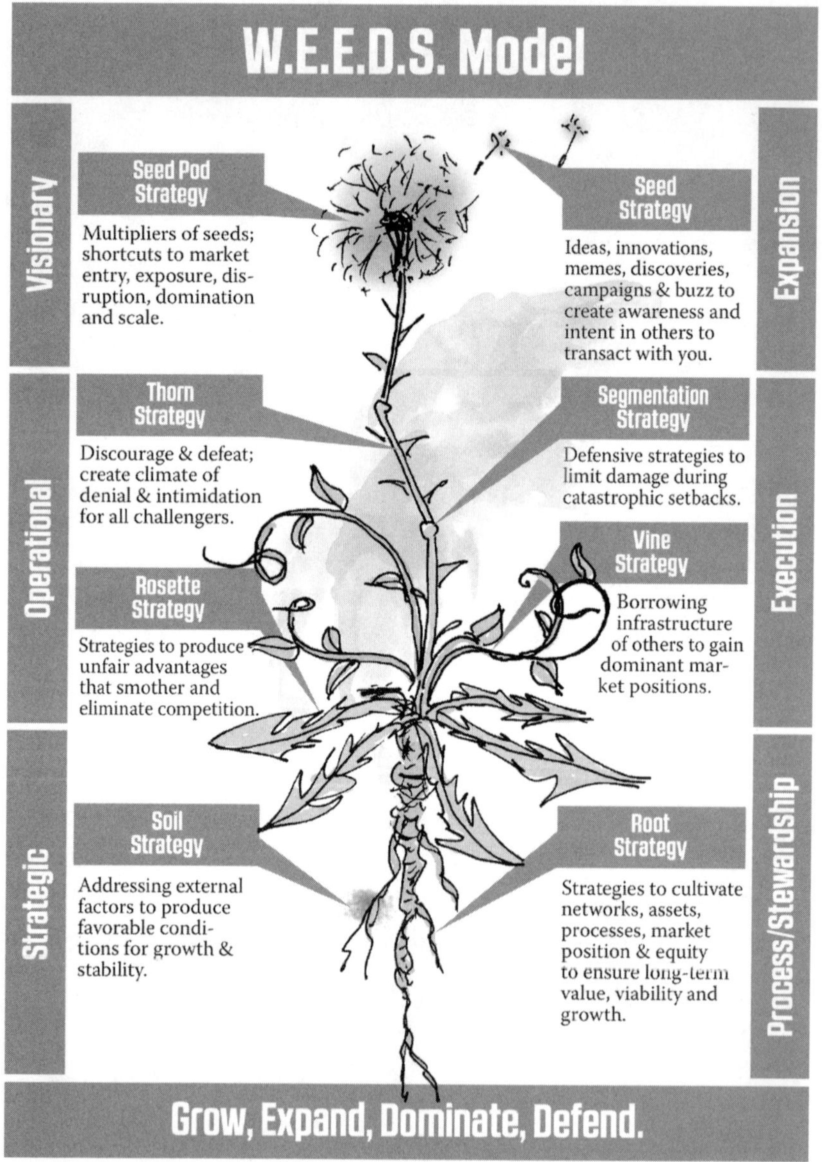

credit: © Stu Heinecke

11

SEED STRATEGY

Water hemp (*Amaranthus tuberculatus*). A supremely invasive species, water hemp has invaded farmlands across North America in recent years. Individual plants can produce as many as 4.8 million seeds, ensuring wherever it lands, *Amaranthus tuberculatus* is there to stay. credit: © The Board of Trustees of the Royal Botanic Gardens, Kew

THERE ARE PLENTY of tough, bad weeds out there, but none more extreme than water hemp. A recent unwelcome guest in farmland across North America, it has taken root with a vengeance. In just four years, *Amaranthus tuberculatus* has raced to develop full immunity to RoundUp, leaving farmers very few remaining choices for eradication. Soon, it will be immune to every herbicide available to agriculture.

Even more extreme is the plant's seed production. A single plant can release as many as 4.8 million seeds, barely a millimeter in diameter. They have no tufts to carry them airborne, but the seeds are so plentiful and tiny they get into everything, including farmers' machinery. Giant combines become one of the primary spread mechanisms, along with waterfowl, who eat and then excrete the seeds far and wide. The tiny seeds also travel in flowing water—or they stay put in the soil surrounding the plant, ensuring there is no way the water hemp will ever leave.

The plant serves as an interesting example for our study of seed strategy for our businesses. Because it is an annual, meaning each plant lives and dies in a single-year cycle, it's in a rush to produce massive growth. Rapid evolution is also a part of its plan, allowing it to circumvent farmers' herbicides and other threats.

All of this is served by the plant's massive priority on production of seed. Dandelions produce fifteen thousand seeds throughout their five- to ten-year lifecycle. We have seen them acting aggressively in our lawns, as they spread rapidly thanks to tufted, highly mobile seeds blowing everywhere on the breeze. Now imagine that multiplied by a factor of fifteen hundred to get a sense of the overwhelming cyclone of seeds water hemp unleashes to subdue all competitors and challenges.

I chose the species as the lead to this chapter for a reason: it is an example of seed strategy at its most extreme. And it demonstrates the absolute power of seeds to overwhelm markets, competitors, and any obstacles to growth.

The Salisbury Study

Sir Edward James Salisbury was a prominent British botanist during the twentieth century. The former director of the Kew Royal Botanic Garden from 1943 to 1956, Salisbury was a beloved author of books on plants in the wild and for gardening. He found all aspects of plants fascinating, but had a particular interest in their seeds.

Salisbury was also taken with naturalist Charles Darwin's fascination with weeds, noting they were an example of greatly accelerated evolution. Over a twenty-five-year period, Salisbury studied the output and nature of seeds from 249 plant species, counting and weighing seeds from half a million plants. The work became a celebrated book, *The Reproductive Capabilities of Plants,* which led to a fascinating study of the mobility of seeds and their strategic effects for certain plants.

His study involved setting up a ten-foot ladder in a stilled room, dropping various seeds, and timing their descent. The assumption was the slower the descent, the greater the range of dispersal. He found buddleia or butterfly bush (*Buddleja davidii*) seeds, outfitted with tiny helicopter-blade wings, took just five seconds to hit the floor. The seeds of common groundsel (*Senecio vulgaris*), a close relative to the dandelion, took eight seconds. Coltsfoot (*Tussilago fanfare*) seeds lofted for twenty-one seconds before hitting the floor. The rosebay willowherb (*Chamerion angustifolium*) seeds floated in the air for nearly a minute before touching ground.[19]

Some seeds are meant to travel with the wind, while others hitchhike on or within animals. Birds eat berries and seeds, excreting the intact morsel with a packet of fertilizer throughout their travels. Other seeds attach with sticky filaments or barbed burrs that entangle themselves in fur and feathers as animals pass by. Flowing water can carry seeds for miles while others disperse through explosive action.

Weeds employ ingenious methods and designs to create enormous fields of seed dispersion and rapid expansion of their domains. That is precisely what we need to do for our businesses, too.

Marketing That Spreads

Our mission now is to build a powerful process for growth—our own unique process—in which we can apply the ferocity of the weed mindset in our execution. So far, the weeds have told us to deal with what is and to allow our actions to lead our emotions. They've emphasized that, to win in the field, we must execute with audacity and resilience. And they've been pointing the way toward following our own ferocious process.

The weeds are blunt and simple in their message. And they continue that here, as we develop the first of eight levels of our process within the W.E.E.D.S. model, seed strategy. Their message:

> Spread an overwhelming amount of seeds that bring devastatingly unfair advantages to your business.

In the W.E.E.D.S. model, seeds are anything that creates awareness and intent in others to transact with us. They include products, services, brands, innovations, discoveries, memes, referrals, social and traditional media buzz, reputations, social movements, ideas, concepts, designs, word of mouth, articles, speeches, books, marketing, natural or recurring events, proposals, fascinations, stories, timing, free trials, gifts, interviews, thought leadership, experiences, market upsets, viral content, evangelism, insights, e-commerce, tracking pixels, philanthropy, relationships, sales calls, customer buzz and reviews, podcasts and blogs, names and domains, and courses.

Most of what passes as marketing and sales activity is bland and uninspiring. We see sales reps using automated connection requests and email sequences that are utterly out of touch with the humanity of the people they're trying to reach. Most advertising falls far short of inspiring any of us to take any action. It's just unwelcome background noise that brings zero value to anyone's life.

If weeds were marketers, they would be pushing us to do far, far better. They would tell us to be audacious and offer insightful value in every customer- and market-facing thing we do. They would tell us to reach levels of fascination that none of our competitors can match. That is what gets people talking and thinking and ready to act. That is what gets people excited about who you are and what you have to offer. That is what produces marketing that spreads.

Giving Our Seeds Wings

If we follow the example of weeds, what, in our world, corresponds to the wings weeds give their seeds? What adds special purpose or a more compelling nature to our stories, ideas, products, sales calls, innovations, and more? How do we avoid producing seeds that simply fall to the ground, creating no spread in our marketplace?

Think about the best stories, innovations, products, gifts, free trials, and other marketing seeds you've ever encountered. What made them stand out? Which stories or products have inspired you to bring them up in conversation? There are three critical attributes that cause people to react to marketing stimuli: audacity, fascination, and insight. If a concept, or an article, or an event contains any of the three, it gets our attention. If it contains two or three of those elements, people can't help but continually talk about it.

Fortunately, I've seen a lot of this in action. I've even written books about it and was named the father of a marketing form (contact marketing) that uses all three to great effect. Contact marketing uses micro-focused campaigns to create contact at the highest levels of the companies that can change our scale. The campaigns are certainly audacious. One involved placing a full-page ad in *The Wall Street Journal,* at a cost of $10,000, to reach Oracle founder Larry Ellison. It resulted in a $350 million sale and a 3.5 million percent ROI. Another used a $28 Facebook ad to connect with the right buyer at Walmart headquarters. It produced a $20 million result and a 69,500,000 percent ROI.

Audacity shows courage. It draws people to us. Delivering compelling and useful insight has the same effect. If people learn something just by interacting with us, we become a valuable and trusted resource, someone people are always willing to follow and engage.

Fascinations are also powerful magnets that draw people to us. In my contact campaigns, I often use my cartoons. I'm one of *The Wall Street Journal* cartoonists and have used cartoons in marketing throughout my career, so I use them well. Assuming I've hit the target with the cartoon, recipients keep them for years, perhaps the rest of their careers. Combining audacity with the cartoons, I often deliver them as giant foam boards, featuring a cartoon about the recipient and messaging on the rear panel pushing for a critically important meeting.

Others use visual metaphors. Turnaround specialist and top sales blogger Dan Waldschmidt sends thousand-dollar swords to CEOs of companies that have just missed earning estimates. The sword comes with a handwritten note explaining, "Business is war and I noticed you lost a battle recently. If you ever need a few extra hands in battle, we've got your back." So far, he's getting a 100 percent response to the campaign, generating multiple assignments worth a million dollars or more apiece.

Waldschmidt's swords generate weed-like growth by delivering on the promise of audacity, fascination, and insight. Ditto for the outreach campaigns to Ellison and Walmart. There is an irresistibility to the campaigns, but also to the people behind them. In all three cases, the marketers behind the campaigns simply could have asked for meetings, but those requests would have fallen straight to the ground. Adding wings drastically lifted the spread and effect of their seeds.

My Own Seed Strategy in Action

In the following sections, I share many examples of seed strategy in action. But let's start by examining how it's applied to the marketing of this book.

This is a book about growth strategy as inspired by weeds, but it's also a startup business. To succeed, it must quickly build a recognized brand around the world, and it is in a critical race to generate sales. And like any business using weed strategy to grow, it has some pretty fascinating, unfair advantages built in.

The first of those is the weeds themselves. Weeds are despised around the world, but also admired for their capacity to spread and grow. I believe this casts weeds as the reluctant hero, the archetype that drives many stories. We are programmed to react to characters who start in a tough spot but ultimately triumph. Weeds have that part nailed.

Because of its theme, the early spring release date is significant, timed to coincide with the release of weeds themselves, all over the Northern Hemisphere. The idea is to have all of the weeds in the world act as memes for the book. I want people to notice weeds showing up in their yards and suddenly realize, "Oh yeah, but there's that book . . ." And if that works, I hope to see it renew every year, like Christmas music, suddenly popular again when the right time of year arrives.

It's audacious and ties to our fascination with how weeds grow and spread. And it offers obvious insight and value, because we all want our businesses to grow like weeds.

As we move through the W.E.E.D.S. model in this section, I will explain more about how weed strategy has been applied to the book. But now, let's take a look at how others have given their seeds wings, and applied utterly unfair advantages to their customer/market-facing activities.

Stories: The Ultimate Seeds

The movie industry thrives by telling stories, but really, all businesses blossom by telling their stories, too. And the more their stories read like a Hollywood blockbuster, the more likely we are to engage. Most screenplays start with an unlikely hero setting out on a perilous journey to achieve an impossible goal. Setbacks ensue, and the goal seems even more out of reach. But in the end, conflicts resolve and the hero is redeemed as the goal is achieved.

Can you think of any stories like this in business? Elon Musk immediately comes to mind. Tesla singlehandedly changed the auto industry, showing electric propulsion can work in our lives. And suddenly upstart Tesla became the most valuable car company in the world.

Then SpaceX set out to revolutionize the space launch industry, with reusable boosters that, for the first time ever, return from space, making pinpoint propulsive landings. The hero triumphs once again, greatly reducing the cost of space launches, while beating insurmountable odds from giant competitors Boeing, Northrop, and Roscosmos.

Now Musk has us enthralled with his latest venture, to make humankind a multi-planet species with a new kind of reusable spaceship. If it works, Starship will also revolutionize Earthbound travel with short hops into space, reducing flight times from Los Angeles to London to twenty minutes.

As a seed strategy, Musk's stories are miraculous—and a truly unfair advantage in his marketplace. Consider his competitor for space crew launches, Russian state space agency Roscosmos. Agency director Dmitry Rogozin, clearly smarting from his vanquished status as launch provider to NASA, boasted of the successful recovery of a portion of a Soyuz booster in the remote, frigid tundra of the Yakutia region. "I wonder if gentle SpaceX is able to work in such conditions," he taunted.[20]

But what Rogozin didn't realize, while the rest of the planet surely did, was that SpaceX was already making boosters that land wherever needed, ready to be tanked up and used again. Rogozin only succeeded in giving a boost to Musk's already compelling story. The impressions created by these stories are billions of seeds, floating all over the world. As a result, we're all aware of Elon Musk, his companies, and his dreams for the world. And they create a totally unfair market advantage for all he does.

"Tesla gives ordinary people a chance to become part of Elon's story," says sales thought leader Alice Heiman. "His story creates unbeatable brand loyalty." Growth strategist Stephan Annema agrees, "Saving the planet, traveling into space, Elon gets the entire world population aligned with his goals." The power of a good story that gets people inspired and keeps them talking is truly one of the great unfair advantages in business.

If you have a compelling story, how can you get it out to the world? And how can you give your story wings so that people constantly talk about it with others? The weeds would tell us to make sure it has the proper seed elements, by making it easily passed along. Consult a story expert, organize it, tighten it up. Learn how to tell it. Then use social media and hire a publicist to get the story into mainstream consciousness.

Seed Strategy Tip: Infographics are a great way to give your story an unfair advantage, by putting it in a form that is easily shared in articles and social media. I am using an infographic to spread seeds as part of the growth strategy for this book. Imagine how compelling Elon Musk's stories would be as infographics, and how much they'd be passed around. If you have a story worth telling, this should be part of your seed strategy.

Names Are Seeds

Branding experts have always known giving something a name gives it life, dimension, and personality. If sufficiently clever, a name gives its subject an undeniably unfair advantage in the field. Naming applies to companies, products, services, initiatives, proposals, movements, missions, employee titles, menu items, and essentially anything that can come up in conversation. Giving it a compelling name makes it important, memorable, remarkable.

Alexandra Watkins is president of naming agency Eat My Words and the author of *Hello, My Name is Awesome.* Naturally, she has some thoughts on what makes a good name, and how it can bring unfair advantages to your seed strategy. "A good name is disruptive," she says, adding, "It can cause the impetus for a sale to spread throughout a company."

It's difficult to track the ROI from naming, but Watkins points to a recent assignment for a Manhattan hotel's wedding catering department. They wanted more exciting names to compete with some of the hipper hotels nearby. Watkins went to work on their services menu, and suddenly the rehearsal dinner was renamed "Meet the Parents," the post-reception bar rental became "Last Call for Alcohol," and the coed wedding shower "Shower Together." The new names caused sales to shoot up 25 percent.

Naming can infuse objects with fascination, insight, and intrigue, just as companies can be transformed with the right name. Consider these examples: Google was originally called "Backrub," Pepsi started as "Brad's Drink," and Nike was once "Blue Ribbon Sports."[21] While the names Google, Pepsi, and Nike don't tell you what the companies do, they're distinctive, easy to remember, and more likely to pop up in conversation.

Just as names can steer fortunes, domain names can as well. When Nova Scotia–based Outshine president Andrew Breen started his company, the best domain name he could find was *outshineonline.com.* Working under that domain, it became apparent the name was creating the wrong impression. "We were working with advertising agencies," he explains, "and it was clear our domain name had no star power. It didn't sound professional."

Breen discovered *outshine.ca* was available at an asking price of $20,000. After negotiation, he paid $2,000, eliminating the troublesome "online" portion of the company's Internet address. But the ".ca" designation still limited the company's perceived scope to Canada. It was still seen as a local player, not an international powerhouse. Finally, he broke through to the owner of *outshine.com,* after years of outreach, and they reached a deal.

"Immediately, we saw the new domain helping," Breen says, and adds, "People look at things like domain names as a way to determine the value of your services." He paid $20,000 for the domain, but says it's been worth every penny. "With top-tier advertising clients in San Francisco and New York, you have to seem like you belong," he says.

Names can work internally, too. Watkins recalls Make-a-Wish Foundation asking its employees to create their own titles. "They became happier and more satisfied with their jobs," she says, "and they talked more about what they do."

Still, there are many ways to fail with names that conjure unintended meanings. Who can forget stories like the time Rolls-Royce was ready to launch a new model with the name "Silver Mist"? They quickly discovered the word *mist,* in German, is slang for manure. They avoided rolling out the new Rolls-Royce Silver Shit in the nick of time.

The same unintended consequence befell Chevrolet's "Nova" when released in Puerto Rico. In Spanish, the name translated to "no go," which is not a good name for a car in any language. Ditto for the Ford Fiera and Pinto, which failed in Brazil, saddled with names that translated to "ugly old woman" and "tiny penis" in Portuguese. Whether or not translation to a foreign language is a factor, all names carry the potential for unintended meanings.

Seed Strategy Tip: Use a naming agency to assist with creating monikers that become truly unfair advantages. They'll help steer your search away from unintended meanings and potential trademark issues and toward acquisition of the best domain names. Or, for a quick infusion of ideas, try using name-generator sites such as Shopify's Business Name Generator, Wordlab's Business Name Generator, or GoDaddy's Business Name Generator.

Branding as a Seed Strategy

The best brands are a promise between companies and their customers. They are a beacon of trust in a crowded marketplace, drawing new and repeat customers with products and services that work as advertised. Brands are also a conversation between companies and their markets. Brands like Four Seasons Hotels or Cartier communicate values of luxury and exclusivity. Costco, Walmart, and Amazon are brands that promise enormous selection at best-possible prices.

Brand Intervention author David Brier says an effective brand is one that captures the disruptive spirit of a company. "The best brands are synonymous with resiliency and ingenuity," he says, and adds, "They communicate that you're alert to opportunities, and always connecting dots that others miss." In this way, brands humanize companies, giving them distinct personalities people relate to and want to interact with. "They give life to the potential of what can grow," Brier says, pointing to an aspirational dimension of branding. A good brand shows us who we can become, motivating people to talk and act on our behalf.

Thus, our brands are a necessary part of our seed strategy. So how do we build a world-beating brand? Former supermodel and branding authority Kathy Ireland says, "It's a building process that takes time and dedication, but there's no product on the planet that wouldn't be enhanced with the power of great branding."

Ireland recalls starting her branding company in her kitchen after realizing she didn't simply want to fade out as an aging supermodel. Today, kathy ireland Worldwide (kiWW) is a multi-billion-dollar branding empire that multiplies the scale of products for "All things home," including lighting, home office furnishings, home decor, and, now, affordable housing developments. But she didn't get there right away. "We started with a single pair of socks as our first product," she recalls. "We were building from the ground up, with a desire to create something of quality that would go on long beyond our lifetimes."

Ireland's focus on quality is a foundational element of her branding signature, but her true passion is service to the world, all of which stands out to her market. Kathy is a person of integrity, passion, and drive, but also humility, caring, and philanthropy. She creates an irresistible presence in the business world, and consumers respond. Her brand, applied to her collection of products, becomes the unfair advantage the weeds advocate.

There is also an element of layering that cultivates unfair advantage. Millions of us know Kathy Ireland as a glamorous figure from the world of modeling and fashion. Her personal and product branding are boosted by her story and household name. These seed elements don't occur in a vacuum. There are usually several elements working together, and the more layers there are, the greater the unfair advantage. In the world of branding, Kathy Ireland certainly has insurmountable advantages her competitors won't easily match.

We don't have to be former supermodels for layering to work for the rest of us. From the earlier sections in this chapter, take inventory of your story, both personally and for your company. Work with a consultant to give it structure and polish. Layer it with a compelling name that says the right things to your audience. And write out the tenets of your belief structure. Together, these become your promise to your marketplace, their reason to trust and engage and find you and your company utterly fascinating. That's what gets them talking and what builds an unfair advantage into your entire seed strategy.

Seed Strategy Tip: Without periodic renewal, brands become stale. They're meant to be reinvented. Delta Airlines, McDonald's, Uber, Mastercard, United Airlines, and many other major brands are constantly updating and, at times, reinventing. We can do it too, adding a perfect opportunity to reintroduce your company, its story, and new innovations to your market. Do it yourself or hire an agency that specializes in rebrands.

Designs and Innovations as Seeds

Great design can build empires. Ferrari and Lamborghini automobiles are beloved for their sleek beauty, penned by designers such as Sergio Pininfarina, Sergio Scaglietti, and Marcello Gandini. As seeds, nothing can beat the viral passalong images their creations inspire. If you're interested in cars at all, the names Countach, Daytona, Testarossa, and Dino inspire daydreams and fantasies. Perhaps one of these even resides in your garage.

Henrik Fisker knows the power of great design well. He penned the lines of three modern classics—the Aston Martin DB9 and V8 Vantage and BMW Z8—and was recently named one of the ten greatest car designers in automotive history.[22] He is also one of the great modern automotive entrepreneurs, having founded, then losing, Fisker Automotive to the great recession, then resurrecting his company as Fisker, Inc. The latter is the world's first digital car company, in which all production assets are digitized, enabling his cars to be built anywhere in the world by subcontractors.

"Design can make us happy, make us smile," he explains. "It can cause you to like something without knowing what it is or how it works." Fisker masterfully uses design to draw us in, to make us curious about his products and create the desire to buy into his story. Design creates a dream that everybody can buy into. As photos of the designs propagate across the Internet, they can generate billions of viral impressions that act as seeds within a seed strategy.

No one knows the value of great design better than Apple. The world's first trillion-dollar company built its empire on sleek designs and simplified interfaces that seem to drop into our laps, straight out of the future. iPhones, iPods, iPads, and Macs define the high end of each product category. The build quality and engineering are excellent, but it is their design that has us tracking every rumor and lining up to purchase copies of each new iteration of the devices.

Apple's former head of design, Jony Ive, explains, "Apple's goal isn't to make money. Our goal is to design and develop and bring to market good products." The design and quality of the product causes the market to respond. The money follows the design. "When something exceeds your ability to understand how it works," he says, "it sort of becomes magical."[23]

The same can be said for innovations: batteries that power cars for thousands of miles on a single charge. Flying cars. Elon Musk's Starships. New developments that will soon bring the future to hand are always fascinating. As seed strategy elements, they're irresistible

Seed Strategy Tip: Design can take physical form, as in a new product, but it should also be infused throughout your seed strategy. It should apply to all external communications, websites, and social media posts. The unified impression it will make will be worth the investment, as good design communicates competence in everything you do. Make good design part of your business philosophy and an unfair advantage in your seed strategy.

Business Cards as Highly Mobile Seeds

For many, the concept of the business card is dead. In my own recent survey on LinkedIn, half of respondents said they don't use business cards. Instead, they trade phones and type in their contact details or connect on LinkedIn. Whether they use cards or not, they're all missing out on important opportunities to create marketing impressions that spread like weeds.

If someone types their name and details into someone else's address book app, their identity and information are likely to be lost. Who was that again? It all disappears into a fog of perhaps thousands of other entries. When we connect on LinkedIn, there is nothing memorable about the action, thus nothing remembered about each new contact. Even when we do hand out cards, we're using a dead-end strategy. Cards end up in drawers or the trash, so in all cases no connection is made. And a potentially valuable opportunity is forever lost.

If weeds used cards, there would be some sort of unfair advantage involved. Card companies are convinced the solution is to add foil stamping, embossing, and exotic paper stocks, but they're just producing fancy junk. The cards still go into a box or the trash, never to be seen again. The weeds would tell us to start over.

Google "coolest business cards in the world," and you'll find some truly amazing bits of creativity. There's Kevin Mitnick's card, a chemically etched piece of stainless steel, with an inset of locksmithing tools for picking locks. Mitnick is one of the top IT security consultants in the world, so the lock-picking tools are a clever visual metaphor for the problem he helps clients fix: he prevents hackers from breaking in. There's even a video on Mitnik's site, showing someone using the tools to actually pick a lock. They're legit.

Mitnick's card is almost something else, something I called a "Pocket Campaign" in my earlier book *Get the Meeting*. A pocket campaign looks like a business card, but it's quite different. It starts with an item of fascination. Mitnick's card certainly fits that description. When he keynotes at conferences, audience members climb over each other to get one of his cards.

The tool set adds something regular business cards never match; they have a real purpose. They actually *do* something. Naturally, people want to see them in action, which draws recipients to the video page on Mitnick's site. A true pocket campaign would take it two steps further: set tracking pixels from the video page and run a retargeting campaign.

Thus, the effect of handing out a card is suddenly seeing Mitnick's presence all over the Web.

The components of a pocket campaign are the device (visual metaphor, tool, etc.), a jump offer (go here and see a video to learn how to use the device), a jump page (hosting the video and setting tracking pixels), and an automated persistence campaign (retargeting ads follow recipients around the Web). Suddenly, those lost connections and opportunities from chance meetings become fully optimized, with no contact ever lost to meaningless social media friend requests or foggy recollections of who just typed their details into our phones.

Sometimes pocket campaigns can produce results with just the initial device alone. Paul Nielsen's pocket campaign did just that, with a set of "business cards" printed on a stretchy rubber sheet. The cards were printed with his name and details, but first placed on a jig and applied while the cards were stretched. Once the ink cured, the cards were removed and returned to their original shape, squeezing the printed details together. In order to read the card, a recipient would have to pull each end to stretch it.

When Nielsen hands out the cards, out comes the floppy piece of rubber. Recipients give it a stretch, then discover Nielsen is a fitness trainer. And guess what? He already has you exercising! Recipients become so excited they show the cards off at work and to friends. Every time someone stretches the card, it recruits more clients for Nielsen. On average, every card handed out produces three new clients.

If weeds had cards, they'd surely use pocket campaigns. They'd probably be printed on rubber, too. As we know, weeds don't do anything without an unfair advantage.

Seed Strategy Tip: I devote an entire chapter to pocket campaigns in my earlier book *Get the Meeting.* Find suggestions for devices and how to produce your own pocket campaign in Chapter 9.

Movements as Seeds

Comic-Con founder Gareb Shamus understands the power of creating international movements. In fact, you might say it's his superpower.

Growing up with a fascination for comic book heroes, Shamus was consumed with taking on superpowers of his own. “I was basically a nerd,” he recalls, “but later in life, I discovered my superpower was to help nerds become cool.” Thus began his quest to help the downtrodden find their own true purpose in life. His quest was to help others discover their own superpowers.

Shamus's passion soon became a business, publishing his first magazine about comics while in college. It grew quickly, achieving a high rate of passalong. Several factors powered the growth. Shamus touched a nerve with many others who, like him, loved comic books and superheroes, and felt like outcasts. They, too, longed for the superpowers they saw in the books. The shared experiences and emotions, and the desire for acceptance, produced a seismic response from a worldwide audience ready for change.

The viral passalong of his magazines was also fueling growth. Remember, the point of seed strategy is to produce multitudes of seeds that produce unfair advantages in the field. The most effective forms of seeds are highly mobile, with superpowers of their own to get people talking about us. Shamus's readers were doing the work for him, growing the magazine by sharing it with friends. That creates collective scale.

From the magazine sprang the Comic-Con events known around the world today. It started with a struggling comic book convention, which Shamus purchased. The magazine provided the cash, but it also attracted a rapidly growing movement. Now his readers had a focal point, a safe place to meet up and be themselves.

Today, many of the highest-grossing films are based on comic books, which opened a new opportunity for growth for Shamus. “I always include celebrities at our events,” he explains. “At first the actors didn't want to be too deeply associated with their roles, but they realized we gave them a way to promote their films.” Celebrity tie-ins create a multiplier effect for Shamus's seed strategy, drawing greater press attention and spreading the seeds to their enormous social followings. This multiplier effect is what we'll cover in the next chapter on seed pod strategy.

Movements are a powerful seed strategy, but where do they come from? The comic book/superpower movement ignited by Shamus tapped into a social need experienced by millions of people around the world, but also a burgeoning celebrity culture.

To start your own movement, focus on how you can change people's lives. What are the insights behind what you do? How do they tie to the larger world around you? How can you empower others to be more effective, more successful, more fulfilled?

Seed Strategy Tip: As you define your own movement, give thought to whom you can draw in as partners, sponsors, and seed spreaders. Are there companies that might benefit from an association with your movement? Would anyone pay for sponsorship to be involved? Can you recruit celebrities and social media influencers to amplify your cause? Movements that inspire passion can last a long time and open many new opportunities for growth.

Trust, Reputation, and Positioning as Seeds

Trust and reputation are the anchor points of social interaction. They define who we are to others and determine our success, socially and, of course, in business. If we've earned trust—if we've built a solid reputation—people want to work with us. They recommend us to others. Trust and reputation spread like seeds on the wind.

Michael Roderick is a CEO and Broadway producer, but by reputation he is a super-connector. He says reputation and positioning start with trust. "Trust is accelerated instantly if you do things," he explains, "just by doing what you say you're going to do, and by doing it quickly." His comment echoes the weeds' emphasis on urgency in this book. Urgency creates importance, results, and trust.

Roderick feels our reputations—what we're known for—are our most critical asset in business. It's what creates ever-increasing awareness of who we are and what we do, but also whether or not people will engage with us. Reputation, then, becomes the foundation of all seed strategy.

Ideally, Roderick says our reputations are multilayered, which, again, fits with the nature of the W.E.E.D.S. model. There is great overlap between the eight levels of strategy. The more they overlap, the more purposes they serve toward our growth. "What are you known for?" is the key question

Roderick sees in the cultivation of a strong reputation. "Vin Diesel is known just for action movies," he explains, "but the Rock is known through wrestling, acting, movies, and television. He's in more parts of your brain."

Roderick uses a fascinating tactic to network and raise his profile on the Broadway scene. He regularly hosts live panel discussions on various topics of importance to the community. The onstage panel is a handful of legendary producers with Roderick as the moderator. In the audience are many more producers and useful contacts. He says being seen on stage with the legends of the business has repositioned him as someone who belongs with the best. That, in turn, opens many unforeseen opportunities for his business.

Seed Strategy Tip: Use Michael Roderick's question "What are you known for?" to define the components of your reputation. Get unfiltered feedback from clients and those in your target market to check alignment. Then go about building the reputation you want. Key point: The more layered your reputation, the more compelling and unique it becomes.

What Is Your Seed Strategy?

This chapter could continue indefinitely and still not capture the full palette of possibilities for creating awareness and intent. I have focused on earned rather than paid sources, because organic growth is how weeds grow and conquer new ground. A seed strategy based on guerrilla tactics becomes self-sustaining and relentless.

But even in the world of mega-budget marketing, the principles are the same. Every seed should be equipped with unfair advantages, and every activity should be focused on delivering extraordinary value and fascination that gets people talking about your company's goals, movements, aspirations, concepts, designs, and brand. It should compel people to participate in your story, by becoming clients, followers, referral sources, and evangelists. Paid or not, our seed strategies should always be focused on marketing that spreads.

As we move through the eight levels of the W.E.E.D.S. model, you'll see how they overlap, but also how easily they disrupt our focus. Each is compelling enough to be a primary go-to-market strategy for any business, but don't allow yourself to be drawn to just one or two. The most effective growth process includes all eight levels, in perfect balance.

Let's start that new process by brainstorming your new seed strategy. How will you create unique expressions to your market, drawing more and more people into your story, your brand, your offerings? Take time now to record initial thoughts for your seed strategy, then move on to seed pod strategy.

What Is My Seed Strategy?

- What are my uniquely unfair advantages for gaining awareness in my marketplace?
- Is my story well-honed and ready to tell, by any member of my team?
- Are my company and its products well-named, or can they be improved with professional help?
- Does my brand dominate my market? If not, how can I rebrand to take that top position?
- Are my proposals set up for rapid response and viral pass-along? Is my process a one-time shot or an ongoing campaign to win business?
- Are my designs and innovations used as seeds? Should they be?
- Are my business cards stale and inert, or are they dynamic campaigns to create ongoing engagement?
- Am I able to create an international movement based on my approach to my market?
- Is my company trusted in our marketplace? What is our reputation? How can we improve it?
- What else can we do to release millions of highly mobile seeds into our marketplace?

W.E.E.D.S. Model at a Glance

1. Seed Strategy

Spread an overwhelming amount of seeds that bring devastatingly unfair advantages to your business.

Points to Remember

- In the W.E.E.D.S. model, seed strategy is analogous to anything that causes people to become aware of and form the intent to transact with us in some way.
- The essence of seed strategy: Spread an overwhelming amount of seeds that bring devastatingly unfair advantages to our enterprises.
- We should give our seeds wings—unfair advantages to spread our marketing message—to maximize our reach in our markets.
- Our personal and company stories can act as powerful seeds in the field.
- Names act as powerful seeds, giving ideas, products, services, and companies greater life and visibility in the marketplace.
- Our brands are our promise to our customers, present and future, for a better life.
- Designs and innovations are seeds that capture our attention and keep us focused on their originators.
- Movements are powerful seeds that can create a deep sense of engagement and loyalty toward our companies, all over the world.
- Trust, reputation, and positioning are force multipliers in the marketplace.

12

SEED POD STRATEGY

Shotweed (*Cardamine hirsuta*). A member of the mustard family, *Cardamine hirsuta*, or shotweed, is known for its peculiar method of seed dispersal. As its seed pods dry and stiffen in late summer, they become spring-loaded, scattering seeds at the gardener's slightest touch or the brush of wind. Shotweeds are unusually aggressive in their growth cycles, which occur throughout the year.[24] credit: © The Board of Trustees of the Royal Botanic Gardens, Kew

SHOTWEED, SPITWEED, POP-IN-THE-EYE weed, wild cress, hairy bittercress, western bittercress, little bittercress, popits, jumping Jesus, bombarding bittercress—*Cardamine hirsuta* is known by many names. It's probably known by so many names because of the impression it makes when spreading its seeds.

Cardamine hirsuta has devised an utterly fascinating mechanism to ensure its propagation. Its seeds are formed in a pea-pod-like fruit in an orderly, single-file line. Sealed with spring-loaded lids that open from the bottom and suddenly, explosively, curl upward, the pods scatter seeds up to fifteen feet away. The maddening thing is, the seed pods pop open at the slightest provocation. For the gardener, pulling the weed means planting dozens more with every pop.

We know weeds never do anything without involving some sort of unfair advantage. As discussed in the previous chapter, they equip their seeds with fluffy wings to ride the wind, and burrs and adhesives to stick to fur and feathers, or they encase their seeds within berries that hitchhike on long rides with birds and animals in their digestive tracts. Some seeds fall straight to the ground but are designed to be carried by water or machinery or whatever happens by.

But the most clever weeds also give their offspring a forceful launch. We're familiar with the dandelion's fluffy geodesic spheres that so effectively loft their seeds into the wind. Thistle and others do the same. The rosebay willowherb, whose seed floated for nearly a minute in the stilled air of Sir Edward James Salisbury's experiment, produces a long, perfectly deployed web to send its seeds skyward.

We can see that seed pods are a critical part of the weeds' strategy to outcompete other plants for turf, by spreading their seeds further. The formula is to produce seeds that are highly mobile and give them the best launch possible.

Legacy Media as Seed Pods

When we think of gaining leverage for our marketing message, legacy media are an obvious choice. While not as powerful as they once were, the world's top magazines, newspapers, broadcast media, and industry publications are still potent platforms to send our seeds skyward.

When my cartoons appear in *The Wall Street Journal,* they reach an audience of 2.1 million readers. Because I am a contributor, I have the opportunity to repeat that exposure over and over. And because my cartoons appear in *The Journal,* I'm not just a cartoonist, but a *Wall Street Journal cartoonist.* It creates an enormous advantage for the other things I do.

Becoming a regular contributor to *The Wall Street Journal,* or *Inc., Fast Company, Forbes,* and the *Harvard Business Review* is not easy. But if you have specific expertise or unusual experiences, you may qualify. These and other news outlets constantly use outside experts for perspective pieces, or as quoted sources.

The challenge with legacy media has always been gaining access. You either pay for it or earn it. If you have the budget to hire a publicist or run an advertising campaign, you're already in an advantageous position. But that's not the focus of this book. For the weeds, using paid media would be like paying a crop duster to spread their seeds. Their focus is always on organic methods that can be counted on consistently, forever, without cost and without fail. That is our focus here, too.

To gain the attention of editors, you'll need to mount an outreach campaign. These will be different from the contact campaigns I've written about in my earlier books, *How to Get a Meeting with Anyone* and *Get the Meeting.* There, we use often outlandish methods and devices for breaking through: swords, giant cartoon boards, live pigeons, and more. Editors are likely to see those as desperation, not worth considering.

I will be engaging legacy media as part of my seed pod strategy for this book. I'll start with the message "Everybody knows what it means to grow like a weed, but how does that apply to our businesses?" The contact piece will be a basic, short copy letter, but with a few twists. Attached to the letter, a classic nursery seed pack, filled with dandelion seeds, will serve as a visual metaphor, offering a live demonstration of weeds at work.

The letter will be written on plantable paper, so if they want, editors can plant it in soil and grow wildflowers. The outer mailer will be made with corrugated cardboard and printed with antique botanical illustrations like those featured at the head of each chapter in this book.

I'm not suggesting you use these components. They're directly suited to my mission of spreading marketing seeds about this book. But you can easily use all sorts of visual metaphors, jewel boxing, video, and more to convey the value of your proposed content in a compelling way. If you want help with this kind of campaign, I suggest reading my books or joining our online course.

Your outreach to editors should not include a pitch for a feature article on your company. Your positioning should be strictly as an expert source of compelling and relevant insight. The outcomes you seek are to become either a regular contributor of articles, or an ongoing source for expert commentary and quotes. If there is the slightest hint you're instead seeking publicity, your outreach goes into another pile, the one that gets emptied into the dumpster out back.

There are a couple of shortcuts as well. Subscribe to the HARO (Help a Reporter Out) newsletter, which publishes requests from reporters for quotes, commentary, and interviews, often from large news outlets. And if you seek publicity, try submitting a news release to *newswire.com, ereleases.com,* or *PR.com.* Although there is never a guarantee any news sources will pick up the story, they are worth a try.

Seed Pod Strategy Tip: Everyone's sending press releases and hiring publicists to connect with legacy media. Instead, try sending a twelve-words-or-fewer statement via email or social media, and ask if it would be of interest. Consider those twelve words carefully, so it actually is of interest. Don't have their contact details? Check articles, mastheads, Nimble, Seamless.ai, or RocketReach.

Seed Pods and Podcasts

Podcasts are a natural way to amplify the reach of our seed strategy. We can either host our own or jump on countless others for guest interviews. Both can grow your social network and keep people tuned into your seed strategy indefinitely.

Investor and podcast host Jay Kim explains, "My podcast is my seed pod. If I need a favor, if I'm starting a relationship, it builds goodwill." Kim says offering a chance to tell their story gives him open access to anyone or anything he needs. "Your network is your net worth, " he says, adding, "If you need a favor, you get to stack the odds."

I have also written about podcasts as contact campaigns, something I have experienced firsthand. The interview process creates camaraderie. After spending an hour together, you feel like you know each other. Hosts often talk of a "golden hour" at the conclusion of the interview. The interviewee is excited, there is a bond, and, as their host, you can ask virtually anything. "If I wanted to call on the right person for what I do, who would I call? Can you introduce us? Do you know so and so? Can you make an introduction?" The answer is almost always yes.

When my most recent book launched, I was interviewed on podcasts nearly every day for months. Guesting on other people's podcasts generates valuable exposure to their networks. Audience size will vary, but the appeal of podcasts isn't sheer numbers. It's who is in the audience. The shows tend to attract specific groups of people who are interested in the subject or followers of the host. They tend to be far more concentrated and responsive than mass-media audiences.

The nature and format of podcasts is changing rapidly, so be prepared. Some are audio, others video, some are recorded, others are livecast. Your signal quality is critical, so invest in a good mic, lighting, and camera. Set up a corner of a room in your home or office where you can build an interesting background. Bookshelves make great backdrops, as you can arrange all sorts of elements, including books, products, samples, and photos.

As a guest, be ready with a quick link, no more than two, where audience members can connect with you. Typically, that's your primary website and a social media account. First-timers often make the mistake of giving too many ways to connect. That creates audience overload and kills response.

You should also have a gift to offer at the end of the show. A PDF summary with links mentioned during the show, an ebook, or an infographic works well. I often offer a sneak peek into one of my books. The object is always to get interested members to sign up for your email list. That's how you'll fulfill the gift, but also how you'll grow your list for further offerings.

Finally, when guesting on someone else's show, be prepared to promote it to your audience, too. The host is exposing you and your story to their audience, and reciprocity is expected. At the very least, participate in their posts about the upcoming show with likes, comments, and responses to others' comments.

Seed Pod Strategy Tip: Some podcasters are easy to connect with, others are not. Try sending a coffee mug decorated with their show card or podcast logo, with a two-sentence note about why you'd be a great guest. Ask to have a cup of coffee together on Zoom to get to know each other.

Influencers as Seed Pods

Podcast hosts are a subset of a larger group, social media influencers. Former Hershey's CMO Peter Horst says influencers and micro-influencers can be powerful multipliers of seed strategy. "Touch one influencer," he says, "and that radiates out to 28,000 touches."

Horst prefers working with micro-influencers whose reach is one hundred thousand to a million followers. "Their followers are much more engaged," he explains, "and they will click, follow, and buy with more rapt attention than the mega-influencer." He warns that influencers are also easily offended, but if you're on their good side, micro-influencers especially will allow you to get reach with far more relevance.

So how do you get their attention? That can be tough, but start with a meaningful partnership to offer. This requires research. Find out what the influencers are saying, what makes them excited, and, most of all, what they're selling. If you can help move their products to your audience, they're more apt to respond.

Horst says when working with influencers, you'll be expected to have digital assets for their feeds. Compelling videos, PDF booklets, and landing pages are all part of the mix. Horst reminds us to place social media links on everything. The point is to borrow the influencer's reach and influence, but also to grow your own following and email contact list.

Seed Pod Strategy Tip: Influencers love to have their egos stroked. Send something that compliments them in an off-handed or clever way. (Check out this video of one of my contact devices being opened by an influencer's assistant: *https://vimeo.com/461937868.*)

Social Media's Fickle Reach and Amplification

So much is written about social media, about the insulting barbs exchanged, but also astonishing kindness and insights. Social media encompasses all of humanity—every thought it has, all of its debauchery and hate, and its kindness and wisdom. Is it a place to magnify your seed strategies? Well, maybe.

There is no doubt social media is a forum for connecting with potential clients, collaborators, and inspiring folks. But it can also be an addicting time suck. And the rules seem to be constantly shifting. Amplification pods are an illustrative example. They popped up a few years ago, as a neat trick to get LinkedIn to promote posts. Based on the assumption ten or more comments in the first hour would trigger the algorithm, pod members agree to drop comments quickly to kickstart each other's posts.

Initially, the pods worked well. My posts would regularly generate 5,000 to 25,000 views, with one topping 200,000. Then everyone else started using the same tactic. I was inducted into a dozen groups myself, each requiring every member to immediately read other members' posts. Most of the posts would take a minute or so to read, but a lot of them included videos or links to articles.

It quickly became an unsustainable time-sink, but it got worse. Every time a post was boosted by the group, the same monotonous responses would show up, always from the same people. "Great post," "Boom," and "Spot on" from each pod member on every post is not engagement. It's a waste of everybody's time, while your real network withers.

There are many books written about profiting from social media, especially LinkedIn, where we assume most professionals are found.

Many have secret formulas for making that happen. Not this book. Here, I'm encouraging three steps. First, invest time in your network, the people you know and respect, by engaging with their posts. Not every day, and not within the first hour to game the platform, but to genuinely show up with thoughtful comments. Your contacts will appreciate you and, most likely, return the favor.

Second, post your own, original content on a regular schedule, consistently, so those who want to follow you can do so easily. Set a day of the week and a regular time to start sharing your message. That will begin to amplify your seed strategy.

And third, start engaging with the people you find most fascinating. You may never connect with Mark Cuban that way, but others will see your comments and you'll find some of his network becoming part of yours. In the end, just like humanity itself, social media is not something to be gamed, but something that responds to honest engagement and insights.

Seed Pod Strategy Tip: Today's biggest influencers swear by square-format videos. They allow space above and below for branding, progress bars, and captioning. Or produce a square-format, multi-page PDF. Both make compelling content that can cause viral passalong and amplification by the platform.

The Red Draco Seed Pod

If you don't know the Flying Cowboys on YouTube, you might want to check them out. Well, if you're fascinated by planes that land and take off in a hundred feet, by adventure, and by guys landing STOL (short take-off or landing) planes on mountain tops, river sand bars, and more, you might want to check them out.

The Flying Cowboys are a group of Carbon Cub pilots in the Western states who fly the way Harley riders ride. There is one member who stands out from the rest: Mike Patey. A serial entrepreneur, Mike and his twin brother, Mark, operate several businesses from their man-cave hangar at the St. George, Utah, airport, where they also engineer and build planes for fun.

One of Patey's builds, a turboprop-powered light single called "Turbulence," is a world speed record holder. But it was his next project that captured much of the world's attention. "Red Draco" started as a Polish-built high-wing Wilga with a regular old piston engine. Its praying-mantis looks already made it a head-turner, but Patey had much more in mind.

He replaced the 300 horsepower (hp) piston engine with a 700 hp jet-based turboprop and a giant four-blade propeller. Then he modified the landing gear for an even more extreme stance, with thirty-inch balloon tires and exotic new suspension bits. The wing was modified, lights and ground-loop appendages added, and a bigger tail plane installed. Red Draco suddenly had its own distinctive look, just sitting on the ground. Each time it leaped into the air, it clawed its way skyward at a thirty-degree pitch and still gained speed.

Before long, the plane and Patey became Internet and media sensations. Sponsors called and wanted to pay money to add their brands to the plane. Toy manufacturers called, wanting to clone the plane in miniature. Red Draco was on the cover of *Popular Mechanics* and gaining more and more television time. And Patey's YouTube account exploded with more and more followers. Patey meticulously documented the entire build, drawing in the audience even more. They saw Red Draco come to life, but they also got to meet their hero, as they watched him overcome obstacles, finish the project, and fly one adventure after another with his Flying Cowboy buddies.

Sadly, Red Draco eventually crashed, but that just solidified Patey's heroic character to his followers. He was soon back at it with a new build, "Scrappy," another extreme bush plane built from scrap parts (mostly), sporting a four-blade propeller from an Everglades airboat, an 800 hp, eight-cylinder race engine, Baja dune-buggy-style suspension, and more. That build, too, has been faithfully recorded in a series of YouTube episodes.

All of these are Patey's passions. He'd be doing it even if YouTube wasn't watching. He just loves flying, pushing limits, and building extreme examples of everyday vehicles. But here's the seed pod strategy of it all: Patey's company produces airplane tugs, appliances that help pilots move their heavy aircraft in and out of hangars. Draco and

Scrappy have made Patey a celebrity in not only the flying scene, but his tug company, too.

Draco and Scrappy are enormous seed pods—powerful multipliers of Patey's seed strategy—not because he calculated the plane builds as promotions, but because they aren't promotions at all. Patey and his planes are the real deal. He is a genuine aviation hero. His story and his planes legitimately push boundaries in aviation. But aviators are his target market, and he's dominating the entire field like a weed.

That's probably another reason you might want to check out the Flying Cowboys on YouTube, especially Patey's channel: you'll get a front-row seat to see just how building real fascinations into your business can multiply the reach of your seeds.

Seed Pod Strategy Tip: If you're a solopreneur, try to turn one of your hobbies or fantasies into a project video series. If you have an engineering team, is there a world record to beat somewhere? A quirky theme and a bit of luck may turn you or your operation into a social media star.

Referrals and Refer-Ability as Seed Pods

One of the first things we're taught about sales is always to ask for referrals. It's basic sales 101. It's also one of those bits of advice we hear so often that it loses its meaning. The weeds suggest we take a fresh look. The act of being referred is the process of people talking about you, mentioned in the previous chapter as the unfair advantage we attach to our marketing seeds. We want people to pass our story along virally, and referrals are one way to make that happen.

Referrals can take a lot of forms. A client recommending you to a friend and a professional recommending another to provide a related service are classic forms of referrals. Viral passalong, word-of-mouth, testimonials, online reviews, social media buzz, and affiliates are as well. The net result is a lot of people doing your marketing for you—spreading your seeds further, with the spreader's endorsement.

Sales thought leader and trainer Alice Heiman advises starting with clients, who she says are our best sources of referrals. "A referral is when someone introduces you to people you would want to know, from someone who believes in you," she says. "Cultivate loyalty so your clients will scream from the mountain top and spread your seeds." Cultivating loyalty makes sense, as well as fascination, admiration, and relevance. If we inspire all of these, our "refer-ability," as super-connector Michael Roderick calls it, becomes multiplied.

Our refer-ability is the measure of the value we bring to the target of the introduction, as well as to the person making it. But it also refers to how easily someone can make that introduction. Think about the psychology of it all. When we share a favorite service, product, or supplier with a friend, we want to share something astonishing and useful, something that affects their lives for the better. And when we do that, we want it to reflect positively on us. Giving a referral is doing a favor, and, for those keeping track, favors score points.

So for us to earn referrals from clients, friends, colleagues, followers, and fellow social media inhabitants, we'd better have some impressive seeds to spread around. In the W.E.E.D.S. model, referrals are the spread of our seeds by others, but they are also how we reach greater scale. Our job is to make our seeds—our stories, brands, innovations, products and services, and more—compelling for others to spread.

Our seeds should also be incredibly easy to spread. Michael Roderick says that is a matter of shrewd packaging. "If I give you a pile of apples versus a bag of apples, there's a good chance you'll drop them in a pile," he explains. "Our brains are the same way." Roderick says if our concepts are unwieldy, people will forget parts of them and not know what to do with them. Thus, we must package our seeds for ease of spread by others.

Imagine the effect of a beautiful, compelling, three-minute video that introduces you and what you do. Or a tightly produced infographic that can be shared in email and on social media, and spread throughout the Internet. Making yourself refer-able means becoming someone who people want to talk about, feel comfortable recommending, and can easily pass along to others. When we do that, we're on our way to creating collective scale for our enterprise.

Seed Pod Strategy Tip: Create a list of potential referral partners, and produce a refer-ability kit of spread elements. This will supercharge your seed pod, seed strategy, and vine strategy as well. Videos, infographics, your own books, and contact campaigns should be ready to go as you ramp up your weed strategy.

Multiplying Your Reach

Seed strategies are all about creating reach with millions of impressions. The point is to spread an overwhelming amount of seeds that bring devastatingly unfair advantages to the field. Seed pod strategies command us to:

> Multiply the effect of our seed strategy by borrowing the reach and influence of others.

There are many outlets for extending our reach. They all involve teaming with others for far greater spread, which multiplies the effect of our seeds. We see this in our use of publicity and social media, in the borrowing of networks of others for referrals, and so much more.

Comic-Con founder Gareb Shamus uses the draw of celebrities, superpowers, and cosplay to multiply the scale of his events. People flock from all over the world to act out their own comic book fantasies, while attending panel discussions with live actors from their favorite movies. If seed pods multiply the reach of seeds, celebrities can surely act as seed pods. Many show attendees come specifically to see their favorite actors in person, making the press also more apt to pay attention.

Niche Down author Christopher Lockhead says when we create our own categories, people can't stop talking about us. Septuagenarian rocker Alice Cooper is still doing concert tours and people are still filling stadiums because he was the originator of the shock rock genre. It's a witnessing of history to see him perform. Elon Musk has created several distinct categories of one, as the electric car impresario, and as the high flying, visionary entrepreneur who is redefining space commercialization and exploration. People and the media are drawn to their stories, but also to their historic categories.

Forbes columnist Kare Anderson points out even social outrages and news story tie-ins can serve as the basis for seed pod strategies. Just find a way to link yourself to the story. Are you an expert who can offer commentary? The media might want to know, and if they feature you, they'll spread your seeds. Even if *Forbes* doesn't snap up your insights, start a YouTube channel and start broadcasting. If your topic is on everyone's minds, and if you're consistently there with daily comment during the crisis, an audience will find you and grow exponentially. That's also a seed pod.

Let's continue the W.E.E.D.S. process now, by creating your seed pod strategy. Ask yourself the following questions and write out your thoughts on how you will amplify the reach of your seeds.

What Is My Seed Pod Strategy?

- What are my unfair advantages for borrowing the networks and reach of others?
- Do I or anyone else I know have connections within the media?
- Do I know any social media influencers or celebrities who can help spread my message?
- What are my special skills for communicating on a mass basis to my audience?
- Whom do I know that could become a referral source for my business?
- How will I attract others to start referring new business my way?
- Are there shortcuts for building a massive referral network?
- What can I provide that will increase my refer-ability?

W.E.E.D.S. Model at a Glance

1. Seed Strategy

Spread an overwhelming amount of seeds that bring devastatingly unfair advantages to your business.

2. Seed Pod Strategy

Multiply the effect of your seed strategy by borrowing the reach and influence of others.

Points to Remember

- The essence of seed pod strategy is to multiply the reach of our seed strategies by borrowing the reach and influence of others.
- Weeds release highly mobile seeds, but they increase their spread with the use of ingenious seed pod launch strategies.
- Shotweed does this, for example, by flinging its seeds from explosive pods that are triggered by the slightest touch of a gardener or gentle breeze.
- Legacy media, although diminished in reach, is still one of the most powerful ways to multiply the reach of your seed strategy.
- Podcasts are also a powerful way to reach highly specialized audiences.
- Social media influencers can extend your reach immensely, but it can be tough to get their attention.
- Your own social media activities can add greatly to the reach of your seed strategy, but beware of dead-end "shortcuts" like amplification pods and automations.
- Special side projects can create immense interest, thus amplifying your seed strategy.
- Referrals come with the added benefit of carrying the spreader's endorsement of you and your company.
- Make yourself easily refer-able by packaging your story in a form that can be easily passed along.

13

THORN STRATEGY

Stinging nettle (*Urtica dioica*). Found in most parts of the globe and especially prevalent in the Pacific Northwest, stinging nettles are known mostly for the painful wound they inflict on transgressors. The plant's stem and leaves are covered with hollow hair-like spikes filled with a toxin that causes itching, pain, and skin irritation. Oddly, nettles are also prized as a source of food and tea.[25] credit: © The Board of Trustees of the Royal Botanic Gardens, Kew

THE STINGING NETTLE is a fortress of a weed, bristling with dangerously loaded weapons. Covered with hair-like hollow spikes, the tips break off at the slightest touch, converting to hypodermic needles that deliver chemically induced pain. There is no ambiguity to the message here: don't even *think* of messing with us.

Some weeds follow an expansionary vision, depending on seeds, seed pods, and root systems to conquer new territory. Others, like the stinging nettle, stake their claim and vigorously defend against any incursion. They're offensive and defensive strategies that are highly complementary. As any football fan knows, you need both.

Elsewhere in this book, we've seen other brilliant examples of weed defenses. The spiny amaranthus (Chapter 7) bares its fangs with ultra sharp two-inch spikes. Himalayan blackberry (Chapter 6) mixes rampant growth with hooked thorns that inflict multiple, painful scratches from the slightest contact. Other weeds emit toxic aerosols or, like poison ivy (Chapter 8), coat their leaves with an oily substance that causes weeks of anguish. Gympie gympie (Chapter 1), a weedy tree covered in the same trichomes found on stinging nettles, inflicts a painful sting that can last for weeks.

Expansion strategies backed by seeds require massive action, energy, and resources, but defensive strategies are quite different. Spikes, thorns, and toxins only have to be used once or twice for the real effect to take root. We've all experienced painful wounds from thorns, and as a result we avoid those plants. The display is part of their function. They'll hurt you if they get the opportunity; otherwise, they'll intimidate to prevent further disruptions.

Toxins work the same way. How many of us have suffered through a summer bout with a poison ivy–induced rash? It quickly causes us to avoid the plants whenever we're next walking in the woods. The credible threat of injury or anguish keeps all potential challengers in line.

Thus, the purpose of thorn strategy in the W.E.E.D.S. model. We've examined how to produce seeds that spread mightily on their own, and how to give them even greater range with seed pod multipliers. Those two strategies are what we'll use to create a visionary expansion of our enterprises. But now we'll shift to examine how we can apply the defensive strategies of thorns to deter our aggressors, as part of our process.

Patents, Trademarks, Copyright, and Contracts

In order to protect our turf, we must first stake our claim. In the world of weeds, it's done with brute force and cunning moves. In ours, it's done with legal instruments. And then brute force and cunning moves. Patents protect innovations, trademarks protect brands, copyright protects original content, and contracts define and enforce the terms of our agreements. They all work together to protect our intellectual property, assets, deals, reputations, and viability. They are our thorns.

Unlike weeds, thorns don't come naturally to us. They require vigilance, effort, and resources. For that reason, these vital measures are often overlooked in our business processes. We know they're necessary, but they're easy to postpone, like avoiding the dentist until we have pain. And when we have a crisis, we pay the consequences of our inaction in multiples.

Patents, trademarks, copyright, and contracts are necessary to effectively build and conduct a business. If you have nothing to protect, you have no reason to be in business. Weeds never release seeds without equipping them with unfair advantages. As they stand their ground, they employ multiple unfair advantages that make them nearly impossible to defeat. The most effective businesses hold many unfair advantages, but those must be protected.

I'm stating the obvious for a reason. I expect I'm pretty typical of business owners. I focus on the things that excite me. I'm an expansionary, visionary thinker. But there are some parts of operating a business where my focus is forced. I imagine the same is true for you.

The W.E.E.D.S. model insists we broaden our focus. As business owners, we operate in a hostile environment. Our rights may be trampled at any time, and there are at least a thousand reasons why someone might suddenly want to sue us. The U.S. Chamber Institute of Legal Reform revealed in a recent study that at any given time, nearly 43 percent of small businesses were threatened with or engaged in legal action.[26]

While we may not be able to stop all litigation, we can avoid much of it by ensuring our patents, trademarks, copyrights, and contracts are in top order. Those form the foundation of our thorn strategy. Together, they create a powerful bulwark, but as we're about to see, the most effective defense is the one that never has to be used.

Thorn Strategy Tip: Think of your attorney as your company's dentist, and meet at least every six months for a checkup. Make sure your intellectual property is properly protected with a thicket of thorn strategies.

The Prince of Thorns

Dr. Nathan Myhrvold is known as the world's most notorious patent troll. He is co-founder of Intellectual Ventures, a holding company with more than thirty thousand patents, held mostly in the tech space. Myhrvold gets right to the point. "Hidden thorns are nowhere near as effective as publicly known thorns," he asserts. He backs that up with aggressive action in court to make the point. When someone breaches one of his patents, *they will pay.* The patents are thorns, but Myhrvold's primary strategy is to cause extreme pain and humiliation when tech giants violate his patents. Thus, his true weapons are a reputation for fearsome aggression and the panic it triggers in transgressors.

Startup strategist Pierre-R Wolff says in the tech world, patents have a negative connotation due to what he describes as "patent thickets," specifically referencing Myhrvold's operation. But Myhrvold counters, "Imagine if someone built a home on property they don't own," adding, "We need to have a defensible business to do well. Warren Buffett calls it the moat around the castle." Myhrvold says it's the thorns that prevent a business from being gobbled up and taken away.

In a sense, Dr. Myhrvold could be thought of as a twenty-first-century Robin Hood. His business is based on helping the little guy versus the Goliath tech companies. "Invention is the closest thing to magic we have in the real world," he explains. "Some IP may be developed too early, but could be valuable later. When the market catches up, if it's not under patent, oops."

Patents are vital to society. They protect ideas and secrets, so they can be invested in and shared with the world. Otherwise, important advances are lost when the owner dies. Myhrvold points to Stradivarius, the famed eighteenth-century violin maker. "They were the best violins ever made, but the family kept their secrets so secret, no one knows how they did it. Their work has been studied extensively, but no one has figured it out, so it's just gone."

Trade secrets and protected intellectual property can have enormous value, both to the patent holder and licensees. Myhrvold cites the developer of a technology that was too early to the market, who eventually licensed it to Intel for $300 million. Even though the company had ceased operation, the IP remained viable and valuable. Without a patent and someone like Myhrvold to shepherd it through the claim process, hundreds of millions of dollars would have been lost.

Myhrvold also cites the example of touchscreen technology, which had become old and boring and was considered over as far as the tech community was concerned. Once the iPhone appeared, touchscreen technology was suddenly hot again. "The technology had a huge first run," he says, "and then suddenly it had a second run that was also huge." Without a patent, the developers would have missed the second lifecycle of the technology. Converting it to dollars required a patent and someone willing to make it stick—and hurt—in court.

He says when patents are perceived as less thorny, it creates an inhibiting effect on innovation. "In the early days of my business, they all did licenses willingly," he explains, "but patent law changed so it created the perception that patents were no longer thorns."

There is always a danger when the protections offered by patents grow weaker or when a closely followed patent suit is unsuccessful. "If Qualcomm had lost its case with Apple, it would have made patents less powerful." Still, Myhrvold notes, most companies want to obey the law. Fear of punishment is enough to keep order. We don't need lots of people experiencing the thorns if they see someone else suffering the embarrassment and consequences of their transgression.

I admire the weediness of Nathan Myhrvold's mission. His prosecution of breached patents helps society maintain order in the business world, and, in that way, he helps us all. At the close of our interview, I paid the highest compliment I could give. "You are a total weed," I told him. His unfiltered reply: "Yeah, I'm the prince of thorns!" Prince of thorns is a fitting moniker for a guy fighting to protect the value of IP everywhere.

Thorn Strategy Tip: Use Dr. Myhrvold's spirit and approach as a prototype for your own IP stewardship. When someone moves in on your property, hit them hard and make sure it's well publicized. Your reputation as a fierce player in your market will deter others from making the same mistake.

Negotiate like a Weed

We have to wonder, with the fierce nature of weeds, how might they approach a negotiation? The weed mindset tells us they would be aggressive and urgent; they'd be tough adversaries. But weeds also give great priority to cooperation. In later chapters, we'll see how they always push toward collective scale, which only happens with massive cooperation.

Thus, there are two modes of negotiation: adversarial and expansionary. In an adversarial negotiation, as in addressing the patent disputes above, aggression and perhaps a touch of apparent insanity are what give one side the advantage. One side has to feel there's no way they're going to win. There is always a winner and a loser.

In an expansionary negotiation, the parties seek a union that strengthens them all. There should be no losers, only winners. I sense the weeds would thrive in these negotiations, combining the urgency and aggression in the weed mindset with their penchant for spreading expansionary seeds to ensure the desired outcome. They might borrow elements of their approach to proposals from their seed strategy, injecting features that cause the impetus for the deal to grow within the target organization. Those elements, coupled with aggressively urgent waypoints and deadlines, would be a powerful approach to getting deals done. Here they are in greater detail.

Exploratory conversation: Two parties agree there is potential, but what exactly is it? The weeds would prescribe a brief meeting with both sides well prepared with notes and forethoughts. Keep it less than fifteen minutes. Urgency creates importance. Instigating party commits to delivering a term sheet in outline form within an hour. Parties arrange their next talk within a week (longer if necessary, but no more than two weeks). Better still, arrange standing weekly call to report progress and develop next steps. Constant movement is paramount; a stalled deal is no deal at all.

Term sheet: It's important to keep the spirit of urgency and aggression alive throughout the process. Term sheets are desirable because they're fast and informal: just an outlined set of parameters and opportunities. Use your notes to write it out. Send it as text in an email, but send a branded PDF copy, too. The PDF makes it easier to share with colleagues on the other end. Always inject competitive pressure. They won't want to lose the deal to a competitor. Term sheets should be delivered within an hour of the exploratory call. Urgency creates importance.

Spread elements: Borrowing from the proposal section in Chapter 11 on seed strategy, weeds propel their growth with seeds that spread. And we want the impetus for the deal to spread throughout the other party's organization in a positive way. Develop templates for infographics or produce an astonishing video that explains the rationale for the proposed deal in deeply persuasive terms. As discussed in the refer-ability section of Chapter 12, make your spread elements easy to pass along. Send them to your contact and invite them to share the assets with stakeholders and other decision-makers.

Contract: Whereas the term sheet needed to be quick and agile, the contract should be produced with utmost seriousness. It should be aggressive but also cooperative. It needs teeth. No more letters of agreement, which scream, "I am not professional, I just want to get this part over," and which tag you as a pushover if there is conflict later. An enforceable contract shows you mean business, and if the other party breaches, you'll come after them. If they transgress, they will pay. Meanwhile, both sides share a happy journey toward greater growth and prosperity.

Thorn Strategy Tip: Everything should have a deadline, especially if exclusivity is involved. If the other party wants exclusivity, give them thirty days to complete the deal. Or charge a fee that is forfeited if no deal is made by the deadline, or credited against later earnings if the deal is completed on time.

My Own Application of Thorn Strategy

Think of this book as a startup. It introduces a new technology, weed strategy, in the form of the weed mindset and the W.E.E.D.S. model and scaling like a weed. The book is a product, but it is also a seed, set to germinate a training, consulting, and franchise operation. It has its own set of seed, seed pod, segmentation, rosette, vine, root, soil, and thorn strategies in place, along with partnerships and other relationships designed to create multi-channel scale and collective scale.

Intellectual property (IP) first. The book, of course, is copyrighted. "Weed strategy" and "W.E.E.D.S. model" are under pending patents, and the terms and other key phrases are trademarked. No one else can use them without my permission. Relevant domains are registered and trademarked. A series of titles has also been trademarked, and a domain for the online course registered. All intellectual property is covered by patent, trademark, and copyright protections. If any other portions or terms in this book come into unauthorized use, the book serves as first-use grounds for stripping away interlopers.

The technology introduced in the book—weed strategy—is applicable to the growth of any business. Growth is a lucrative sector of the consulting market, and, following the weeds' advice, the business model behind the book is to create collective scale. That means cultivating a team of consultants, with a range of specialties, to create a franchise. Only duly appointed franchisees and licensees will have the right to offer and sell weed strategy consulting services.

I've got it pretty well locked down. The thorns are out. If you want to sell anything to do with weed strategy or its derivatives, you have to come through my organization.

Thorn Strategy Tip: Take an inventory of your intellectual property and meet with your lawyer to review all available protections. You probably have more than you thought, and your IP may not be fully protected.

Can Open Sourcing Be a Thorn Strategy?

Open sourcing is a term derived from the software industry to describe the sharing of source code to foster collaboration and create a stronger platform. But the term has been liberalized to describe the open sharing of anything for the purpose of collaboration and collective development.

Elon Musk open sourced his Hyperloop concept, for mass, hyper-fast transit in giant vacuum-filled tubes stretching from city to city. The pods in the tubes are said to be capable of traveling at jet speeds. Others are using the concept to invest and develop their own Hyperloop designs, with no ownership stake for Musk. Can this be considered a thorn strategy?

I believe so. I did something similar with the term *contact marketing* from my earlier books. I intentionally avoided trademarking it, because I wanted it to spread throughout the sales and marketing community. And it has. Meanwhile, the American Marketing Association named me "the father of contact marketing," and I have founded the Contact Awards as the official award for best achievements in the practice. Not trademarking the term allowed it to become a movement.

As the author of the books that introduced the term, and as the father of the genre and founder of the official award of contact marketing, I still have a lot of say about how it's used. But I also have a worldwide network of people practicing contact marketing, bringing it forward as a legitimate marketing genre.

That may sound more like a seed strategy, and partially it is. But there is also a protected realm that helps me market my services and products. No one else can lay claim to the term. I coined it; I'm the father of the genre. The whole thing burnishes my reputation and builds my brand, so there are benefits similar to trademarking.

Thorn Strategy Tip: Legally protecting IP or opening it to the public can both create advantages. As you can see from my two examples, open sourcing contact marketing has led to a worldwide movement credited to my books, while the thorn strategy for the IP from this book is locked down, so only my team can offer it as a service. Set up a pro/con list for both approaches for your own intellectual property and decide which is a better fit for your mission.

Closing Thoughts about Thorn Strategies

Angel investor and attorney Ron Braley says being the best in our fields is the simplest form of thorn strategy. "If you're selling a product, make sure it's far superior to any other in your market," he explains. "Being the best intimidates most challengers." But if a challenger is not deterred, Braley says strictly deep pockets and a big legal department are the ultimate thorns. "Microsoft developed an aggressive legal department to shut down patent trolls. They send a PowerPoint deck showing how much they'll spend and how much Microsoft is willing to pay to get rid of their claim." The deck is a spread element as described in the "Negotiate like a Weed" section above.

Still, Braley points out the threat of stalling a planned expansion or forcing a change of course due to infringement can be enough to win the battle. "It might result in a large sum of money for the patent holder, but still a small amount to the interloper." Attorney/entrepreneur Scott Penick sees thorns as a matter of perception, a sentiment echoed by Dr. Myhrvold, the Prince of Thorns, above. "If you threaten someone who knows your thorn strategy has no sting, it doesn't work very well."

Penick points to Himalayan blackberries as an example. "Blackberries execute their threats well, so it works." He adds, "If you're going to sue, be willing to do it well and know how it works." He advises using aggression thoughtfully. "If you treat people respectfully, they won't get their guard up," but if you encounter someone who is unusually disagreeable, Penick advises countering thorniness by being grounded, not negative. In negotiations, he says, "I'm always protecting my mindset. I'm always careful about what I expose myself to."

Tech executive Judy Buchholz agrees with Penick. "I try to avoid dealing with ornery people," she says, "but if you're taking it on, make sure you have the determination to deal with it." Aviation entrepreneur Mike Patey says there's no joy in executing a thorn strategy, but if someone's trying to take our property, we must put our guard up. "I once had a kid steal a horse from me, then his lawyer sued me for three million dollars," he recalls, "So I armored up with a private investigator and my attorney. They thought I would bow down, but I didn't. When you try to steal my flowers and petals, my thorns will come out."

Sometimes the intended theft is property, other times it's clients, but as Nimble founder Jon Ferrara says, "Great relationships leave no room for competitors." The weeds would say in any of these scenarios, adopting the weed mindset will make us more aggressive, urgent, perseverant, adaptive, and resilient than our opponents. Overpowering an interloper means being more of a weed than they are. Because in battles of attrition, weeds always win.

What Is My Thorn Strategy?

- What is my inventory of intellectual property?
- How is my IP protected, and what are my blind spots?
- Am I scheduling a regular review of my legal coverage?
- Where else in my processes and innovations might there be hidden IP to protect?
- When in expansive negotiations have I developed systems to quickly produce spread elements?
- Is my proposal/negotiation process optimized for urgency, spread, and airtight contracts?
- Am I prepared to be my own Prince of Thorns in my legal dealings?
- On the whole, am I seen as someone others don't mess with, or an easy target?

W.E.E.D.S. Model at a Glance

1. Seed Strategy

Spread an overwhelming amount of seeds that bring devastatingly unfair advantages to your business.

2. Seed Pod Strategy

Multiply the effect of your seed strategy by borrowing the reach and influence of others.

3. Thorn Strategy

Use all available legal protections to safeguard your IP, develop a reputation for using them, and negotiate like a weed.

Points to Remember

- Thorn strategies seek to inflict pain occasionally, creating a psychological barrier in others against intrusion.
- Patents, trademarks, copyrights, and contracts are the foundation of our thorn strategy to protect our intellectual property rights.
- Think of your attorney as your company's dentist; schedule an IP protection checkup every six months.
- Patents play a vital role in society by protecting IP, thus ensuring a constant stream of innovation.
- Many patents cover innovations and technology that may not yet be viable, but may become valuable at a later time.
- Hidden thorns are nowhere near as effective as publicly known thorns.
- In successful expansionary negotiations, urgency, spread, and strength are essential elements.
- Proposals can be designed to spread like weeds throughout an organization.
- Consider open sourcing as an alternative strategy to thorns. Can your IP create a worldwide movement that gives an even greater benefit to your company?
- Having proper protections, along with a reputation for a willingness to use them, will allow you to always negotiate like a weed.

14

SEGMENTATION STRATEGY

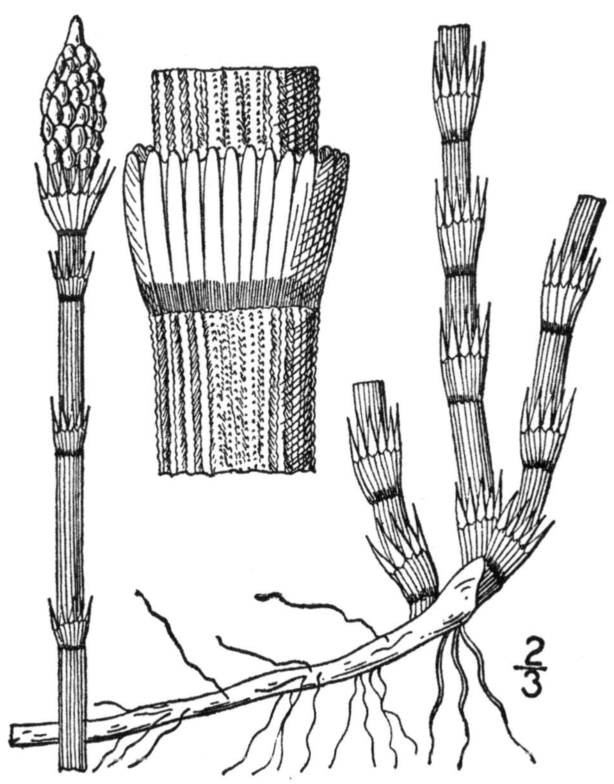

Horsetail (*Equisetum hyemale*). Found in North America, Europe, and northern Asia, *Equisetum hyemale* is a primitive plant related to ferns, distinguished by tall, segmented stalks. Juniper-like leaves grow in a ring pattern around each joint in the stalk. The plant does not produce flowers. Instead, it spreads through the release of spores and vegetative reproduction sprouting from extensive underground root systems with runners that reach past virtually any barrier.[27,28] credit: © The Board of Trustees of the Royal Botanic Gardens, Kew

HORSETAILS ARE NATIVE to many places, including the Seattle area, where I live. Appearing like a tall, thick grass in areas with high moisture content, they quickly fill spaces where they're not wanted. A closer look reveals an ancient plant, a relative of the fern, with a primeval appearance.

Since they show up where they're not wanted, it's natural for backyard gardeners to attempt to yank them from the ground. And that's when we see their ingenious defensive innovation at work. When you grab a handful of the horsetail stalks and pull, all you get are tiny sections of the plant. Its segmented architecture is strictly a damage-mitigation measure, designed to prevent the plant from being uprooted. Even without segmentation, horsetails are ready to battle to the end before relinquishing their claimed turf.

Horsetails could easily have been featured in Chapter 17 about root strategy, because their root systems are also an ingenious, unfair advantage. When horsetails are found, they're usually part of a large outcropping, but the appearance is deceiving, because each grove is usually just a single plant, linked by a thicket of roots and horizontal runners. The backyard gardener has no chance of removing this pest without the help of heavy machinery.

Observing these kinds of measures, the extensive, interconnected root systems, and segmented upper portions, gives us a powerful example to follow in our own enterprises. Weeds constantly employ unfair advantages, in the way their seeds are equipped to spread across great distances, flung into the air with ingenious launch mechanisms and with thorns and spikes and toxins that repel transgressors. We can see they also extend unfair advantages to the ways in which they mitigate risk and damage when they, themselves, are disrupted.

The weed mindset describes a set of behavioral attributes that help weeds win battles in the field. They are persistent, aggressive, and urgent in many ways, but the attributes of adaptability and resilience truly show up in the way weeds gird against disruption. As guides for our own businesses, horsetails remind us to include countermeasures in our weed strategy processes to be ready to respond to disruption quickly.

As business owners, we face constant sources of disruption, from competitors, changing trends, and new technologies, but also from shudders in the economy. The boom-recession cycle occurs as regularly as the seasons, but many are caught in every cycle with little to prevent downfalls. Recession-proofing our businesses is the wish of every owner but rarely is accomplished with any real success.

The weeds tell us we should be better prepared for disruptions. Weeds like the horsetail show us how it's done, with planned measures to limit damage, while constantly pressing on for new ground. They're telling us to disruption-proof, recession-proof, and pandemic-proof our businesses, by building new unfair advantages into our strategies and processes.

Recession-Proofing Your Business

In recession-proofing our enterprises, we often think of businesses that don't seem to be affected by downturns. When the economy sours, businesses still have to maintain liability coverages, so commercial insurance always seems to do well. There may be some disruption as companies shop for cheaper coverages, but they don't stop buying.

Restaurants always seem to do well, because people don't stop eating during recessions. Fast food chains offer adequate fare at low prices, so they continue to prosper when times get tough. Commercial real estate continues to thrive, at least in terms of existing leases that continue to pay out. After all, businesses seek stability during tough times, and changing their addresses is not a desirable move. Gyms are often cited as the ideal setup for a recession-proof business, with members paying monthly dues under strict long-term contracts, whether or not they use the facilities.

But during the pandemic, these were some of the worst-affected sectors of the economy, with the exception of insurance. Suddenly, we were restricted from leaving our homes, and eating in crowded restaurants, exercising in crowded gyms, and working in crowded offices became the definition of super-spreader events. Restaurants, gyms, and office-building owners, usually paragons of stability in rough seas, were the first to start sinking.

Some companies were spectacularly suited for the new work-from-home trend and produced explosive growth. Peloton was already charging ahead with its home-gym model, with sophisticated and high-priced stationary bikes and a connected, worldwide community of users on video screens. Classes are subscription-model sessions with a well-cast ensemble of fitness models and instructors, all pushing riders to achieve more. It was an addictive mix before the pandemic, but once everyone started working from home, Peloton became the go-to source for housebound gym rats. And their revenues immediately soared.

Zoom is another pandemic-driven, work-from-home success. Before COVID-19 changed our lives, Zoom was a rapidly growing videoconferencing platform, but unknown beyond its business user base. Still, it was perfectly positioned when we all set up offices in our homes. Unlike other videoconferencing platforms, Zoom was simple to use. Just click the link and you're talking with someone on the other side of town, or the other side of the world. No software was required, and there were no clunky quirks to the platform. It didn't matter what kind of computer or phone you were using. It just worked in a wonderfully unfettered way. And it was ready to explode into the COVID-19 locked-down world. As a result, Zoom's revenues immediately rocketed nearly 500 percent over the previous year.

Meanwhile, restaurateurs, gyms, and office-building owners were left with an ultimatum: pivot or perish. The results have been eye-opening. Some restaurants were not equipped to absorb the jolt, other than to lay off staff, close their doors, and hope for the best. Others quickly adopted a take-out model and were able to continue reduced operations that still kept the restaurant businesses alive. Some restaurants had been proactively capturing emails all along and were already in constant contact with their patrons. They were best equipped to pivot to new models and ask for their customers' support.

Segmentation Strategy Tip: We know recessions are coming, and we know we need an emergency plan. In addition to the basics, try interviewing clients about their emergency plans and look for ways to fit in. The best hedge is to become indispensable throughout the normal boom/bust cycle of business.

Creating a Balanced Stance

The restaurant sector response to the pandemic demonstrated a crucial element of meeting sudden challenges: pivoting requires a balanced stance. Just as in martial arts, the combatant can only strike or defend effectively from a balanced position. The building of online relationships with patrons is what gave restaurateurs the balanced stance needed to pivot and strike with new food-delivery models. The weeds tell us, in our own segmentation strategy, we must find ways to create evenly balanced stances.

Franchisee Paul Harrison seems to have the perfect approach. He owns a digital marketing franchise and multiple locations within a car wash franchise. Even though they're entirely different businesses, Harrison figured they would mix well. The marketing agency is dynamic; when the economy is booming, companies line up for his services. But when the economy falls back, most business owners immediately cut their marketing spend.

But that's all part of the plan for Harrison's operation. During boom times, he focuses more on his marketing business, but when times get tough, he puts more focus on the car wash locations. He's never ignoring one business for the other, but his process shifts based on economic conditions. During tough times, people like to keep a clean car as a last, affordable luxury. So he shifts more of his marketing focus toward his car wash business.

This is a brilliant approach. The two businesses are completely different but, it turns out, highly complementary. One is dynamic, in that it generates lots of revenue during boom times, whereas the other is stable, generating revenue regardless of economic conditions. But Harrison can easily increase revenue by applying his marketing focus to the car wash.

Harrison specializes in taking over distressed car wash operations and turning them around. So his strategy gains even more ground as other washes become available. They do well in recessions, but only if they're managed and marketed well, so there is always opportunity for more growth.

His mixed business has one other unfair advantage: as a franchisee, Harrison gains a network of aligned entrepreneurs working on the same challenges, constantly sharing new strategies. When one franchisee finds a new way to win, it's quickly shared with the others. And, as car wash locations become available in his network, he gets special consideration to buy in, before they're offered to the outside.

As a marketer, Harrison is used to offering his expert services to clients, but there is a sense he'd much rather apply them to his own business. Marketing exists to help businesses grow. As he speaks about his car wash business, it's clear he approaches it with the growth mindset of a marketer. "The first thing we did was offer $11 car washes in exchange for customers' email addresses," he says. "Nine times out of ten, they come back at full price. It has allowed us to build a large database, which we consider the root system of the business." When sales dropped by 30 percent at one location due to nearby construction, Harrison tested various offers and blew up the business. "We tested $19 and $29 price points and found we got a better class of customer at the higher level."

This is not the language of someone who simply likes to work on cars, but of a true marketer. The layering of expertise creates an unbeatable combination that translates into a truly unfair advantage. And it keeps both operations busy, regardless of what's happening in the economy. It is an effective segmentation strategy.

Segmentation Strategy Tip: In downturns, remain solidly connected with your customer base, yes. But a balanced stance requires more than one leg. Expand your network. Expand your footprint to complementary markets. Your stance will automatically become more balanced by executing the full W.E.E.D.S. model.

Setbacks and Resets

It's obvious there are different levels and natures of disruptions. Harrison's well-conceived strategy to prosper during predictable recessionary setbacks makes sense, but what about other kinds of disruption that cannot be foreseen or even imagined? A recession is a setback. But we know recessions are coming, we can predict their effects, and we know where they'll do the most damage.

To be fair to the many restaurateurs who are very smart businesspeople and who were driven out of business during the COVID-19 pandemic, the conditions they suffered were not predictable. Similarly, the taxi industry couldn't have known, when Uber debuted, their market was about to collapse. These are resets of markets, and perhaps entire economies, that leave them permanently changed, until the next reset comes along. But the question is, could these have been anticipated and mitigated by the restaurants and taxi and car rental companies after all?

The weeds might suggest that, even though we can't foresee future events, there is a lot we can do to ensure the balanced stance necessary to pivot in any circumstance. The restaurants that proactively cultivated email lists and relationships stayed well ahead of their competitors during the pandemic. They were the ones best positioned to change the way they addressed their customers' needs. They still wanted to eat, and were still willing to patronize their favorite restaurants, but only if given appropriate new solutions. Restaurant owners were compelled to innovate, but only those with online relationships had the necessary access to successfully shift their businesses to new models.

Certainly, they could have foreseen the value of collecting email addresses, knowing they'd find many new ways of connecting with and serving their customers. Similarly, when was the last time you had a good experience in a taxi? The drivers are gruff and disinterested, their cars are disgusting, and we never really know, although we suspect, they're often taking us the long way to drive up the fare. And then they argue if you want change.

The taxi companies might not have seen Uber coming, but their customer service frictions were problems they should have fixed long ago. Instead, *they* were were the problem Uber fixed. They were begging to go out of business. And when the disruption came, their mistreated market gladly walked away. There was never any loyalty or special advantage to riding in a taxi versus a private, clean, well maintained vehicle with a courteous driver. Uber drivers never argue about giving change, because there's no exchange of money. It's all in the app. Uber was the assassin's bullet and and the cabbies were sitting ducks waiting to be picked off.

If these two examples can impart a usable lesson, it is to connect with our customers in ways that inspire loyalty, trust, and uninterrupted contact. We should always be pivoting and reinventing. We don't need disruptions, setbacks, and resets to prompt us to action. We should be taking action constantly. Restaurants and taxi companies should have taken action long ago.

Segmentation Strategy Tip: Preparing for disruptions that haven't yet been imagined is nigh impossible. But keeping the fundamentals in shape—strong customer relationships, an ever-expanding network, and an old-fashioned email list for regular communication, but also emergencies—makes you better prepared to face whatever may come.

The Art of the Pivot

Branding guru David Brier says he has witnessed many recessions and setbacks, and sees a key indicator for success. "Marketing gets cut first in tough times, but is that really a good idea?" he asks. One of his clients, a pet food company, invested in a rebrand campaign during the most recent recession, to complement a total reinvention of the company. "They saw a 200 percent increase over the year before, a shocking result during a deep recession."

Brier says during tough times, many owners essentially give up. But the few who redouble their efforts are the ones who thrive. Consider the story of *MeetUp.com,* the vast network of groups who regularly gather for in-person meet-ups. When COVID hit, it threatened to swiftly put the company out of business. But CEO David Siegel had a plan already in mind, to shift the meetings to an online platform.

"The goal was community and staying connected," he says, "and we realized it was needed even more during the social isolation." As a result, MeetUp shifted from an in-person meet-up platform to an online platform and *grew* exponentially during the pandemic. "We went from zero online meetings during our first eighteen years, to over a million online events that first year. Our unfair advantage was our network of people who care about each other and want to help each other."

The Marketing Book Podcast host Douglas Burdett echoes Siegel's assertion: "To pivot successfully, you must know and understand your customer." He cites the examples of the landscaping company that shifted to hanging Christmas lights when their regular business is in hibernation, and the tree company that sells firewood. "These companies see opportunities others are missing. Martin Lindstrom talks about a particular restaurant that pivoted during the pandemic," he says. "They shifted to a home restaurant supply house so people could stock their homes instead. Without understanding your customers' shifting needs, that doesn't happen."

Knowing our customers is part of striking a balanced stance, but Outbound Edge founder Chris Ortolano says it's just as important to know our competitors. Competitors are a constant source of disruption, even more so in a downturn. Thus, Ortolano says, "Know who your competitors are, be able to articulate your value proposition against theirs, and get ready for their traps." He also emphasizes the importance of being known as the best within a specialization as a segmentation strategy. "Niches make more sense than thinking you can sell to anybody. Define your customers, then defend your market share."

A critical element of defending market share during a pivot is to be indispensable. Angel investor/attorney Rob Braley says, "You've got to be the *sine qua non* (the essential element) of whatever you're doing. Make yourself irreplaceable." Turnaround specialist Dan Waldschmidt says during times of setback or reset, we must simplify. "Weeds are simple. They have a mission and they execute," he says, adding there are two rules to follow in any turnaround. "Rule one, be incredibly easy to do business with, and rule two, be so awesome, people ask for more."

Knowing and understanding our customers, and being awesome and indispensable are useful attributes, but brand strategist Ian Rhys Palmer says if we really want to spark loyalty, start a movement. "With some companies, you can sense the lack of belief," he says, "but if they're part of a movement, people stay, they give more. It also attracts thousands of customers who want to be part of the movement, too."

Creating loyalty through a movement or excellent customer experience is critical throughout the lifecycle of a business, and it produces a willingness to remain connected during a pivot. But movements spring from ideas worth pursuing, so how do we build the necessary element of discovery into our process?

Super-connector Michael Roderick says we should constantly be creating and testing promising new ideas. Roderick, also a Broadway producer, likes to use stumble throughs—a term unique to theater—to walk through an idea to determine its merits. "It allows us to see how the idea works, and figure out what we actually have." His point is to continually explore new ideas—new ways to pivot when and if needed.

Attorney/entrepreneur Scott Penick says, "Counting pennies and hunkering down is not the way to deal with a downturn." His solution is to always have a side gig brewing. "My wife and I have been nutrition and health enthusiasts," he explains, "and we're a fan of Tim Ferriss's *4-Hour Workweek*." Penick decided to take action when the economy was good and to create stability when the inevitable next disruption hits. Their side gig turned into a fully outsourced business that continues to produce orders from around the world, twenty-four hours a day. "We just didn't want to be thinking, 'Well let's see how this works out before acting.'"

SaaS entrepreneur coach Dan Martell advises "right-sizing" throughout a company's lifecycle, and particularly in response to seismic shifts. "In a downturn, it's important to cut enough, but not too much," he says. "It's important to strike the right balance." A balanced stance seems to be the key element to pivoting and planning effectively.

Boxing legend Mike Tyson, who made his living by striking from a balanced stance, perhaps says it best: "Everyone has a plan till they get punched in the mouth."[29] Our job is to always be agile and balanced. It is the essence of segmentation strategy, and of thriving through every circumstance that comes our way.

What Is My Segmentation Strategy?

- What can I do to become indispensable to my clients?
- How can I remove friction from my customers' experience with my company?

- How can I create a balanced stance in my business, so I'm always ready to reinvent and pivot to new ways of serving my customers?
- If the worst happened, am I in a position to quickly address my customers directly?
- What am I doing to create a stronger relationship with each of my clients?
- What is my plan to thrive during the next recession or other forms of disruption?
- How can I diversify my offerings to spread risk and expand my markets?
- How can I deliver my service or product in new ways, perhaps to a larger portion of my market?
- What are the blind spots that can obliterate my business during disruptions?

W.E.E.D.S. Model at a Glance

1. Seed Strategy

Spread an overwhelming amount of seeds that bring devastatingly unfair advantages to your business.

2. Seed Pod Strategy

Multiply the effect of your seed strategy by borrowing the reach and influence of others.

3. Thorn Strategy

Use all available legal protections to safeguard your IP, develop a reputation for using them, and negotiate like a weed.

4. Segmentation Strategy

Strike a balanced stance, prepare for disruptions, be ready to pivot decisively.

Points to Remember

- The segmented stalks of *Equisetum hyemale* are a defense mechanism to mitigate risk and damage to the plant from physical disruption.
- As business owners, we face constant sources of disruption, which we must mitigate through our own segmentation strategy.
- Recession-proofing our businesses requires striking a balanced stance and developing options for pivots to new models and modes of delivery quickly.
- Knowing and understanding our customers is also critical to understanding how we must pivot to meet their needs.
- Restaurants and gyms are often cited as recession-proof businesses, but they suffered terribly during the pandemic.
- While most floundered, some restaurants did a masterful job of adapting to the new reality by changing how their product was delivered.
- In order to pivot effectively, we must be ready and willing to act.
- Mike Tyson reminds us, "Everyone has a plan till they get punched in the mouth."

15

ROSETTE STRATEGY

Canada thistle (*Cirisium arvense*). A relative of the dandelion, Canada thistle is considered one of the most invasive weeds in the world. Its leaves and stem are covered in razor-sharp spines, with a thick radial rosette of leaves at ground level. Each stalk produces multiple florets, which convert to dandelion-like seed pods, launching highly mobile, wind-dispersed seeds.[30] credit: © The Board of Trustees of the Royal Botanic Gardens, Kew

WEEDS NEVER DO anything without an unfair advantage. Their seeds are nature's engineering marvels, designed for maximum spread. Their seed pods amplify that reach with jutting platforms and explosive casings that launch their seed cargoes far and wide. Their thorns, spikes, toxic hypodermic needles, and aerosols create unfair advantages to defeat disruptors.

Virtually everything in this book describes some form of unfair advantage, covering every aspect of life for weeds. They don't just hold an advantage in one area; weeds are covered with them. The Canada thistle is a good example. The entire above-ground portion is covered with razor wire. There is no place for the gardener to take grasp without suffering painful wounds.

The thistle's floret is similarly armed, and when it goes to seed, it releases tiny kernels attached to parasols of wind-catching fuzz. Underground, *Cirisium arvense* deploys an extensive lattice of roots looped together with horizontal shoots that launch new instances of the plant, acting as a secondary form of reproduction.

As a member of the *Asteraceae* family, Canada thistle is a close relative of the dandelion, and it shares an ingenious trick of competitive advantage. Both plants form radial fans of leaves at their base, a rosette, a thatch so thick no sunlight or rainwater can penetrate. When we find mature dandelions and thistles in our yards, removing them leaves a ten-inch hole in the lawn. It is a total block of local competition, an entirely unfair advantage—which is just the way the weeds like it.

As we progress through the W.E.E.D.S. model, you'll see more overlaps. Everything in the book is interconnected. The highly mobile seeds, ingenious seed-pod-launching devices, thorn and segmentation strategies, vines for borrowing the infrastructure of others to fuel growth, root systems that store and protect the life force of the plant, and more are all designed to produce unfair advantages that allow the weeds to spread, conquer, and dominate.

The weeds are telling us we must do the same. From now on, we must never do anything without invoking unfair advantages. We don't do things simply because that's the way things are done, we examine every possible opportunity to stack the odds in our favor. Our purpose in this chapter is to identify and maximize every possible factor that can bring unfair advantages to your operation.

Layering and the Nature of Unfair Advantages

Legendary investor Warren Buffett once summed up the nature of competitive advantage. He said the trick is to find a way to stand on a box while everyone else is straining on their toes to get a better view, and not have anyone notice what you're doing. The advantage becomes unfair when there are no other boxes around. Unfair advantages are differentiators, but also moats. By their nature, they cannot be easily duplicated. Those are the unfair, competitive advantages we seek to grow like a weed.

When Kathy Ireland started kathy ireland Worldwide, she had a strong personal brand, a legacy from her modeling days. But she was not known as a brand in housewares. Still, she was able to parlay that earlier source of recognition into something new. She had always been interested in fashion and design, and her face and name were already trusted entities.

Ireland used layering to produce her unique brand in a new space. She was a famous model, and suddenly, she also became a famous brand in home fashion, by overlaying the second dimension onto the first. The result is a space only she can inhabit, a brand uniquely her own. It's also a powerful, totally unfair, brilliant advantage.

Layering is something we can all do. I once met a financial advisor, Joe, who was struggling to get meetings with his target market. As we spoke, I asked what he loves to do outside of work. It turned out Joe was a former golf pro. I asked if he'd ever considered mixing the two, by offering a free golf lesson as a way to connect with his prospects. Layering the two suddenly made him utterly unique and irresistible to meet with. That became his unfair advantage, his differentiator and moat, because very few financial advisors are also ex–golf pros.

Archangel founder Giovanni Marsico says we all have superpowers. We just have to find them. Just like the classic comic book superheroes, we tend to reject our special abilities until we discover their utility in the world. Layering is just like the process of discovering superpowers, by taking stock of our abilities and discovering ways in which they can be overlaid. We can assemble a pretty compelling set of advantages for ourselves, just as Joe did by integrating his ex–golf pro background with his financial advisory practice.

Business books have always been a source of unfair advantage for those who read. The most successful among us read constantly. Many CEOs report reading a book a week. Consider the collective wisdom they absorb, and the effect it has on their operations. If you're not treating yourself to a weekly fare of wisdom and insight, consider compiling your own top one hundred list of books—and get reading.

Warren Buffett says unfair competitive advantages are so important, he only invests in companies that have them. "The key to investing is not assessing how much an industry is going to affect society or how it will grow," he says, "but determining the competitive advantage of any given company and, above all, the durability of that advantage."[31] Durable advantages that differentiate and deny entry are the essence of unfair advantages.

Rosette Strategy Tip: Take stock of your outstanding abilities, achievements, and attributes. How do they layer together to form your unique story, brand, and offering? How can they be combined to create new categories of products, services, and markets? Curate these carefully, as they are the building blocks of your uniquely unfair advantages.

Are Unfair Advantages Found, Made, or Acquired?

The answer to this question is obvious: it's all three. As conditions around us change, ideas and opportunities constantly emerge. Finding new unfair advantages is a product of constantly connecting dots, of observing what has changed and what can be made of it. Of course, the act of finding anything is also a matter of luck.

Unfair advantages are also acquired, by learning a new skill; merging with companies holding unique complementary, technological, or market advantages; or gaining rights to anything that differentiates us in a positive way. The trick, as Warren Buffett reminds us, is to find an advantage that also functions as a moat. Exclusivity is essential for competitive advantages to become unfair ones.[32]

Retired four-star general Barry McCaffrey, who knows the nature of unfair advantages in military operations, today serves as a business advisor. The Pentagon doctrine is one of avoiding a fair fight and, instead, "overmatching" adversaries. In business, McCaffrey says that translates to "barriers to entry significantly high enough to make a fortune."

Entrepreneur Jim Pack sees competitive advantage in similarly militaristic terms. "I prefer a beachhead strategy when entering markets," he explains. "I look for the things larger players don't want, I do what nobody else wants to do." By establishing a presence surrounded by a moat of indifference by potential competitors, he creates his own exclusive advantage.

SaaS founder coach Dan Martell says, in the tech world, unfair leverage often comes from early access to an API (application programmer interface), an exclusive license, or a first-mover advantage. "The best companies are monopolies," he says. And that is the whole point of unfair advantages: to create *de facto* monopolies in our markets.

Early access and exclusive licenses are acquired forms of unfair advantage, but being a first mover is strictly a result of hard work. It is an advantage built by a company's founders, from the ground up. These are the most interesting forms of advantage, because their existence is completely under our control. Neither luck nor lack of capital play any role in leverage we create on our own.

Rosette Strategy Tip: If you have a team, get them involved in your search for unfair advantages. Open lines of communication to allow ideas to surface. Sometimes the simplest suggestions can add new efficiency to your process. Always remain vigilant for new opportunities to connect new dots.

Dominant Reputation and Brand

Beyond layering, the simplest path to unfair advantage is through the careful cultivation of reputation and brand. After all, we're in charge of the quality of our innovations, work, and interactions with clients. The strength of our reputations and brands can act as an inhibitor to our competitors.

Weed ecologist Anthony DiTommaso likens the effect to allelopathy, when a plant infuses surrounding soil with toxins that prevent other plants from moving in. "The black walnut does this very effectively," he says. "Nothing grows near it." Walnuts aren't the only species to use allelopathy, as some grasses emit toxins that prevent the growth of trees in order to preserve their access to sunlight.

Angel investor Ron Braley defines it this way: "Become the go-to person for your area of specialty. That's your unfair advantage." Environmentalist Marilyn Heiman says, "Your reputation can become your unfair advantage." She recalls encounters with elected officials who already knew her reputation for being tough but fair. "Build a relationship," she says. "Find ways for a win-win."

Insurance entrepreneur Sam Watson even has a word for reputation, at least in the insurance industry: *persistency.* Persistency is the length of time someone remains actively paying premiums on an insurance policy. And Sam's persistency rates happen to be the highest in the industry. "My persistency is a rosette with insurance carriers," he explains. "It allows me to call any CEO in the industry and ask for just about anything. They know my numbers and they want my production." Sam's persistency is his unfair advantage, a self-built position that no other producer can match.

Forbes columnist Kare Anderson says rosette strategy is about becoming what author Joe Calloway describes as "a category of one" in his book *Becoming a Category of One.* "Philz Coffee is in that category," she says. "Nobody goes to any other source of coffee. They've become a community center." It's that sort of brand dominance, whether local, regional, national, or international, that produces the black walnut effect. No viable competitors ever emerge, thanks to the smothering effect of an unassailable reputation and brand.

MYOB chief sales and support officer Daniel West cites a similar example in Christopher Lochhead, who pioneered category design in his book *Play Bigger.* Lochhead argues that, to achieve what we would call a rosette strategy, it's fruitless to compete in the same old way with everybody else. Instead, Lochhead prescribes inventing a new market category and dominating it from the start. West says owning your category is a totally unfair advantage, in that it can establish an Amazon-like brand dominance anywhere.

Entrepreneur Josh Steimle says Amazon has probably the most weed-like presence in the world today, with a solid rosette strategy. "Amazon shows up in the number-one position on Google for almost any product," he says, "which allows them to dominate every consumer market. It leaves no room for Walmart [or others] to compete."

Speaker/author/connector Jeff Sheehan also points to Amazon Prime, which gives faster delivery times and other benefits for $99 annually, and leaves other retailers unable to compete. Amazon is actually bristling with unfair advantages in every aspect of their business. They are currently the most weed-like business in existence. That's fine for Amazon, but for the rest of us, building brand dominance has to happen on a much smaller scale.

Sales trainer and thought leader Alice Heiman says achieving brand dominance only requires ingenuity. "Dominant brands like Apple, IBM, and Coca-Cola are ubiquitous," she says, "but anyone who speaks at an event employs a rosette strategy. They get most of the attention and everyone knows their message. That's just as dominant. Nobody's thinking about Apple, IBM or Coke; they're thinking of you."

Rosette Strategy Tip: Building a brand today means standing out in an oversaturated world. Posting on social media has little effect, because it's what everyone else is doing. Instead, try forming new alliances with influencers, event organizers, and media to get other people raving about you.

Innovations and Designs

Henrik Fisker knows the power of innovation and great design. "When I designed the Z8, I was up against a paradox," Fisker explains. "You can fall in love with a sculpture, but there is engineering, marketing, and you have to shave out cost, add more headroom. But that would ruin the proportions. With the Astons and Z8, there were no compromises. That's what causes strong emotional appeal."

Fisker explains that design can make us happy—make us smile. "You don't have to own it to enjoy it," he says. "Architecture, a beautiful old car, or a beautiful bathroom enhance your life and make you feel good." The strong emotional appeal of design is also what can trigger an unfair advantage for the producer.

Apple has taken advantage of our love of uncompromised design for years. We can see that it creates a strong emotional bond, like the Astons and the BMW Z8 have. "We're creating dream machines," he continues. But Fisker is an exception in the automotive world, precisely because he produces the designs he displays at car shows, when most concept cars never make it to production. "It builds a certain trust," he says. "If I say it's good, it's good. And consumers believe me."

A fantastically designed product captures our attention because it gains easy exposure. The media love to pick up stories with an overwhelming visual hook, which is how we all come to know the product. So the design produces a seed pod effect, while also producing an unfair advantage, because it uniquely belongs to one company or designer.

Amazon head of sales strategy Sid Kumar says we're not guaranteed a dominant advantage simply because of an innovation. The technology and model have to fit an urgent need. "Uber took off because they solve an acute pain point," he says, "but lots of apps aren't moving a problem or providing an engaging experience." As General McCaffrey points out, "Are we offering a product that people desperately need? If not, we're in trouble."

Rosette Strategy Tip: Invest in industrial and graphic design services from top creatives to produce products and communications that inspire conversations. A thoughtful, beautiful design communicates deep competence and inspires trust.

Physical Presence

In the United States, we think of Amazon as having a dominant worldwide brand, but that isn't the case everywhere. Dutch growth strategist Stephan Annema points out that in the Netherlands, *bol.com* is the big player in online retail. Surprisingly, *bol.com* has successfully repelled Amazon's advance, precisely because it is based where it operates (Holland).

"They imitated Amazon," he says, "but they focused strictly on the Dutch market, which created a dominant market advantage." Annema explains that *bol.com* takes advantage of the fact that the Dutch are always proud of Dutch companies. "It's a matter of convenience and foot print and they make it easy," he explains, "so for the moment, Amazon is kept at bay."

So physical location can be an unfair advantage. In *bol.com*'s case, its presence sparked nationalist pride, but there are many other expressions of location serving as an unfair advantage. "Look at Starbucks," *Eat Their Lunch* author Anthony Iannarino says. "They're on both sides of the road, every mile or so." He's right.

Their strategy of being omnipresent, including always being on both sides of the road and always having right-turn access, makes them the obvious stop for coffee and warmth. Their location strategy truly is a weedy, unfair advantage. Starbucks also plays perfectly into another weed strategy: operation within collective scale, covered later in the book. Collective scale is a strategy, but also an utterly unfair advantage.

The location advantage can also stem from the state of mind it inspires. "Just living and operating in New York is a rosette strategy," brand strategy guru David Brier says, "It's a post-graduate study in hard knocks." Brier says the tough, competitive New York environment trains people to become more resilient and more resourceful. The famous New York state of mind, it turns out, can be an unfair advantage when competing beyond the city limits.

London-based Reachdesk founder Alex Olley has found his location to be particularly advantageous. The gifting platform competes with bigger players from the United States, but for the European market, his UK location has been ideal. "No one was doing what we're doing," he explains. "We built a platform that can be used in all of the languages across Europe. Is your goal to grow in Europe? We're the only platform that can do that."

Rosette Strategy Tip: Explore how your location—or multiple locations—might effectively layer onto your market and offering. Are there unfair advantages to be exploited? Can you claim special status because of your location?

Relationships

Hong Kong–based investor Jay Kim sees a link between location and relationships. "If you're a small business or a startup, it's critical you do business-development on a local basis first," he says. "If you're starting a garden shop," he continues, "you need to do bus-dev even with other gardening shops. Even though they may be your competitors, you can still do cross-promotion."

Kim suggests finding ways to benefit each other and find synergies. Again, this fits two strategies later in the book concerning operating at collective scale and vine strategy. It all makes sense, but it first requires strong relationships and alliances. "I did this with my podcast, too," Kim explains. "I reached out to all the other podcasters and we had each other on our shows. It turns out listeners like to listen to multiple podcasts."

Australian carwash franchisee Paul Harrison recalls the critical nature of developing relationships with car dealerships early on. "Starting out, we wanted as much wholesale traffic as possible," he says, "so we created relationships with the major car dealerships in Melbourne." Those relationships served as Harrison's initial rosette strategy, effectively locking out competitors from the dealership market. Another unfair advantage.

But Harrison says the ultimate rosette strategy is with his retail customers. "We're out there on the driveway talking to them," he says, "as soon as they come on the lot. When a customer comes in with a $200 paint scratch, we don't have to sell them on it, they're already sold. That's the power of relationship."

Nimble founder Jon Ferrara runs much of his business on relationships. "Be the best you can be," he says. "The market decides who wins." He says when strong relationships are paired with a dominant brand and maybe even fame, the cascade of unfair advantages is too great to overcome. "Why would anyone compete?" he asks.

Rosette Strategy Tip: The weeds naturally gravitate toward expanding networks of relationships, and you should, too. Look for new sources of alliances, even with competitors. Find ways to create mutual benefit. But also burnish your brand and reputation so there's no room for competitors.

Always Build Unfair Advantages

There are many ways to find, acquire, or build competitive advantages. Unfair advantages are even better because they imply exclusivity. Unfair advantages ensure no one can intrude in your space.

As we look across the span of strategies, attributes, and tools weeds use to win in the field, we can see they never do anything without attaching unfair advantages. Their seeds are super-spreaders. The seed pods add even greater force to their spread. The way weeds protect themselves, deny territory to others, the way they seek out alliances and steward their species, and certainly the way they grow and spread like a weed, all function at such a high level because of those unfair advantages.

The purpose of this chapter, and of rosette strategy, is to elevate our thinking about how we approach every aspect of our businesses. The weeds are telling us never to make a move without injecting unfair advantages. These should be the first words out of our mouths when considering new moves or shoring up our present business: What are our unfair advantages?

What Is My Rosette Strategy?

- What are my present unfair advantages?
- What can I do to make them even stronger and apply them in more ways?
- Am I building unfair advantages into everything we do?
- What are the books in my top one hundred list?
- What courses can I take to add new layers of skills?
- Where else can I find more unfair advantages?
- How can I acquire exclusive new advantages?
- What is my story, and how can I turn it into an unfair advantage?
- What am I known for?
- What do I love to do?

- Who do I know?
- How can I layer all of these factors into new unfair advantages?

W.E.E.D.S. Model at a Glance

1. Seed Strategy

Spread an overwhelming amount of seeds that bring devastatingly unfair advantages to your business.

2. Seed Pod Strategy

Multiply the effect of your seed strategy by borrowing the reach and influence of others.

3. Thorn Strategy

Use all available legal protections to safeguard your IP, develop a reputation for using them, and negotiate like a weed.

4. Segmentation Strategy

Strike a balanced stance, prepare for disruptions, be ready to pivot decisively.

5. Rosette Strategy

Cultivate and integrate unfair advantages into everything you do.

Points to Remember

- The Canada thistle bristles with unfair advantages, including razor-sharp spines, highly mobile seeds, and an expansive root system that doubles as a secondary method of reproduction.
- The Canada thistle serves an example for our businesses, which should also be armored with multiple unfair advantages.
- Canada thistles also produce a radial fan of leaves at their base, known as a rosette, which completely blocks sunlight and water from surrounding plants.

- Rosette strategy is based on producing those same results in our marketplaces—using unfair advantages to make it impossible for others to compete.
- Unfair advantages are competitive advantages with a moat, as Warren Buffett describes.
- Unfair advantages can be found, built, or acquired.
- Exclusivity and first-mover leverage can field new unfair advantages.
- You don't have to be Amazon, IBM, or Coca-Cola to enjoy the benefits of a dominant brand in your field.
- Becoming "a category of one" creates new opportunity to be the first ever and dominant player in a new market of your making.
- The purpose of rosette strategy is to always be cultivating and integrating unfair advantages into everything we do in our businesses.

16

VINE STRATEGY

Chinese wisteria (*Wisteria senensis*). A native of Japan, China, and the eastern United States, wisteria is a striking, flowering vine often cultivated for its ornamental beauty. A twining vine that can grow to gargantuan proportions, the largest known example is located in Sierra Madre, California, occupying more than an acre and weighing 250 tons.[33,34] The plant can quickly grow out of control, toppling trees and damaging buildings and anything else within reach. credit: © The Board of Trustees of the Royal Botanic Gardens, Kew

THE MOSCOW RULES author Jonna Mendez knows something about masked intent. As the former head of disguise for the CIA, she specializes in misdirection as a strategy. The goal was always to make the operative unremarkable: the "gray man who gets into an elevator and you can't describe him." Of course, it was also the CIA's job to spot the other side's spies. Both sides know that when a bad actor is unnoticeable, they're free to do a lot of damage.

Mendez has lived on the same forty-acre spread for more than twenty years. Mostly forested, there is a large clearing for house and yard, with many mature plants and trees nearby. Off to one side was a hardy but relatively small planting of *Wisteria senensis* that constantly bloomed with massive, draping strands of fragrant violet flowers. It was one of Mendez's favorites.

She and her husband decided at one point to transplant it to the edge of the yard, near a stand of grand old oaks. In the new spot, the plant suddenly sprang to action, scaling the trunks of several mature oak trees. What Mendez hadn't realized was her wisteria was capable of growing ten feet per year and quickly reaching as high as seventy feet. When she discovered her oaks were under attack, swift action was required.

"When we realized it was about to topple one of the trees, we had to get rid of it with hatchets," she recalls. She also noticed the wisteria was following classic spy technique. "You're always trying to go unnoticed until it's time to finish the operation," she explains, "and there comes a time when you have to declare yourself. You're under the radar until you're not." This is exactly what the plant did.

Spy stories aside, vines are the perfect adaptation for explosive growth, making vine strategy critically important in business. It is the essence of cooperation and partnership, allowing companies to borrow the infrastructure of others to gain access to vast new sales channels, followings, networks, intelligence, relationships, brand dominance, credibility, buyers, funding, IP, and other resources. Such alliances are a substantial portal to growth—for weeds and businesses.

When there are nearby structures to climb, vining plants use a brilliant strategy for fast growth. Rather than investing in growing thick trunks, the plants focus on life-sustaining root structures that always supply water and nutrients, while foraging vines do an entire tree's worth of photosynthesis with simple leaf-bearing tubes. It is the very definition of operating beyond 1:1 scale and will be our immediate strategy for expanding our businesses.

A Truly Nimble Strategy

As we move through the W.E.E.D.S. model, we see how each level intertwines. Seeds already equipped with great modes of mobility become even more effective when combined with ingenious launch mechanisms. Meanwhile, roving vines constantly probe for vertical structures to instantly elevate the weed's position for sunlight. We see it in nature, but what would that look like in the business world?

It would look like Jon Ferrara's free-trial strategy. Ferrara is founder and CEO of Nimble, a software as a service (SaaS) customer relationship management (CRM) platform for social media. The system tracks activity, but also gathers contact details, key interests, and other information that's helpful when forming relationships. Ferrara's target audience is literally everyone using social media.

If he had unlimited funds, he could simply spend untold millions building his user base. But the weeds tell us there is a much faster and easier way, by using a vine strategy *at no cost.* Ferrara's featured free trial strategy has achieved that and more, by gaining access to two of the world's largest Internet user bases. Suddenly, Nimble's free-trial offer was placed within Microsoft Outlook and Google Workspace platforms. That put it in front of more than *three billion users.*

This is brilliant. As a seed strategy, free trials make a lot of sense, especially for SaaS platforms. The only cost is a sliver of processor time, rendering a service temporarily for free, then moving users behind a paywall. Ferrara says the free trial not only leads to up-sells, but expands throughout an organization once someone starts using the platform. "Nimble is a Trojan horse," he explains. "You'll bring it back to your business and become an evangelist."

Placing the offer on platforms used by more than three billion users, each creating multiple daily impressions, amounts to a massive spread of seeds. As a seed pod strategy, it's hard to imagine a more impressive force multiplier. And as a vine strategy, meant to borrow the infrastructure of others to gain greater access to markets, you can't beat a pair of partnerships with Microsoft and Google. It all binds together neatly, creating a delightfully weedy, totally unfair advantage for Ferrara's operation.

Focusing on the vine element alone, Nimble's example shows how we can probe for opportunities to team with others, to borrow their infrastructure to gain access to vast new sales channels and networks, creating a suddenly greater scale for the business. The right vines, as Ferrara discovered, can create an instant change in the hierarchy of businesses vying for customers, revenues, new markets, greater market penetration, and funding. In the business world, these are the equivalent of sunlight. And we can never get enough of that brand of sunshine.

Vine Strategy Tip: Who are the dream partners who have the power to change your scale overnight? Create a vine strategy program with compelling spread elements, make yourself utterly refer-able, and reach out. See if you can get some of those dream partnerships to take root.

Borrowing the Infrastructure of Others

Vine strategy is based on teaming for the mutual benefit of the involved parties. It's pretty simple. Each side brings something valuable to the other to create a sum greater than its parts. The relative size of the participants doesn't matter. Fortune 500 companies can team with single proprietors and each side can gain tremendous value. But as the party seeking weed-like growth, we should focus on partners who have unique force multipliers to offer.

Nimble's free trial serves as our prototype. As a startup, it was a coup for Ferrara to achieve product placement in the Microsoft and Google platforms. The company has since grown, but Nimble is nowhere near the size of the two giants. That a small startup could form partnerships with Google and Microsoft, and gain access to their three-billion-member user base, should embolden all of us in formulating our own vine strategies.

Reachdesk founder Alex Olley used his own version of a vine strategy to launch his company, a gifting platform that helps sales teams get meetings. "Our buyer is a B2B salesperson," he explains, "so we started hanging out where they are." Olley and his team headed straight for every industry event he could find, stopping by every booth, where his target audience was waiting. "We'd go to all the events and talk to our core audience for free," he says.

In Olley's vine strategy, he borrowed the infrastructure of event producers to reach their audience, which also happened to be his audience. There was no need for a partnership agreement; there was simply an opportunity to visit industry shows at no cost and talk to everyone running the booths. Those were the sales reps who needed the Reachdesk service. They were also the buyers and influencers Olley needed to launch his business.

He leaned heavily on the reach of LinkedIn, too, which became part of Reachdesk's vine strategy. Olley's team ran competitions on the platform and rewarded winners with their product. "At one point, we asked, 'Want to send a Halloween box?' The post generated over 1,500 tags and suddenly our inbound business didn't cost anything."

Outbrain president Andrew Breen says his company grew quickly as a result of vine strategy. "When we started," he says, "all of our growth was through vines." Outbrain provides analytics and data-enhancement for digital advertising, used to optimize campaign results. It's a service used by ad agencies to enhance their offerings and performance, so naturally, they were happy to recommend Outbrain to their clients. The more the agencies teamed with the company, the more successful their campaigns became.

This is a classic example of vine strategy. Outbrain needed customers and growth, and the agencies needed a competitive edge that would enhance client results. They provided complementary services, and each enhanced outcomes for the other. Their relative size didn't matter. What did was the synergy of their pairing. Their shared outcomes were greater than the sum of their parts, so naturally, the advertising community was ready to lend their infrastructure to gain their own unfair advantage.

Tech sales executive Bill Scott discovered the power of vine strategy in his first sales job, selling educational books door to door. "We would drive into a new town, set up shop, and break into the market," he explains. "It was always a matter of building references, then presence." Scott's process was to develop a vine strategy quickly, by building a network of referral sources. The vine strategy elevated Scott's reputation all over town, providing quick access to the warm sunshine of fast sales.

Borrowing infrastructure can take many forms. It can be access to vast user bases, as in the case of Nimble and Outbrain. It might involve a formal agreement, or it could be under the radar, as with Reachdesk's start. Or it could look like Bill Scott's quick market entry process, establishing referral relationships that lead to more and more opened doors. It can also take an entirely different form, if we consider networks and followings as infrastructure as well.

Vine Strategy Tip: As you make your list of potential dream partners, figure out not only who can bring benefit to you, but whom you'd bring unmatched value to as well.

Borrowing the Networks of Others

Social media created a new brand of referral source: the influencer. Influencers have been around since the dawn of humankind, but social media has intensified their reach dramatically. Their significance is exploding while legacy media wanes. Borrowing an influencer's infrastructure can mean reaching millions of people ready to follow their leader's recommendations.

MYOB chief sales and support officer Daniel West recalls his own growth trajectory as a sales enablement influencer. Growing his following by borrowing the networks of other influencers, he launched an effort to guest write for others' blogs and appear on other people's podcasts. "I didn't want to go through the effort of building my own podcast or blog," he explains. "My vine strategy paid off with a significant uptick in my social media presence."

SaaS founder coach Dan Martell says borrowing followings as a vine strategy is a lot like drafting on a bike. The idea is to borrow the momentum of others to build your own. "It's done all the time in the SaaS community," he explains. "Shopify used their distribution for separate apps and found they could quickly spin them off to attach to other platforms and explode their growth." Martell says vine strategies play a crucial role in allowing tech startups to "bootstrap" their way to success.

Speaker, author, and connector Jeff Sheehan says it's easy to connect with influencers, but we must be careful to connect with the *right* influencers. "The Fyre Festival had a lot of influencers involved," he says, "and look how that turned out." (Not well.) Still, for those who fit your mission, Sheehan says connecting is a simple matter of helping them out. "It always comes back as an incredible advantage."

Investor Jay Kim says while social media can waste a lot of time, it can still be a fantastic source of borrowed infrastructure, to connect with people and form relationships—especially with other influencers. "I'd been following Gary Vaynerchuck for years," he explains, "and I'd always wanted to get him on my podcast." But rather than ask right away, Kim engaged in a long play. "I watched his videos, commented on his posts, and responded to his tweets," he recalls.

Suddenly, he saw his opportunity when Vaynerchuck released a new book. "I bought some of his books and posted that I couldn't wait to pass them around in Asia." That got Vanyerchuck's attention and raised the level of their relationship. Vanyerchuck has since helped elevate Kim's profile and business into that bright sunshine we're all seeking: explosive growth of our businesses.

Marketing CEO Jack Kosakowski points to a slightly different kind of influencer, not necessarily based in social media. "Build advocates," he says. "That gives you the fastest way of growing." It makes sense and is a central feature of building collective scale, discussed later in this book. An army of advocates constantly recommending your product or service is a fast path to explosive growth. "A lot of businesses make the mistake of spending a lot to build their own audience," he explains, "but it's much more effective to spend time with your influencers to create scale."

WE Trust co-founder Cherie Ware adds, "When you have referral partners recruiting other referral partners, your network grows like a weed." The key, she says, is building a dominant reputation. "We take care of our clients like family members and word spreads fast," she says. "We've never needed a sales team. They sell for us."

Broadway producer and super-connector Michael Roderick prefers influencers he can connect with in person, activating what he calls "associative leverage." He explains, "If I'm associated with someone, the brain goes directly to assuming I'm on the same level as that person." Roderick uses associative leverage constantly in his theater production practice, regularly convening industry panel events.

"Most people at a high level want to leverage their time at scale," he explains, "so I invite them to sit as an expert panelist." Roderick has used the method to attract some of the biggest names among Broadway producers as panelists, appearing before an audience of his peers. "When they see me on stage moderating the discussion," he says, "everyone starts thinking of me as one of the top producers, too." In this way, Roderick borrows the prestige of the top producers to reach the warm sunlight of having his own productions financed and launched. His borrowed status becomes actual status, and his process amounts to an unfair advantage.

Vine Strategy Tip: Include influencers in your vine strategy partner list, too. They may not have vast channels of customers, but they can certainly produce vast amounts of customers for you. Power the partnership with compelling spread elements and a generous rev-share plan.

Borrowing Down

In nature vines don't grow downward, but in business, they can. "Amazon supports many vine strategies," says startup strategist Pierre-R Wolff. "By building a distribution framework anybody can take advantage of," he explains, "they create enormous scale for their own business." When the vine strategy involves two mismatched businesses in terms of size, the smaller company is always looking for scale through the borrowed infrastructure of the larger company. That usually involves access to vast new sales channels.

But the larger company gets a big payoff as well, by accessing valuable intellectual property held by the smaller ones. Amazon does this with every product, every book, every business storefront hosted on their platform. They're aggressive, master-of-the-universe digital marketers and distributors, holding many uniquely unfair advantages in their space. But the platform is nothing without interesting and useful wares to sell. In this way, Amazon gains powerful leverage by reaching downward in their vine strategy.

It's interesting to look at vine strategy from the other side. I'm always thinking in terms of partnering with someone who can provide more sales. But if we're the smaller partner in the equation, we're required to bring compelling, unique intellectual property that is well protected with a robust vine strategy. Perhaps I can share my own circumstance as an example.

In addition to being an author, I own a marketing business, which includes an image bank of more than fifteen hundred cartoons. What's unique is all of the cartoons are created with personalized captions, for marketing applications. There is no other collection like it in the world. And then the cartoons are part of a system backed by millions of dollars worth of utterly unique test experience. I am the world's leading expert on the use of personalized cartoons in a range of marketing applications, and the content is protected.

That certainly qualifies as unique, well-defended intellectual property. And it gives me unfair advantages when seeking partnerships or direct business with some of the largest companies in the world. It allows me to partner upward for an utterly synergistic effect. It gets even better when the cartoon devices are coupled with strategies to maximize marketing results. As I've mentioned, I'm also known as the father of contact marketing, through the publication of my earlier books, *How to Get a Meeting with Anyone* and *Get the Meeting.* So this utterly unique cartoon asset becomes a vetted solution to help sales teams get more meetings with top decision-makers, or to get a mailing to perform better, or to double open rates in email.

I have positioned my business as a unicorn whose IP, when deployed against the infrastructure and processes of much larger companies, becomes their new unfair advantage. As a result, I form partnerships quite easily. If your company is the smaller of the two, your vine strategy will also require the development of uniquely unfair advantages and IP, carefully protected through your own thorn strategies.

Former *Forbes* chief insight officer Bruce Rogers agrees. "Partnerships are a way for smaller companies to throw more seeds out there," he says, "while allowing larger companies to be more agile." Both sides benefit. "But," he cautions, "what good is a partnership if it doesn't create something new you couldn't do by yourself?" The benefit to both sides and the sense of synergy are required for any partnership to succeed.

Venture capitalist Esther Dyson points to the software and computer business as an example of a successful downward vine strategy. "Value-added resellers (VARs) are essential in the computer business," she says. "Oracle, EDS [Electronic Data Services], CSC [Computer Sciences Corporation], PwC [Price Waterhouse Consulting], Salesforce, and HP all start marketplaces for their VARs and app developers." They have all recognized creating thriving sales channels for their downward partners is essential to their own growth.

Vine Strategy Tip: When you reach out to companies bigger than your own, you're asking them to partner down. You should be doing the same, by partnering with smaller companies or standout individuals who can bring unique unfair advantages to your operation.

Elements of Effective Vine Strategy

Mutual benefit: A viable vine strategy must provide mutual benefit to all parties. Each partner should be excited by their potential gain from the relationship.

Symbiosis, synergy: The partnership should serve specific needs for both sides, and the sum of the resulting benefits should be greater than the individual contributions of each side. It should produce a magical combination—something utterly unique in the marketplace.

Unique value: Differentiating features of the partnership should result in an unfair advantage for both sides in the marketplace. Otherwise, there is no reason for the partnership to exist.

Do no harm: In their cooperative venture, partners must strive to protect each other's businesses and reputations. Vine strategies should bring mutual benefits, not mutual destruction.

Vine strategies are based on the borrowing of infrastructure to create uniquely unfair advantages for both parties. It allows each participant to instantly elevate their place in the hierarchy of their markets. In nature, most plants cannot change their height; they grow as tall as they grow and that's it. Vines are the only structure in the plant world that are able to change their height, creating dominant access to sunlight.

Like the Nimble example, an effective vine strategy can change everything about the scale of the business. The effect of a vine strategy should be like popping through the clouds in an airliner; suddenly, you're out of the dark, gray fog and into the bright sunshine of a lot more sales, revenues, and profit. It's the kind of sunshine we all need to grow our businesses like a weed.

What Is My Vine Strategy?

- Which companies would be our ideal partners to open vast new sales channels?
- What is the ideal profile of companies we can benefit the most?
- What kinds of partnerships would help us grow fastest?
- Can we establish exclusivity with our partners to block entry by competitors?
- What are the critical IP and resulting unfair advantages we have to offer a larger partner?
- Is there a benefit to reaching down in our vine strategy?
- Whom would we reach down to?
- Who are the influencers who could become our partners?
- What unique unfair advantages do we have to offer to influencers?
- Who are our competitors securing vine strategy relationships with and how can we replace them?

W.E.E.D.S. Model at a Glance

1. Seed Strategy

Spread an overwhelming amount of seeds that bring devastatingly unfair advantages to your business.

2. Seed Pod Strategy

Multiply the effect of your seed strategy by borrowing the reach and influence of others.

3. Thorn Strategy

Use all available legal protections to safeguard your IP, develop a reputation for using them, and negotiate like a weed.

4. Segmentation Strategy

Strike a balanced stance, prepare for disruptions, be ready to pivot decisively.

5. Rosette Strategy

Cultivate and integrate unfair advantages into everything you do.

6. Vine Strategy

Borrow the infrastructure of others to gain dominant access to critical resources in your market.

Points to Remember

- Vines are the only structure in the plant world that enable upward mobility to gain dominant positions to gather sunlight.
- Businesses can do the same by establishing vine strategies that provide dominant positions for sunlight in their markets.
- The basis of vine strategy is borrowing the infrastructure of others to gain new, elevated market positions.
- Vine strategies can come as the result of a formal partnership, the use of open infrastructure at no cost, cooperation among

companies with complementary offerings, or informal referral relationships.

- Networks and followings are the infrastructure of influencers, which can be borrowed to great effect.
- Advocates can volunteer their own networks to spread seeds and generate growth in our businesses.
- We can borrow the prestige and status of others through associative leverage, causing others to think of us as having similarly high prestige and status.
- We think of vine strategies as always reaching upward, but they can also reach downward for great effect.
- If we're the junior partner in a vine strategy, our unique value comes in the form of our protected intellectual property.
- An effective vine strategy is like lifting out of the clouds during takeoff and emerging into the bright sunshine of more sales, revenues, and profit.

17

ROOT STRATEGY

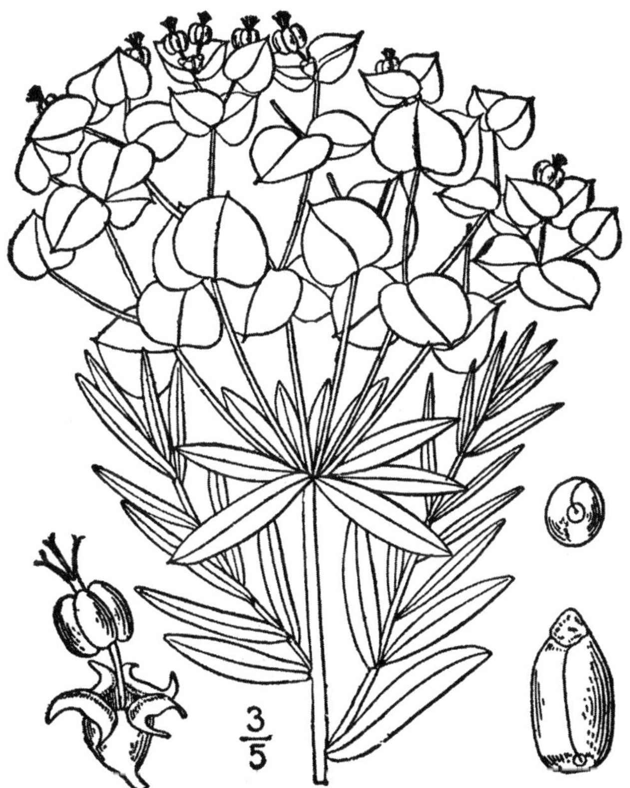

Leafy spurge (*Euphorbia esula*). Native to Eurasia, leafy spurge is an invasive species that has spread across grasslands in North America. It reproduces through seeds ejected from explosive pods, and from an extensive root system that sprouts new plants from shoots. It outcompetes native species by growing dense, massive root systems that can span fifteen feet across and nearly thirty feet deep, providing superior access to water and blocking ingress to competing plants.[35,36,37] credit: © The Board of Trustees of the Royal Botanic Gardens, Kew

IN NATURE, ROOT systems are often the determinant of which species wins the battle for turf. Deep taproots amount to strategic weapons, providing critical access to water. During dry months, when water supply tightens, the plant with the deepest roots wins.

But roots don't just extend downward. They can extend laterally, creating stealthy columns of attack or impenetrable thickets that deny entry. Roots can also act as a secondary form of reproduction, with vertical shoots piercing the ground, emerging as new instances of the plant. Some lateral shoots can reach great distances, allowing the plant to escape any barrier, reaching under roads, retaining walls, and residential structures from below.

Roots forage and permeate, but also store nutrients, sustaining the plant throughout the year. Other than gathering sunlight, the subterranean portion of the plant is nearly self-sustainable, and that's by design. Roots are the strategic seat of the plant, the vault safeguarding its life force.

Leafy spurge is a weed with an ironclad root strategy. Above ground, the plant barely reaches a few feet in height, but down below, it can stretch nearly thirty feet. At that depth, *Euphorbia esula*'s taproot keeps it well stocked with water while other plants perish during dry spells.

The root system not only runs deep, it can become massive and dense, reaching as much as fifteen feet across for a single plant. The thicket becomes a fortress against any possible competitors. Although the plant's reproductive strategy makes use of seeds ejected from explosive pods, its roots are also part of the plan, popping up new shoots everywhere to create instant collective scale.

Leafy spurge's root strategy is so extensive, it's the plant world's version of an iceberg, with 90 percent of its mass submerged. The result is a weed that grows in dense clumps, perfectly adapted to a predatory life on grassy plains. Its greatest defense is its massive network of roots that make it nearly impossible to remove or control.

In the plant world, roots are the repository of value and life force. In business, root strategy maximizes real, lasting, rapidly growing, transferrable value in the business.

The Nature of Root Strategy

As entrepreneurs, our sacred mission is to create and accumulate value. That comes in the form of products and services that enhance our clients' lives and businesses. But what really matters is real, transferrable value in the business itself. Our quest is always to increase the *worth* of our enterprises.

That is the purpose of root strategy in the W.E.E.D.S. model: to steward resources and stores of value in order to *keep the business running while growing its worth.* Financial advisors often have the unenviable duty of informing clients of the true nature of their own businesses. They often arrive with fanciful values in mind, but most have done nothing to build actual worth. The advisors end up telling them, "What you've built is a job, not a business."

What's the difference between building a job and a business?

In our world, the measure of value comes in the form of revenue metrics, process, intellectual property (IP), reputation/brand, networks, relationships, channels, and real assets, including cash, real estate, equipment, natural resources, and commodities. But in the weeds' world, it's much simpler: Do I have the resources I need to operate at a high level, and what is my process for generating growth? Resources and process.

Throughout this book, the weeds have been sharing their message of simplification and focus. In some instances, like optimism in the weeds mindset, the message is "Let our actions lead emotions." In the W.E.E.D.S. model, it's "Don't just focus on your favorite or most comfortable areas, operate equally on all eight levels." And in root strategy, it is, simply, "To build worth, focus on process and sustainability."

We humans tend to overcomplicate things, which leads to inaction. And in business, inaction leads to disaster. We have all sorts of considerations to take into account. Assets depreciate, and there are hard costs such as leases and insurance. They have significant tax implications depending upon how they're structured. Cash can be invested and managed in so many ways. And then there are stock options, ownership stakes, classes of shares, and so much more. The weeds are telling us to simplify concerning building worth.

Root Strategy Tip: If you don't have a financial professional in your operation, get one involved in forming your root strategy, concerning building and maximizing worth in your business.

Process, Sustainability, and Growth

In the weeds' world, worth is measured by dominance in the field. It's measured by wins in battle and the ability to persist. As we have seen throughout this book, process enables weeds to win consistently. And they're always operating under careful management of resources to ensure sustainability across growing seasons, across times of abundance, scarcity, and crisis.

In business, process is how expertise and experience are accumulated, organized, and shared throughout the organization, enabling each member to function at a high level of expertise and efficiency. And this is where the worth of so many businesses is often lost.

Process consultant Leanne Hoagland-Smith estimates 75 percent of mid-size businesses and 95 percent or more of small businesses have absolutely no recorded process. This means they're failing to build worth, while creating massive inefficiency in their operations. Every onboarding of new team members must be reinvented every time it's done. Operations take longer, needless mistakes are made, and customers are lost. This is a massive blind spot in business and a major failing to accomplish our mission as entrepreneurs.

Again, weeds make it simple. Their process is automatically passed along, baked into their DNA. There is no need for training or documentation. It's all automatic—and all part of their process. It needs to become part of the way we do business as well. It's as essential as charging for our products and services. If it isn't happening, the business isn't functioning. In fact, it isn't even a business. Not yet—not until process is recorded and efficiently shared across the organization.

All of this is quite similar to the way the military and even the CIA operate. "The military is a giant training machine," explains General Barry McCaffrey. "It takes ordinary people and turns them into people of heroic capability." McCaffrey recalls the time his chief of staff was transferred twenty hours before the launch of the Desert Shield offensive in the Iraq War. "Because of the depth of training in the military, I knew all three replacements would be qualified and could step into the job within hours."

Process is ultimately a plan, but with full flexibility to adapt to new conditions. "It's usually better to grow where you're able to go," explains former CIA station chief and *Rebels at Work* author Carmen Medina. "Follow the terrain rather than following a master plan." Medina is describing the mechanism that allows weeds to count on the existing process, while always in a balanced stance, ready to pivot in new ways and add new elements to the process.

If that reminds you of segmentation strategy, it's not by mistake. Every level of strategy in the W.E.E.D.S. model, every attribute in the weed mindset, and every element of scaling like a weed are all part of the process weeds use—and we'll use—to grow, expand, and dominate in our markets. But only if we commit to documenting and using our process.

As process is key to building worth in a business, root strategies must also build sustainability. Root systems gather and store water and nutrients from the soil, and automatically distribute what's needed, balanced against future needs, as conditions change. It may happen automatically, but it's also a complex management process, involving inventories, expected intake, and calculations of time and change.

This is a constant battle for businesses—for example, something as basic as keeping sufficient cash on hand for day-to-day operations and contingencies.

Root Strategy Tip: Start recording your processes immediately for all areas of your business. You can write a manual, but simple video works, too. Put one of your team members in charge of gathering and recording established processes. Organize process assets so they're easy to navigate. Use them for onboarding new team members.

Your Root Strategy Think Tank

In business, there are dimensions of worth beyond the process and raw resources of the weeds' world. Weeds live a simpler life than we do. They don't juggle things like patents, copyrights, trademarks, or ever-changing relationships, channels, networks, reputation, and brand equity. Still, their message of simplification is alluring: *Don't overcomplicate things. As we generate assets, whatever they may be, our job is simply to curate and optimize.* They're talking about curating and optimizing the essence of the plant and its life force.

We already addressed protection of intellectual property in Chapter 13. But protection and curation are not the same thing. Think of your portfolio of intangible assets—IP, relationships, and brand—as a priceless art collection, to be displayed in a high-end gallery. They're irreplaceable works of art, so of course they're protected against theft and damage.

But if those assets are going on display, they must be curated as well. Groupings of complementary art—themes among the pieces, where each artist's work belongs in the gallery—have great impact on the success of the show. It all depends upon the quality of curation of its components.

Cultivating and curating our portfolios of IP, relationships, and brand are essential to the expansion of worth in our companies. The collections require constant attention, to ensure they're always put to their highest use. Conditions are always changing in the field, which brings new threats and new opportunities. The function of root strategy is to monitor those and curate accordingly. As things change, are there new opportunities to make use of our IP? Do our innovations suddenly fit new markets? Are new licenses possible or desirable?

The mission of curating and optimizing company worth is a top-line responsibility. There is no more important job in the enterprise. And there is an obvious temptation for the owner to reserve this domain as theirs alone, but weeds would suggest otherwise. Later in the book, we'll examine the weeds' simplified approach to building scale. They eschew 1:1 leverage, always approaching their mission as a group. They always operate within the tremendous leverage of teamwork.

So the weeds would advise getting stakeholders involved, as a group—and forming a root strategy board. Different from a board of directors, this would be an internal think tank composed of executives, managers, and key employees. Every participant should have a stake in the outcome, and perhaps stock options or bonuses tied to increases in company value. This could even be extended to all employees, in the form of a suggestion funnel, in the quest for improved process and unrealized uses of company assets.

This is not the way things are usually done, particularly in the curation of company worth, but the weeds are clear about this. Their success and competitiveness derives from flawless execution and working as a collective. Warren Buffett seems to agree. In a recent letter to shareholders, he explained, "My job as chairman is simply to (a) treat operating managers well, (b) stay out of their way, and (c) allocate the capital they generate."[38]

Buffett seems to be saying the same thing the weeds are: the team builds worth, not the individual.

If there is a team, empower them to be part of the collective scale of the company and to participate in the rewards. If there is no team, build one. Imagine the power of a think tank constantly sharpening process, curating assets, and optimizing the worth of the business. That's the essence of root strategy.

Root Strategy Tip: Give thought to who you want as part of your root strategy think tank—and have fun with it. They can be from within the company or they can be outside experts and thinkers—or you could go really wild and invite a favorite author or business personality.

Annuals and Perennials

Time to add a bit of complexity back into the equation. No two businesses are alike. Same for their processes. Elements may be similar, but the collection of expertise held by any given company is unique. Complicating matters further, there are two modes of growth trajectory—rapid and continuous—just as there are two distinct types among plants: annuals and perennials.

Their lifespans, missions, and strategies couldn't be more different. Annuals, as the name suggests, follow a one-year plan that has them germinating, flowering, seeding, and dying off every twelve months. There is an apparent strategy here that treats the entire species as a single, aggregate creature, while the individual plants serve as the cells of the plant. The species lives on, renewing itself with completely new cells every year. An obvious benefit is the rapid path it provides to evolutionary adaptations.

Annuals are under tremendous pressure to reproduce in sufficient numbers, just to maintain their turf, requiring a massive seeding effort. Canada fleabane and water hemp, both discussed previously, are vivid examples of the annual strategy in action. They're seeding superstars, with water hemp producing as much as 4.8 million seeds per plant, and Canada fleabane's nearly quarter-million seeds capable of traveling more than 300 miles in any direction. Meanwhile, their rapid evolutionary arc has allowed them to become immune to most herbicides, including RoundUp, within the past few years.

Annual plants live life fast and, each year, face the possibility of total extinction. But their processes have been beating the odds for millions of years, each and every year. Perennials, by comparison, are the more sedate variety. Their lives span multiple years, and their mission is to build more permanent life force repositories.

As annuals place their strategic focus on seeds, perennials put it in their roots. These plants don't perish during senescence. They're built for continuity.

The two approaches to evolution, process, sustainability, and growth are obviously quite different. And they give us useful insight into the use of weed strategy in startups versus, say, privately owned businesses, which are ultimately destined for quiet succession or acquisition. The correlation is the pace of expected changes in ownership.

Startups are meant to pass through quick changes of ownership as they go through rounds of funding. Their arc from angel-funded seedling to IPO maturity and beyond is meant to be a short one. Investors want their money multiplied quickly. They are the annuals of the business world, with weed-like attributes and rapid scaling. They live fast, adapt fast, and move fast. Many die off, but some become the "unicorns" we all hear about (the Ubers and SpaceXes and Zooms).

Perennials are the companies that take a different route to prominence. They're still in a hurry to scale, but usually through organic growth, with or without outside investment. They're much more likely to bootstrap their way to the top of their fields, building worth as they go along.

We can see that seed strategy will be the heart of growth for startups, just as it is for annuals in nature. And root strategy will be more prominent for privately owned companies that are not seeking IPO launches. But in either case, the mission of building and documenting their processes is critical to success in their missions. Root strategy remains central to that process.

Root Strategy Tip: Velocity of ownership dictates different approaches, but processes must always be developed and recorded to generate worth in the business. If you don't want to record it yourself (most entrepreneurs don't), hire a consultant to do it for you. One way or another, get it done.

Closing Thoughts

So two elements (process and sustainability), two actions (curate and optimize), two classifications (annuals and perennials), and one mission (create transferrable worth). When we're talking something as complex as growing the worth of a business, the weeds have given us simplicity and clarity. And within that simple framework, we see the complexity in a new light.

When someone like branding maven Kathy Ireland says, "We earn trust every day," we can easily slot that into process (what we do to earn trust every day), sustainability (trust builds brand strength, attracting more customers and revenue), and curation and optimization (greater brand strength builds greater worth in the business). When executive officer Tim Minert talks about the syncopated marching of a college band or the critical nature of a pilot's checklists, we can easily file that under process and optimization.

When MYOB chief sales and support officer Daniel West tells about the nearly $1 trillion economy Salesforce built around its platform, we can bank that in the curation and optimization accounts. When career coach Jonathan Schober talks about the utility of multiple income streams, we can see it serves our sustainability mission. When Insurance Office of America CEO Heath Ritenour or sales thought leader Alice Heiman talk about putting the client first and cultivating customer success, we understand how that goes directly to curation of relationships and optimization of value.

Whether we're talking about shooting-star startups, rock-steady privately owned SMBs, giant public companies or solopreneurs, everything we can conceive that builds worth into our businesses falls neatly into one of the four interlocking quadrants of root strategy: process, sustainability, curation, or optimization. It makes it easy to understand how to build true worth in our companies, so we never have to hear "All you've built is a job." Jobs don't have roots, but valuable businesses surely do.

What Is My Root Strategy?

- What is my exit strategy?
- What are the assets in my company?
- What do I hold as intellectual property?
- What are the key relationships that sustain my business?
- What is my network, and how can I add more of the right people to it?
- What is my company's reputation, and how can we enhance it?
- How would someone in my marketplace describe my brand?
- What can we do to enhance the value of our brand?
- How can we curate and optimize our assets to produce more worth?
- Who should be part of my root strategy think tank?

W.E.E.D.S. Model at a Glance

1. Seed Strategy

Spread an overwhelming amount of seeds that bring devastatingly unfair advantages to your business.

2. Seed Pod Strategy

Multiply the effect of your seed strategy by borrowing the reach and influence of others.

3. Thorn Strategy

Use all available legal protections to safeguard your IP, develop a reputation for using them, and negotiate like a weed.

4. Segmentation Strategy

Strike a balanced stance, prepare for disruptions, be ready to pivot decisively.

5. Rosette Strategy

Cultivate and integrate unfair advantages into everything you do.

6. Vine Strategy

Borrow the infrastructure of others to gain dominant access to critical resources in your market.

7. Root Strategy

Use process, sustainability, curation, and optimization to cultivate the highest possible worth of the enterprise.

Points to Remember

- As entrepreneurs, we have a sacred mission to create and accumulate value.
- The purpose of root strategy is to steward resources to maximize value.
- Process is how expertise and experience are recorded, organized, and shared throughout an organization, enabling each member to function at a high level of expertise and efficiency.
- Process is the key ingredient to building a business that has transferrable worth for succession or acquisition.
- Sustainability allows the organization to allocate real assets as needed to perform at a high level across time.
- Curation is the artful combining of assets to create new permutations, new opportunities, and new value for the company.

- Optimization enables the organization to maximize the collective value of assets, producing greater worth for the business.
- Root strategy should be addressed by a think tank of stakeholders within the company, not just by the owner or CEO.
- Everything that builds worth into our businesses falls neatly into one of the four interlocking quadrants of root strategy: process, sustainability, curation, or optimization.

18

SOIL STRATEGY

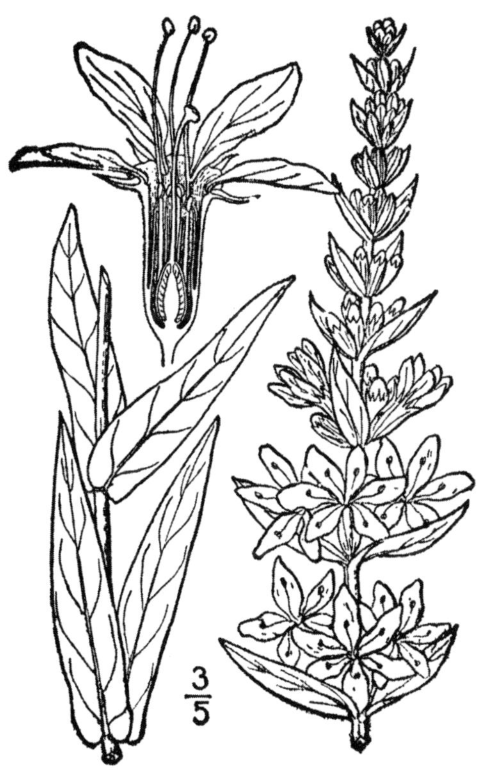

Purple loosestrife (*Lythrum salicaria*). Purple loosestrife came to America in the 1800s in the bilges of cargo ships dispatched from England, where it lightly decorates riverbanks and bogs. In its native home of Europe and Asia, its growth is held in check by other native plants, but in America, it has become invasive, choking waterways with alarming ferocity. Each plant can produce as many as 2.7 million seeds annually. Preferring wet soil habitats, its thick, woody roots can also thrive in several feet of water or in dry soil near the water line.[39] credit: © The Board of Trustees of the Royal Botanic Gardens, Kew

TALL SPIKES OF brilliant flowers disguise the aggressive intent of purple loosestrife. It is a beautiful plant that adds a colorful flourish to riverbanks and wetlands in its native habitat of Europe and Asia. But in America, where it has no natural competitors, it is an aggressive weed, choking off all other species' access to waterfront turf.

The plant's growth strategy profile is aggressive, with monstrous seed production and a fortress-like root architecture. Each plant produces up to 2.7 million seeds, while thick, woody roots form a lattice that supports massive growth. But the purple loosestrife's greatest unfair advantage is its broad tolerance for soil conditions.

When a plant's seeds are dispersed, by wind, water, animals, or humans, the seeds land where they land. The plant has no choice where its seeds will set down their roots. Its soil strategy is to make the most of wherever it ends up. Still, there are limits. If a dandelion seed lands in water, it won't germinate. Ditto if it happens to summit a snowy peak or land in the ocean. But pretty much anywhere else, it will thrive.

The presence of too much water is a significant barrier for most plants, but not for purple loosestrife. The bell curve of chance dictates 2.7 million seeds will drop into a range of soil conditions, even while confined to a narrow band of wetlands turf. Most seeds will plant themselves optimally on the shoreline, others will set down in several feet of water, while others will find themselves on dry land. This weed does them all with equal prowess, from water's edge to several feet of water to dry land. Purple loosestrife thrives no matter what.

The technical challenges of this are immense. Just imagine, landing in either several feet of water or on dry land, and living the rest of your life there. You'd be two completely different species. The ability to adapt to a wide range of living environments is purple loosestrife's unfair advantage. And it's one we're going to explore now, for ourselves.

The Nature of Soil Strategy

Weeds don't get to change the conditions they find themselves in. Wherever their seeds land is where they take root, and they are prepared to make the most of it.

So in a sense, they do control their soil conditions through their weed mindset. They're not going anywhere and they're not giving up. They are wherever they are, to stay and thrive. The purpose of this book is to instill that same weed mindset in each of us, but in this area we humans have the edge.

We have mobility; weeds don't. We can invent things out of thin air; they can't. We have an impact through words and deeds that can change outcomes; weeds have no equivalent options. Still, as we examine the soil strategy options to follow, we recognize that the weed mindset is also what will drive our success.

General Barry McCaffrey talks about the work ethic of soldiers in battle: "They're willing to get killed doing their jobs." There is no greater commitment to winning than being ready to die for a cause. McCaffrey says that is the sort of mindset required to win no matter what. "Do you have a reputation as being someone who is part of the team and with an unlimited capacity for work?" he asks, adding, "Can you be counted on?"

With the right mindset, we can substantially improve the quality of our growth environment. Our areas of leverage include internal conditions of culture, freedom of expression, retaining talent, and creating internal movements. External factors include community, vision, movements, regulatory considerations, and market viability/timing. Let's take a look at how soil strategy can be applied to change outcomes for your enterprise.

Soil Strategy Tip: To change our conditions for growth, we must start from within. This is about investing in team development. Your team is your army. Consider hiring a development coach to foster your team's weed mindset (see Weed Mindset Bootcamp training in the "Let's Connect" section at the end of the book).

Internal Culture

Team members like to know they're in charge of their destinies within any organization. The more impact they have, the happier they are. Their jobs become more fulfilling when they know they're contributing to something that carries them to greater heights in their own careers. And the more invested they are in their jobs, the faster the organization grows.

A vibrant company culture, a feeling of being part of a historic moment in time, is a force multiplier for growth. A team that is energized just by being part of it all is a team that will naturally act like a weed collective. They'll win battles, negotiate like they own the company, and post their excited support on social media. Building a strong internal culture changes the soil conditions for the enterprise, giving it an optimized environment for growth.

Internal culture might be defined as a set of common behaviors and assumptions within an organization, but for our soil strategy purposes, we need an upgraded definition.

Internal culture: A shared mindset among team members of deep belonging and significance to the organization, of being an important part of a momentous time, vision, or story as it unfolds.

Everyone wants to feel like they matter and that their contributions are essential. In 2013, Wharton professor Adam Grant released a study of the Midwest chapter of Make-A-Wish Foundation, as it tinkered with self-proclaimed employee titles. During a trip to Disneyland, staff members noticed Disney employees had been retitled as "cast members." They imagined conjuring their own whimsical titles might help relieve the stress of the job.[40]

Soon, the CEO became the *fairy godmother of wishes* and wish managers became *merry memory makers.* Grant concluded the new titles helped employees feel "a sense of affirmation and psychological safety, reducing emotional exhaustion." Naming guru Alexandra Watkins points out the team's greater happiness and satisfaction "caused them to talk more about what they do" on social media.

If changing employee titles had such an effect, imagine what could happen if given more autonomy in other areas. Former CIA station chief and *Rebels at Work* author Carmen Medina says formality leaves no room for creativity: "I like scruffy, natural gardens." Medina's premise is that leaders should find ways to make their team more comfortable together. "Doing something by consensus squashes creativity," she says. "The intelligence community tends to be formal—hierarchical. I've always wanted to find a different way." The result was a noticeably stronger team culture.

The feeling of belonging and fulfillment is important, but we can do much more to change our internal growth environment. Author and turnaround specialist Dan Waldschmidt says the key to radical internal culture stems from a sense of mission. "Floundering companies are full of process without intensity or purpose," he explains. "The key is to inspire people to reach beyond themselves."

Another way to inspire greater reach is to develop a reputation for being indispensable. Executive coach Angus Nelson explains, "Being a member of the team needs to be a transformation of self. We need to feel we deserve and are worthy of success. One way to do that is to make our product or service indispensable."

So, fulfillment, a feeling of belonging, and making a significant contribution create a winning culture, but is there an even higher expression of internal culture? Yes, there is. Being part of a societal change, a new vision, or a historic moment can change anyone's perspective and create a great sense of alignment.

Soil Strategy Tip: Try hiring a story consultant to define and instill a "moment in time/we're making history" sense of mission and purpose for your team. Or, consider letting your team decide which charities they'd like to support as part of their mission with the company. The point will be to stir passion and purpose, centered around working for your company.

Internal Movements

Former *Harvard Business Review* editor and consultant Kate Sweetman specializes in helping businesses form internal movements. The idea is to create a platform for self-actualization that helps team members fully plug into their jobs and organization. When employees can see they're part of something much bigger than themselves, their work takes on even greater levels of significance.

"3M is a great example of this," she says, in the way the company invites participation from its employees. "Everybody within the company is expected to take a day a week to pursue their own thing." If they discover something worthy of development, they can put together a proposal. In this process, it's possible for any employee to become an intrapreneur and even start their own division within the company.

"That's how Post-it Notes came about," she says. "An employee took a failed adhesive and started using it in church hymnals to mark pages. They quickly realized it was useful everywhere and turned it into a blockbuster product." Opportunities to not just perform a job, but participate as a stakeholder in the business, certainly form strong internal cultures. But it goes well beyond that. It creates a hive of activity on the company's behalf that otherwise wouldn't have been happening. It activates collective scale among employee teams, a very smart approach.

Amazon does it a little differently, but the outcome is similar. Their "Hackathon" events invite participants to join a twenty-four-hour race to explore solutions to specific problems or opportunities. Group sizes are limited to "no more people than can eat two pizzas." Sweetman points out these events create an entire ecosystem of people, from within and outside the company, who become deeply dedicated to the mission.

Tech companies seem especially well positioned to create such ecosystems. "Apple did it with their app store," she explains, by putting out the message "We need your help. We need you to develop apps for this new platform." At last count, there were more than two million apps available for download on the store. Being an app developer became a sweeping movement that touches every consumer's life.

But since we're talking about elements of soil strategy, it's fitting Sweetman would save the best for last: a fertilizer conglomerate in Morocco. At first, the company was facing stagnant growth, which they solved with a quick turnaround program. But the company wanted to dig much deeper. "They thought, 'We can't just be concerned with ourselves,'" Sweetman says. "'We have to be in a weed patch.'"

The company took on an entire community development role, at first creating a university and engineering company. Then they asked employees to take up to twenty-eight days per year to help the community develop. They started small, with entrepreneurial startups, and then funded the build-out of a giant port. They became so successful, the company now represents a 3 percent share of the entire country's GDP.

Their philosophy became "We're trying to develop Morocco, not just our company." Imagine if every company in the world took on the same mission. Soil conditions everywhere would improve for all markets.

Soil Strategy Tip: Empower team members to become collaborators with the company, to create an even greater purpose. Let them tell you what they want to do to make the company better, more efficient, more profitable, and more a part of the community. Consider experimenting with team members creating their own titles. If they make sense and boost morale, make them permanent.

External Movements and Fanatical Followings

Some companies are entirely in the movement profession. And it's really good for business. Wizard Entertainment and Comic-Con founder Gareb Shamus recalls his early years, when he was a self-described nerd, engrossed with comic books and superheroes. "*Geek* and *nerd* used to be derogatory terms," he explains, "but I was fearless. I kept pitching comics and superheroes, and couldn't understand why other people didn't see it." The "it" he was referring to was the coming groundswell that would become today's Comic-Con and superhero phenomenon.

"The characters are what made this so successful," he explains—but also the social movement it ignited, especially among those who felt marginalized by society: the nerds and geeks. Shamus made them cool and gave them a place to congregate and celebrate. Today, Comic-Con is a worldwide movement, welcoming hundreds of thousands of visitors who rub shoulders with actors from their favorite comic book and sci-fi movies. Shamus turned his company into one giant, purposely inclusive cool-kids' party.

Giovanni Marsico is on the same wavelength, having founded Archangel, which is also more of a movement than a just a company. His cause is similar to Shamus's, a recognition that we all have a superpower within. "Any movement starts with the true believers," he says, "and spreads like a weed." Marsico sees movements as necessary for success, but also as an unfair, totally weed-like advantage. Everything becomes community-based, rather than the more transactional and traditional client-based approach to growth.

But Marsico says community building is more than a marketing strategy. "We build based on community first and product second," he says. "When you do that, people will stick with you in tough times. It starts by saying, 'These are the people we want to serve.'" Ultimately, building a community becomes a soil and thorn strategy. "People might rip off your IP, but they can't rip off your relationships," explains Marsico.

Venture capitalist Esther Dyson says a brilliantly disruptive vision can work the same way, attracting a community of investors. "The right vision will attract investors," she says. "They want to get rich." Journalist and METAL founder Ken Rutkowski says the personality of leaders can also create deep loyalty. "I was once interviewing Steve Jobs and asked, 'So Steve, what's the big deal about the MacBook Pro?'" Jobs suddenly handed over his personal laptop and instructed Ken to take it and try it out.

"Before long," Rutkowski says, "I started talking about the Mac and how much I loved it." But there was a problem: Microsoft sponsored Rutkowski's podcast and pulled their funding. "All of a sudden, I hear from [Apple's head of publicity] Katie Cotton, telling me I can keep the Mac." During the conversation, he explained he'd been talking so much about it, Microsoft canceled their sponsorship.

A week later, Rutkowski got a call from Intel, at Steve Jobs's behest, asking if they could sponsor his show. "Steve made a personal call to Intel, asking them to be my sponsor," he recalls. "When you look at the Apple brand back then, it was all about Steve listening and making a difference." Personality, integrity, humanity, and ingenuity can all inspire fanatical followings that provide the best possible soil for a company to grow.

Soil Strategy Tip: When people follow their passions, they do legendary things, which create movements. Are you following your passions in your business? If not, how can you incorporate them now?

The Magic of a Weed-like Mindset

While we have ways to affect our surroundings, others remind us that it's essential to check conditions before setting out. "It's obviously part of due diligence before starting any new venture," says Reachdesk founder Alex Olley. Entrepreneur Josh Steimle says it's basic entrepreneurship. "You've got to know the external, market and regulatory conditions going in," he says. "What's the market size? Is this worth taking the risk?"

But there will always be hurdles and rivals looking to uproot our efforts. Our ability to inspire movements and fanatical followings ultimately stems from having a weed-like mindset. Movements often spring from a mixture of compelling concept and a sense that this is our time—this is our historic moment. Years from now, we'll look back on this and think, "That was extraordinary. That was when everything changed."

That's what it felt like for Harlem Globetrotter Herbert "Flight Time" Lang every time the team landed in another city. "We felt like we were positive ambassadors of goodwill," he explains. "We were the world's basketball team." He recalls, "They would stop wars to have the 'Trotters come in and play." He says the constant feeling of being on a team of destiny changed his teammates, but also the world around them.

Aviation entrepreneur/YouTube sensation Mike Patey says a positive mindset changes the people and conditions around you, but a negative outlook can be just as powerful, albeit utterly damaging. "Disparaging others ends up hurting you," he says. "It shuts down creative thinking and prevents you from getting anything done." His inspiration for positivity is his father, who lost his eyesight when Patey was a teen.

His father's positivity never wavered. "I'm still here. I can talk to you, hold your mom's hand. I can listen to the birds," he recalls. "It's just my eyesight. It will come back." Thanks to new surgical developments years later, his eyesight did return. His faith in his father translated to astonishing creations and feats in aviation, which has created a large following on YouTube.

Patey's not doing it to promote his business. He's built his ultimate lifestyle, which creates a community of aviation enthusiasts who feel great loyalty toward anything he does. And all of it springs from his positive and adventurous mindset. Super-connector and Broadway producer Michael Roderick says having a positive attitude doesn't come from demanding perfection from yourself but permitting yourself to make mistakes.

"I write daily," he says, "and I give myself permission to suck." What he's saying is we can't always be consistently brilliant. There will be efforts that are off target. Roderick says, "Very often, entrepreneurs search for the perfect soil as opposed to just saying, 'I'm going to make a go of it over here.'" He's saying to not expect perfection. Let go of that, and make it your best. That's the mindset of a weed, for sure.

As Kate Sweetman points out, it's never one weed showing up in our lawns. It's many. We change our conditions for growth by working with many, by operating in collective scale rather than just by ourselves. Because *our* soil, after all, is the people surrounding us, our teams and companies, our communities, and the world. The more we make it a better place, the better our own conditions for growth.

Soil Strategy Tip: Let Mike Patey's airplane builds serve as a template for any special project you and your team can rally around. Is there a world record to beat? An exploration to mount? A film to make? Embark on an adventure together to supercharge your team's mindset.

What Is My Soil Strategy?

- What can I do to positively affect conditions for growth around me?
- What is our mission, and how does it benefit the community?
- What do we already do that could ignite a movement?
- How can we get our team more excited about what we do together?
- Is there a charity we can all get behind as a team?
- Who are our government representatives, and what's happening with regulations that affect us?
- Can we start an external recognition award as a team?
- How can we constantly build a more positive mindset as a team?

- What can we do to improve our environment for growth?
- How can we create a "moment in time" around our mission?

W.E.E.D.S. Model at a Glance

1. Seed Strategy

Spread an overwhelming amount of seeds that bring devastatingly unfair advantages to your business.

2. Seed Pod Strategy

Multiply the effect of your seed strategy by borrowing the reach and influence of others.

3. Thorn Strategy

Use all available legal protections to safeguard your IP, develop a reputation for using them, and negotiate like a weed.

4. Segmentation Strategy

Strike a balanced stance, prepare for disruptions, be ready to pivot decisively.

5. Rosette Strategy

Cultivate and integrate unfair advantages into everything you do.

6. Vine Strategy

Borrow the infrastructure of others to gain dominant access to critical resources in your market.

7. Root Strategy

Use process, sustainability, curation, and optimization to cultivate the highest possible worth of the enterprise.

8. Soil Strategy

Create the best possible circumstances for your business to grow, internally and externally.

Points to Remember

- St. Francis de Sales's famous quote "Bloom where you are" pays tribute to weeds' ability to flourish anywhere, in any soil conditions.
- Weeds don't get to change their ambient conditions, but we do.
- We have mobility, we invent things, and we can have impact through our words and deeds. Weeds have none of those options.
- But weeds do control their environment through their mindset.
- With the right mindset, we can control the quality of our growth environment, too.
- Internal culture is a shared mindset among team members of deep belonging and significance to the organization, and of being an important part of a momentous time, vision, or story.
- Creating internal movements can have a drastic effect on the outlook of our teams—and the growth of our companies.
- Internal movements spring from four elements: a shared mission, recognition, creative freedom, and a sense of making history together.
- External movements can transform a company into a cultural phenomenon, producing deep loyalty from its client base—and its employees.
- The better we make our communities, the better our own conditions for growth.

SCALING LIKE A WEED

19

1:1 LEVERAGE AND SCALE

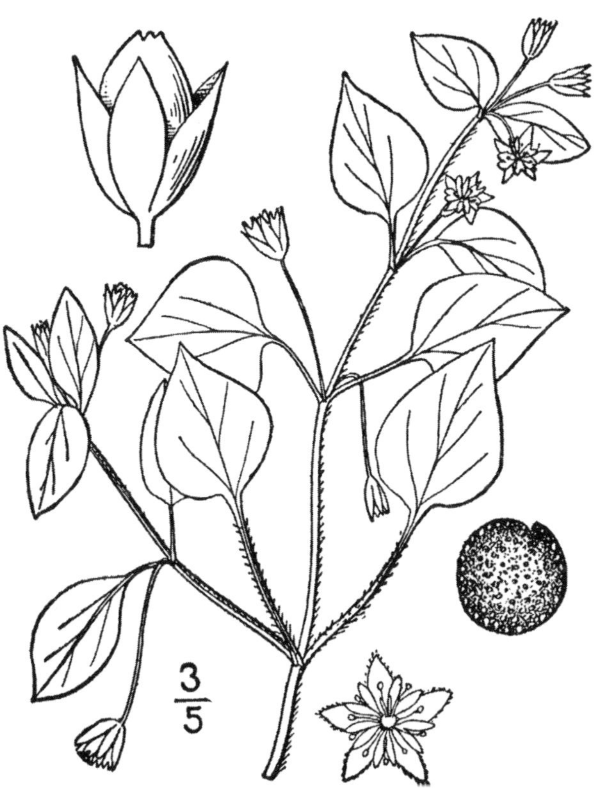

Chickweed (*Stellaria media*). Although known as a medicinal, chickweed is considered an invasive species, especially in farmland across North America and Europe, where it competes with wheat, rye, oats, and barley crops. Its soft, hairy stems grow to a length of forty centimeters, which hug the ground and quickly block sunlight for other plants. Chickweed is unusual in that it adapts to its climate and grows either as an annual or a perennial plant.[41,42,43,44] credit: © The Board of Trustees of the Royal Botanic Gardens, Kew

SOME WEEDS HAVE seeds that travel hundreds of miles on the wind. Some have root systems that extend thirty feet into the ground. Some can reproduce themselves from any shred of a branch or root. Some have seeds that hitch rides with hooks or adhesion. Some detach from their Earthly moorings to roll across the land, spraying seeds as they go. Some are covered with thousands of hypodermic needle-like hairs that inject painful toxins to keep intruders away.

And even with all that, the chickweed holds its own surprisingly unique and unfair advantage in the weed world: us.

For other weeds, the wind, water, rain, animals, birds, other weeds and plants, trees, buildings, fences, toxins, fear, desert sands, sunshine—even cracks in concrete—are their leverage. But for chickweed, we're their ticket. We're their leverage.

Chickweed inhabits six continents (everywhere but Antarctica), and we are entirely to blame. Their tiny dark seeds have no adaptations to fly in the wind, float downstream, or hitch a ride. The seeds are not sticky; they don't have burrs or tufts. They simply find their way into our implements for disrupting new ground.

Chickweed thrives in freshly disturbed soil, so they pretty much follow us around. We provide tilled farm fields, lawns, and gardens, and their ubiquitous seeds find their way into our handiwork. It's a symbiotic relationship, as the species also has medicinal and food value for us. But far from a polite herb, it is a highly invasive weed that suppresses crop growth. When it shows up in a field of planted barley, chickweed quickly germinates, covering the field and robbing seedlings of crucial sunlight. Crop yields can be reduced by as much as 90 percent.

The weed shows its unique adaptability by following us around, but it has another surprisingly unfair advantage. It is generally an annual plant, which means it puts down shallow roots and dies off every year. But in warmer climes, it puts down deeper roots and converts to a perennial. This is one very versatile little weed, but its best trick has been recognizing us as its partner. The weed clearly understands leverage.

The Nature of Leverage

Leverage is the multiplication of force exerted by one object against another, through the use of a lever acting against a fulcrum. The lever achieves mechanical advantage by varying the length on one side of the fulcrum versus the other. A longer length acting against a shorter portion will multiply the original force.

We apply this effect whenever we use pliers or a shovel. If the portion we're pushing or squeezing is longer than the portion on the other side of the pivot point, our force is multiplied. Whenever we use any implement of modern life, leverage is always the objective. We drive to get somewhere faster than walking. We use stairs rather than climbing a wall. We use a stove to cook rather than starting a fire by rubbing sticks together.

Leverage is everywhere. Oddly, in business, the word is mostly used to describe debt. Borrowing funds obviously allows us to multiply our purchasing power. If someone has leveraged an asset, they have borrowed against it. But there are so many other ways we multiply force through leverage in our businesses.

If you're an owner, your team provides leverage; they allow you to do more than you could on your own. Your relationships, alliances, and partnerships provide enormous leverage in your operation. We need to broaden our recognition of leverage not just as debt, but as a force multiplier throughout our businesses.

Leverage allows us to integrate the expertise of others, raising the level of competence in our enterprises. Process is a form of leverage that allows us to infuse our own collective expertise and best practices across our teams, causing them to act with a higher level of competence.

Weeds tell us in order to scale our businesses, we must root out all forms of 1:1 leverage in our thinking, then quickly reorient toward multi-channel scale, and then collective scale. Weed species operate at collective scale, which is part of their core formula for explosive and sustainable growth.

The more leverage we create in our businesses, the more successful we become. Seeking leverage should always be our goal as we build our careers and businesses, but there is an unfortunate paradox blocking the way.

The Self-Reliance Paradox

From the moment we're born, our mission is to become self-reliant. Childhood play teaches us to recognize danger and solve problems. It teaches us to be confident and explore our limits. It teaches us to think for ourselves.

Self-reliance is reinforced through games like musical chairs and team sports. Who can forget the first time the music stopped and we ended up without a chair? It taught us to be aware of our circumstances and proactive in our actions. Team sports taught us to work hard to gain proficiency in order to win.

The problem is, the learning seems to stop there. Even though we're exposed to team dynamics, we seem to remain inwardly focused on beating every challenge ourselves. We learn to teach ourselves new skills and hone them with practice.

Another way of understanding the paradox of self-reliance is examining the leverage—that is, mechanical advantage—it creates. When a fulcrum is equidistant from the two ends of the lever, it produces 1:1 leverage. The amount of force on one end is equal to the force applied on the other. There is zero mechanical advantage; the force achieved is a direct result of our efforts.

> **Self-reliance paradox: The more focused we are on self-reliance, the less likely we are to build scale.**

We're in direct control of our outcomes, but unable to exceed our own strength. To do that, we must increase the leverage. And to do that, we must move the fulcrum closer to the object to be moved. This is intuitive if we're working with a pole braced against a rock. But not so obvious when trying to scale our businesses.

Like chickweed, our greatest leverage in business is other people. There are deeply diminishing returns from limiting our output with our own talent and expertise. It's obvious our collection of abilities can never match the crowdsourced expertise and force of a team.

The 1:1 Leverage Trap

We're taught to be self-reliant, which means we're also deeply conditioned to seek 1:1 leverage. We're told to study hard to get good grades to get into a good college and then get a good job. But jobs are not scalable. We can't have a thousand jobs. We're not taught how to scale. In fact, we're trained *not* to scale.

Our adherence to 1:1 scale is so deeply rooted, we have no awareness of it. It's just the way we naturally think. And it absolutely prevents us from scaling anything.

Everyone who has ever dreamed of starting a business knows working for someone else stifles freedom. There is no pursuit of our passions—no chance to build something of value for ourselves. But 1:1 leverage doesn't lessen its grip once we become entrepreneurs, either.

Many years ago I was laid off from my job as a marketing manager. Still in shock, I pressed ahead, offering my services to my previous employer's competitor. But this time, I went in as the president of my own marketing agency, asking for a retainer, which was twice what I was paid in my previous job. I got the account and was ecstatic.

Soon, they asked me to create a leave-behind device for their sales team. I designed and sourced the production, and marked it up. The profit from that single project exceeded my entire year's salary at my old job. Then I moved on to the publishing industry, picking up clients like Time, Inc., Condé Nast, *The Wall Street Journal,* and *Forbes.* And I was paid $25,000 a shot to write direct mail campaigns. It was equal to what many people made per year back then.

Still, I was blindly mired in the trap of 1:1 leverage. Each client was high-touch, and none of the work was delegable. There was no recorded process. I was doing it all on my own. I was making excellent money and thought I'd built an elite business. But the truth was, I was still working a job, filled with elements only I could do. It was still 1:1 leverage.

I've mentioned earlier the uncomfortable task financial advisors have when consulting new clients. A lot of these clients own businesses, but never executed a root strategy to produce actual worth. The advisors are often the first to tell them their businesses are worthless. In fact, they don't even have businesses. The clients find themselves in this predicament because they never eliminated 1:1 leverage from their operations.

Financial people have a term I will borrow here: *leverage trap.* It's used to reference when investors borrow money to speculate on ETFs (electronically traded funds). If the market dithers, fees accumulate that can quickly wipe out potential gains. In the financial world, that is known as a leverage trap.

Our predicament is different but has the same effect: wiping out value from our hard work. The 1:1 leverage trap prevents scalability and destroys the worth of our businesses. It stems from the inefficiency of doing everything ourselves, rather than distributing the work across a dedicated team.

> **1:1 leverage trap: A self-limiting attitude based on insistence of doing and keeping everything ourselves. By infusing our labor into our process and never sharing equity, we become our own bottlenecks, severely limiting our opportunity to scale or build worth.**

Leverage and process are two sides of the same coin. Process enables us to share our collective experience and expertise across the enterprise. Leverage allows us to multiply the force of our process with the expertise and labor of others, inside and outside the organization, raising our output to higher levels.

All of it produces greater worth in the business, because it can continue without you. Suddenly, you have something you can sell to a willing buyer.

100 Percent of Nothing

My father was a highly self-reliant person. His passion was sailing, which is a true test of wit and skill. He was the kind of person who never took "no" for an answer. And in that way, he was an inspiration.

But my father was also an entrepreneur, although not a particularly successful one. He had grand plans, insights, and innovations, but he was consumed with keeping it all for himself and doing everything on the cheap. It left him in a constant shortfall, always scrambling for more funds. At one point, when things were getting particularly desperate, I asked, "Why don't you take on a partner?"

His reply was immediate: "I don't want to give up the equity." But, equity in what, exactly? If the business was failing because of his refusal to share in exchange for new leverage, then there was no equity, because there was no value. I expressed it to him this way: "If you don't do something now, you'll end up owning 100 percent of nothing." He didn't like the feedback, but it turned out to be 100 percent correct. Sadly, he died nearly penniless.

Imagine insisting on walking everywhere instead of driving or flying. Imagine insisting on learning every possible skill instead of hiring experts. Imagine insisting on doing all jobs in your company rather than building a team. Can you see how this prevents any possible scaling?

When we're operating at 1:1 leverage, it's obvious to everyone around us. Clients sense it, and it decreases their respect. Competitors, vendors, and partners spot it, too. It affects every relationship we have. Those who are succeeding have a rapidly expanding team and sphere of influence. Those who are not are constantly short of funds and always too busy to live.

Success lies in making the leap toward symbiotic leverage, involving other talented and resourceful people, whose shared involvement makes the resulting enterprise much larger and stronger. Fortunately, these things are easily changed, by following the advice of the weeds in the following chapters.

Scaling like a Weed

1:1 Leverage

Root out and eliminate all sources of 1:1 leverage in your operation.

Points to Remember

- Leverage is the multiplication of force exerted by one object against another.
- The further the fulcrum is from us, the greater the multiplication of our effort.
- In business, leverage refers simply to debt, but we can broaden its meaning to include other people: investors, employees, partners, vendors, and more.
- Leverage allows us to raise our performance by drawing upon the expertise, experience, and resources of others.
- The more leverage in our businesses, the more successful we become.
- The self-reliance paradox states the more focused we are on self-reliance, the less likely we are to build scale.
- The 1:1 leverage trap is a self-limiting attitude based on insistence of doing and keeping everything in our operations ourselves.
- By infusing our labor into our process and never sharing equity, we become our own bottlenecks, which severely limits our ability to scale.
- Success lies in making the leap toward symbiotic leverage, and including other talented people in our enterprises, whose involvement benefits all parties.
- To scale like a weed, start by discovering and eliminating all sources of 1:1 leverage in your operation.

20

MULTI-CHANNEL SCALE

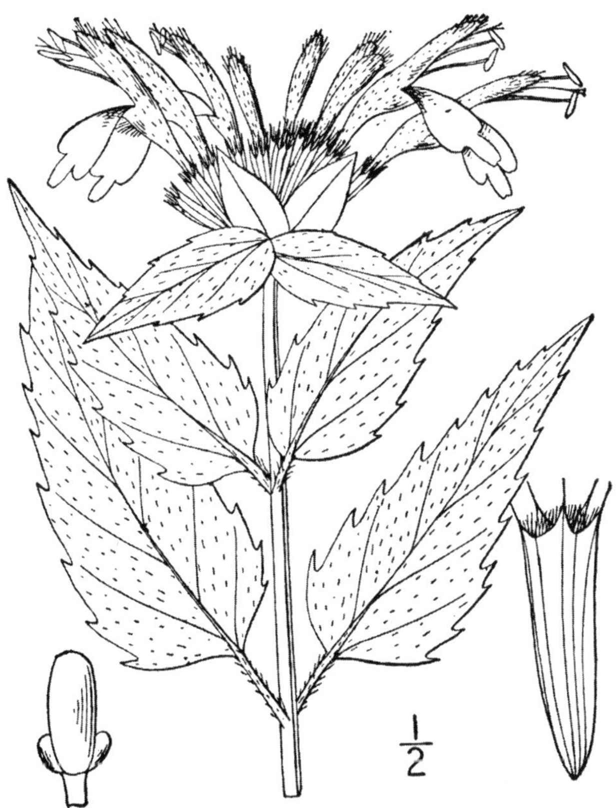

Bee balm/wild bergamot (*Monarda fistulosa*). Bee balm is a favorite among gardeners for its brilliant, fragrant flowers that attract pollinators. A member of the mint family, *Monarda fistulosa* is an aromatic herb whose flowers and leaves are edible in the raw or as a sweet-scented tea. It is also considered invasive due to its aggressive spread from fast-growing runners and shoots that form new plants and breach garden barriers.[45,46] credit: © The Board of Trustees of the Royal Botanic Gardens, Kew

BEE BALM IS not a vine. Part of the mint family, it is considered an aromatic herb. Its stems are upright, reaching a height of four feet. Its seed production is moderate, with no special adaptations for flight or spread, other than dispersal action from birds.

It's not a vine, but it clearly has a vine strategy. Although it will never scale nearby trees or man-made structures to reach great heights, *Monarda fistulosa* has formed a symbiotic partnership with human soil disruptors—otherwise known as gardeners.

Symbiosis is a partnership between two species which creates leverage for both. Bee balm produces striking blooms that look like neon signs to butterflies, bees, and hummingbirds, attracting throngs of pollinators to our gardens. Bee balm also has medicinal uses, and its flowers and leaves can be eaten or brewed into a delicious tea. It's easy to see why gardeners want it around.

Meanwhile, *Monarda fistulosa* count on us to bring them into our yards. They do spread by seed, but prefer to reproduce through shoots from their root systems that emerge as new instances of the plant. For that reason, when gardeners add the plant to their gardens, it's usually a transplant, not a deposit of seeds.

Monarda is so effective at this form of spread, it has also earned a reputation as an invasive species, because once planted, it's hard to contain. Plant it in a neat sector of the garden and it will quickly spread to all corners of the yard.

Still, it is only somewhat aggressive in its expansion, certainly nothing like the other weeds featured in this book. While unruly at times, this beloved plant adds a splash of color to our lives. And it attracts our most favorite visitors from the wild. So it is always welcome in our gardens and yards.

And in that way, bee balm has adapted a useful strategy to gain new ground. It has selected us not only as its vine strategy partner, but as its gateway to multi-channel scale.

Start the Spread

When weeds show up in our lawns, we know they arrive equipped with millions of years of evolution. They're crafty and nimble, aggressive and resilient. They're experts at executing their processes with ruthless persistence. When they show up, they're prepared for battle.

Let's look back at where we've come, because we are assembling the same level of readiness for your expansion. In the previous section, we examined the eight levels of strategy in the W.E.E.D.S. model. And in the previous chapter, the role self-reliance plays in both pushing us forward yet holding us back.

It's a lot to take in—and a lot to put into motion. We start with defining our strategy and building our growth process based on each level of the W.E.E.D.S. model: seed, seed pod, thorn, segmentation, rosette, vine, root, and soil strategies all combine to define an enterprise bristling with unfair advantages, ready to burst on the scene. And this is the chapter where that burst begins.

Activating Your Weed Mindset

To produce explosive growth requires the right strategy and process. But it also requires a carefully cultivated mindset. The coming phase of accelerated growth will focus on intensive outreach, which will be exhilarating and frustrating. And it will change your life. But your potential partners will erect all sorts of unexpected, unwarranted barriers. Nothing will happen according to your timeline. This will be your first test as a weed.

In "The Weed Mindset" section of this book, we examined the attributes that make weeds such formidable competitors. They are irrepressibly optimistic, ruthlessly persistent, brutally urgent, ferociously aggressive, utterly adaptive, and unshakably resilient. They deal with what is, not what they thought they were entitled to or expected would happen.

Kickstarting your weed mindset is surprisingly easy. It's all based on behavioral activation, the structured use of actions to produce desired psychological effects. Although usually used to treat depression, our goal is to increase optimism. Optimism, in turn, will ignite the entire set of weed attributes needed to produce the explosive growth we're after.

The weeds have told us to let our actions lead our emotions. That stems from their flawless execution of their process, without emotions, because they don't have any. If they could speak, they'd tell us to move our emotions out of our way and simply behave the way we would if we were feeling ever more optimistic.

Ask yourself, "What would I do if I were feeling more optimistic than I do now?" Write out the answers and keep them handy. If that means you'd take more walks, take more vacations, or travel more, do it. I suspect most of us would include getting more exercise among our answers. Workouts are the simplest path to behavioral activation, because you can work out anywhere, it doesn't cost a thing, and the rewards are immediate.

Rearrange your schedule to create room for daily exercise. Get up earlier to fit it in, or add daily appointments in your calendar to reserve the time. Give yourself permission to put daily exercise at the top of your priority list. It will make you healthier, but also far more productive and optimistic. If you don't already do it, you'll be amazed at the effect a daily workout routine will have on your mood and outlook.

Next, add this daily affirmation to your routine. Find a quiet space every morning and say the words out loud:

Weed Mindset Daily Affirmation

I am a total weed.
I bow to no one.
I am irrepressibly optimistic.
I am ruthlessly persistent.
I am brutally urgent.
I am ferociously aggressive.
I am utterly adaptive.
I am unfailingly resilient.
I win at all costs.
I am a total weed.

The exercise routine and saying the affirmation out loud are both forms of behavioral activation. They will reprogram your brain and create the mindset you'll need from this point onward. The weeds say these will allow your actions to lead your emotions. But what they're really doing is producing an absolutely weed-like ethos of winning at all cost.

As you activate your weed mindset, it is important to treat it as a material asset. It should be listed in your root strategy as a resource to be maximized and stewarded. Be mindful of others, whose influence either enhances or undermines your mindset, and adjust their access accordingly. Assign a value of at least a million dollars to your mindset. And treat it as though it is actually worth a million dollars. After all, it's what will enable you to achieve the miraculous growth you're about to produce.

Take the Leap

In Chapter 16, we looked at various examples of businesses forming vine strategies, using partnerships to climb to dominant positions in their fields. There was Jon Ferrara's vine strategy that placed a free-trial offer on two of the biggest platforms in the world: Google's Gmail and Microsoft's Outlook. The result was constant visibility among three billion potential customers.

We looked at various examples of borrowing the networks of others to create greater reach and borrowing down to access unique IP, products, and innovations that create unfair advantages. And we examined the elements of effective vine strategy, how alliances create mutual benefit and synergy for each party, and how partnerships create unique value.

In order to form these rapid-growth partnerships, we'll need to know who to approach, and have the ability to connect with maximal effect. We'll need to develop our refer-ability, as Michael Roderick calls it, with hard-hitting branding, a compelling story, and spread elements.

As we develop these elements of our vine strategy arsenal, we also must consider how we balance new growth with the elimination of 1:1 leverage in our operations. That will include producing current deliverables, and carefully culling dead-end clients who may temporarily be necessary to meet overhead. The transition from 1:1 to multi-channel scale will require working in both realms initially, until the larger scale sources allow the removal of unprofitable sources and methods.

This will be our process:

1. Identify all sources of 1:1 leverage; develop elimination plan. Determine all choke points in your operation. These might include areas where your labor is part of the delivery, production, or support processes that constantly tie down your time and attention. Anything that can be delegated should be, while you distill your functions to the things that are uniquely your areas of expertise and value to the company. This will free your focus for growing and building the business. It should also increase the revenue and output of the business. When the "CEO" is also the person fulfilling orders, respect and credibility evaporate. Develop a plan to grow staff and delegate as much of your duties as possible as growth takes root.

There are always clients who demand much, but don't add to your operation. Take a hard look at who's not worth keeping. Some clients will be invaluable to your efforts to grow and will support an expansion of the relationship. Some may also be helpful with referrals to help you grow. Go through your list and determine which will fit your expanded model as you grow and which should be eliminated once new lines of business are established.

Create a clear plan to eliminate all choke points, but don't take action just yet. As you progress through the growth process, check your 1:1 elimination plan constantly, to allow it to evolve with you. If you will be eliminating clients, find ways to do it without losing the relationship. Things can always change, in their operation or yours, and even when deactivated, they may useful.

2. Take inventory of your network; develop multi-channel expansion plan. We started a review of your clients in the previous step. As long as the relationships are good, all of them are possible referral sources. They all know other people and, as you expand your domain, can lend critical support to your expansion efforts. But you also know people beyond your clients. Compile a list of contacts who can become referral, strategic, or platform partners. Find out who they are as people, understand the issues they face, discover what they're talking about. That comes from perhaps a social media/Internet search–sourced "profile scrape," as well as visits to their websites. Use a service like ZoomInfo, Seamless.ai, or Boardroom Insiders to discover stakeholders who will support and influence decisions.

Your list should include centers of influence, existing clients, social media contacts, influencers, and platforms that offer vast customer/user base audiences. Centers of influence may include CPAs, attorneys, consultants, and complementary businesses whose clients may need ancillary services they don't provide. Who are your favorite social media influencers? Who has command of followers that can fuel your growth? And which platforms are a fit for your services or products?

To formulate your multi-channel scale plan, start with your goals for growth. Which markets will you target? What are your revenue and profit goals? How will your offering fulfill the needs of your partners' clients or followers? How will it benefit your partners? You'll need a clearly defined statement of purpose to share with potential partners.

Your plan should also define the nature of the relationship you seek with your partners. Will it involve revenue sharing or discounts to their customers? Is there a special format, product, or service you're proposing? How will your partners benefit from the arrangement? Formulate all of these elements into an easy to read document ready to be circulated and signed.

3. Develop multi-channel spread elements and contact campaigns. In Chapter 13, we covered the act of "negotiating like a weed." If the negotiations are expansive—that is, in pursuit of a project or partnership—we want the initiative to spread like a weed. Our story must be compelling and well-crafted. Our exciting reputation should precede us. And we should be prepared with spread elements that illustrate our proposed journey together and encourage people to share it.

Infographics are excellent spread elements. These long-format, graphical depictions of complex stories make them easy to understand and even easier to share, usually as a jpeg sent via email or posted to social media. Video is also an effective spread format, especially when combined with a platform like Vidyard, BombBomb, or Loom, which can track views and passalong in real time. Spread elements can come in many other forms, too. T-shirts, deep personalization gifts, Zoom wine tastings—almost anything that creates involvement can help spread the excitement for the partnership.

You'll also need to develop outreach campaigns to connect with the contacts you don't yet know. Use mutual connections for introductions and referrals. Create a set of contact campaigns for cold outreach. These can be well-targeted, personalized gifts based on intel from earlier profile scrapes, or more involved, with formally developed creative. I use my cartoons; others have used swords, cupcakes, email, social media, and many other methods for breaking through. (If you're interested in digging deeper, check out my books, *How to Get a Meeting with Anyone* and *Get the Meeting,* or join my online course at *howtogetameeting.com.*)

4. Launch multi-channel expansion. You now have an expansion plan centered on partnerships, a list of people to contact, spread elements, and contact campaigns ready to send. You're ready to start your expansion campaign. Start activating requests for introductions from your clients and other contacts. Start sending your contact campaigns. And start having conversations with potential partners about how you can help one another.

As you run your contact campaigns, break your list into batches of ten or fewer. If they become interested, the work you'll do to secure the deals will be intensive and overwhelming beyond that number. Once you've cycled through each batch, move on to the next. Breaking into batches allows you to test approaches before rolling out to the whole group. The mission is rapid growth, but also not to lose business if you or your team become overwhelmed.

Moving through your expansion plan, you will gain new partners and valuable new contacts. These, too, can become valuable referral sources or new platforms for business. Be sure to explore all possible avenues together, noting that, as things evolve, new opportunities will always pop up. As you move through your growth campaign, be sure to keep good records. Or use a CRM platform to manage the details.

5. Eliminate 1:1 leverage choke points. You identified sources of 1:1 choke points and developed a plan to eliminate them in step 1. Now it's time to activate that plan. Any point in your production process that involves your labor should be eliminated immediately, by recording process elements, delegating, and training your team. At first, the time demands will be unbearable. The temptation to return to old ways of doing things will be fierce.

Resist that temptation and move ahead. The goal is to build a team and a business that can operate whether you're present or not. It's the only form of business that will allow for greater scale.

Next, take a fresh look at your client roster. As you've achieved growth, your process has changed, and your labor is no longer involved in production or delivery of your product or service. In that new light, are the clients still a dead end, or is there new opportunity to grow together? Make sure your efforts to save clients have been exhaustive, but realize some will have to go. Best to measure twice and cut once.

Achieving multi-channel scale will change everything about the way you do business, how you spend time, and the amount of freedom you'll have. Building your team, recording your process, and training your staff will build transferrable worth in your business. You still haven't achieved weed-like growth, but you're on your way.

In the next chapter, we'll explore collective scale, used by the titans of business to capture entire markets and amass fortunes. Welcome to the world of Elon Musk, Jeff Bezos, Warren Buffett, and more. Collective scale is where you will truly become a total weed.

Scaling like a Weed

1:1 Leverage

Root out and eliminate all sources of 1:1 leverage in your operation.

Multi-Channel Scale

Use vine strategy to rapidly scale through partnerships and alliances.

Points to Remember

- Multi-channel scale derives from vine strategy—borrowing the infrastructure of others—to create immediate, explosive growth.
- To transition to multi-channel scale, we must eliminate all forms of 1:1 leverage in our operations.
- Step 1 in the multi-channel growth process is to identify all sources of 1:1 leverage and develop a plan to eliminate them from your operation.
- Step 2 is to take inventory of your network, compile a list, and develop a multi-channel expansion plan.
- Step 3 is to develop tools—spread elements and contact campaigns—to connect with prospective partners and help them spread the impetus for new deals through their referrals.
- Step 4 launches the multi-channel growth campaign, to enlist the help of centers of influence, clients, influencers, and companies with vast sales channels to grow your business rapidly.
- Step 5 calls for the elimination of all sources of 1:1 leverage in your operation.
- Eliminating 1:1 choke points will provide vastly more freedom and start building true, transferrable worth in your business.
- Multi-channel scale will produce an explosion of growth in your business, but it is still just an intermediate step toward collective scale.

21

COLLECTIVE SCALE

Giant ragweed (*Ambrosia trifida*). Giant ragweed is a plant of impressive proportions, growing as tall as twenty feet. Native to North America, it has spread throughout the Northern Hemisphere. In all areas, it is considered a noxious and invasive species, preferring disturbed habitats such as roadside ditches, vacant lots, and farmers' fields. Due to its rapid growth and large proportions, it easily outcompetes agricultural crops. Making matters worse, it has recently developed resistance to glyphosate (RoundUp) and most other herbicides used in agriculture.[47,48,49,50,51] credit: © The Board of Trustees of the Royal Botanic Gardens, Kew

WHAT A PERFECT weed to introduce collective scale. Everything about *Ambrosia trifida* is outsized, including its common name, giant ragweed. A disruptor by nature, it's always seeking newly disturbed turf—usually farmers' fields—where it can quickly move in and dominate any crop.

The giant ragweed's unfair advantage is its ability to rapidly scale. Throughout its lifecycle, the weed towers over other plants in its field. It germinates earlier than crops such as soybean and corn. It grows faster and taller, too, quickly leaving competitors in the shade as it reaches heights of six to eight feet, with some rising as tall as twenty feet.

Farmers notice when a weed wipes out half of their crop yields, but *Ambrosia trifida* has countermeasures in its process. It has already developed immunity to several commonly used agricultural herbicides, including glyphosate (RoundUp).

Meanwhile, we are unwitting partners in its seed pod strategy. Each plant can release as many as thirteen thousand burr-covered seeds that adhere to animals, machinery, and us. We're often the ones who spread it.

Giant ragweed is part of a group of super weeds covered in this book. Remember water hemp? It spreads as many as 4.8 million seeds per plant. Canada fleabane launches its nearly quarter million seeds in a six-hundred-mile diameter. *That's every plant.*

Compared with the standard weed that everyone knows, the dandelion, these are in a class of their own. Dandelions are formidable, and, like all weeds, they operate at collective scale, which is to say, they recognize the power in numbers and the power of a shared process executed in unison. They recognize it as their goal for achieving scale. All weeds do this, but some seem to be especially equipped to achieve mega scale.

But enough about the more polite weeds. Let's see what it looks like when someone operates like a *total weed at collective scale.*

Total Weeds

Elon Musk is a total weed. We've watched as he has disrupted and revolutionized e-commerce, electric cars, and how satellites and astronauts are launched into space. Before he's done, he will have disrupted battery technology, home and municipal power systems, air travel, and Internet connectivity worldwide. And then he'll take us to the moon and Mars.

His development process for SpaceX has been fascinating and illustrative of utter weediness in business. We've watched as the Falcon 9 orbital booster progressed from crude prototypes exploding on the launch pad to the familiar, dependable, awesome rockets that deliver satellites and astronauts to orbit, and then land safely to fly again.

Then we witnessed the birth of an entirely new rocket system, Starship. The four-hundred-foot-tall, self-contained system is racing toward delivering astronauts and settlers to the moon and Mars, and revolutionizing air travel. When finished, Starship will take passengers throughout the solar system, or make the hop from Los Angeles to London in about twenty minutes.

Musk has used the same process as before, blowing up prototypes and practicing the flop/flip maneuvers that allow Starship to re-enter Earth's atmosphere. Just as with the Falcon orbital boosters, their process is left out for the world to see, as they try, fail, try, fail, try—and then succeed at doing something no one ever has done before.

The try-fail-try-fail-try-succeed process is not for the timid. With each iteration, he risked his own capital, but we can assume Musk never thought of failure as his ultimate outcome. He only saw the prize, and measured his ever-decreasing distance from it.

Now, imagine Musk trying to accomplish any of this on his own, without a team.

Collective scale: The optimal size, scope, composition, and culture of an organization to enable it to fully penetrate, dominate, and transform its market.

Jeff Bezos is also a total weed. Amazon started in his garage as the world's first online bookstore, at a time when it wasn't considered safe to purchase anything on the Internet. Bezos told early investors there was a 70 percent chance the company would fail, but three years later, an IPO made Amazon a publicly traded stock.

It was clear Bezos had unusually grand visions for the company. Amazon began sprouting world-first innovations including one-click checkout, a massive affiliate program, and a storefront platform for small- and medium-sized businesses to sell products on Amazon.

In 1998, the company launched an aggressive acquisition campaign to eliminate competitors, while broadening its offerings. Amazon Web Services became the dominant cloud services host, Kindle launched to compete with Apple's iPad, and Amazon Prime has more than one hundred million subscribers, receiving everything from free expedited delivery to free access to the company's eponymous movie streaming service.

Today, Amazon is the world's biggest online retailer and much more. It would be impossible to list everything they sell, because they sell . . . everything. Meanwhile, Bezos's hand is into everything else, from media to AI to space travel and more.

But Bezos couldn't have achieved any of this on his own, either.

Musk's SpaceX unit employs eight thousand, while Tesla's head count is seventy thousand. Amazon employs more than a million people. Musk and Bezos are total weeds, because they are not doing this alone. They have achieved collective scale, supported by massively talented teams, allowing them to succeed beyond anyone's wildest imagination.

Here's a more complete definition of collective scale:

Collective scale: The optimal size, scope, composition, and culture of an organization that enable it to fully penetrate, dominate, and transform its market. Factors include a well-staffed, best-in-industry team, an aggressively honed and adaptive installed process, a ferocious, well-tuned strategy, industry-leading innovations, rock-solid financials, and exclusive force multipliers.

Millionaires versus Billionaires

If millionaires think in terms of market share, billionaires think in terms of capturing whole markets, or inventing entirely new ones. We see that in the way Musk and Bezos have built their businesses, always with the assumption they would dominate, if not own, each market they entered. Everything they do is calibrated for that result.

There is no equivalent to what SpaceX brings to the orbital launch market. No one else on the planet has a constellation of 12,000 Internet relay satellites, other than Musk's Starlink. Tesla, a scrappy startup in the stodgy field of carmakers, still leads the pack by far in electric vehicles.

Amazon's affiliate program produces 500 million visits per month, from the top 300,000 of the 1.24 billion sites on the Web. The Amazon Storefronts platform hosts 20,000 small retailers. The company's share of global e-commerce is roughly 40 percent.[52,53,54]

When I interviewed T. Boone Pickens for this book, I was struck by the scale of his thinking. When he was on a mission to grow Mesa Petroleum, his first acquisition target was a company twenty-eight times the size of his own. And it worked. He then went after the giants of the industry. With each takeover campaign, he and his investors made millions whether they made the acquisition or not.

He had an uncanny ability to spot market trends early and step in with insanely aggressive plans. In one case, he spotted an early trend in the price of natural gas, aggressively bought up futures, and suddenly had control of the entire market.

There are others with similar histories of big plays that either created market dominance or defined entirely new ones. Warren Buffett, Bill Gates, Richard Branson, Larry Page and Sergey Brin, Larry Ellison, Eric Yuan—they're all pulling off amazing feats and utterly dominating their markets.

Some inherited seed money, but most built their businesses and wealth from scratch. But there were always investors and highly skilled teams helping them achieve collective scale.

Does that mean billionaires have different mindsets than the rest of us? It's not as likely as you might think. They do see greater possibilities and pathways to get there. And they are willing to do whatever it takes to realize their plans. But that still sounds like the standard weed mindset we've been discussing. They just crank it way up. The difference is their ability to leverage force multipliers against collective scale to gain greater effect from every action.

We, too, have the option to turn up the volume on our own weed mindsets, and employ force multipliers at collective scale. We decide whether to be a demure dandelion, forcefully capturing new turf, lawn by lawn, or a formidable water hemp, spewing out millions of seeds, rapidly evolving to overcome any challenge, and dominating millions of acres of ground.

I find it deeply encouraging that whether we're solopreneurs, startup founders, SMB owners, publicly traded corporate officers or franchisees, beginners or veterans, millionaires or billionaires, the same system can give each of us new leverage. After all, the mindsets we cultivate and the origin of the strategies we use to grow all come from the same source: weeds.

Collective Scale and Force Multipliers

There is no millionaire mindset—no billionaire mindset. There is just weed mindset dialed up or down. And there is no separate growth model, one for millionaires and another for billionaires. The same eight levels of weed strategy apply to every one of us, regardless of our scale.

The difference is how intensively we want to apply what the weeds are offering us. The same is true for the scale of our enterprises. We choose whether they remain small and relatively insignificant, or grow to great heights, with great significance.

That dial-up of intensity is reflected in how the weed mindset is cultivated and how intensively we flesh out our weed strategies. But the biggest factor is how we scale. We see the great difference between operating at 1:1 leverage and multi-channel scale. That's already a giant leap in productivity and results.

But the weeds tell us the greatest leap is when we combine collective scale with force multipliers. Collective scale centers on creating a ravenous, hard-charging team of motivated investors, experts, and partners, executing and constantly perfecting a fierce process for growth.

The term *force multiplier* comes from military science, referring to any factor that enables a unit to achieve far greater outcomes in battle. Superior technology, weapons, training, logistics, strategy, and mindset all combine to make a military force far more effective, giving them an edge over any adversary. This is as true in modern warfare as it was when

Sun Tzu penned *The Art of War.* The spoils always go to the force with the best set of unmatched advantages.

These are the same unfair advantages cultivated at every level of the W.E.E.D.S. model. Seed strategy helps us gain dominant footholds with overwhelming amounts of awareness and market attraction. Seed pod strategy gives us multipliers of that same awareness and attraction. Thorn strategy defends our positions and IP, and denies entry to rivals. Segmentation strategy keeps us balanced and alert, ready to defend against any disruption. Rosette strategy has us always seeking and developing more unfair advantages. Vine strategy gives us quicker and more dominant access to markets and critical resources. Root strategy stewards assets and maximizes the overall worth of the company. Soil strategy helps create advantages all around us that enhance our growth potential.

They're all force multipliers.

As I have written this book, I have been amazed by how well the weed strategy model addresses everything in business, everything about scaling anything. We are not weeds. We have brains coursing with curiosity, imagination, and invention. We constantly learn new things; we have passions, inspirations, and instincts.

Weeds don't have those things, but curiously, they all fit within the weeds model. The things we produce with our curiosity and imagination, the things we invent, all become part of our unfair advantages, our force multipliers. The alliances we forge, the relationships we form, the access to markets, and the resources we gain are all force multipliers.

What this means is, to scale like a weed, we must take on the weed mindset, apply the W.E.E.D.S. model, replace 1:1 leverage with multichannel and then collective scale, and dial it all up to one hundred. Just like any total weed would.

Scaling like a Weed

1:1 Leverage

Root out and eliminate all sources of 1:1 leverage in your operation.

Multi-Channel Scale

Use vine strategy to rapidly scale through partnerships and alliances.

Collective Scale

Apply collective scale with force multipliers and dial it up to one hundred.

Points to Remember

- Giant ragweed is reminiscent of billionaires in the weed world, because everything about them is outsized, and grows faster and taller than competing plants, absorbing unchallenged positions for sunlight, water, and growth.
- Billionaires are total weeds in that they enter markets to dominate, not just to compete for market share.
- Elon Musk is a total weed for the way he fearlessly pursues goals that everyone else considers impossible. Each of his businesses break traditional market paradigms and, as a result, dominate their markets.
- Collective scale introduces the element of team to growth in the broadest possible sense. Employees, investors, alliances, fans, and followers all work together to propel the enterprise further.
- The key to scaling like a weed is to graduate from 1:1 leverage to multi-channel and then collective scale, while applying force multipliers.
- In the military, force multipliers are superior technology, weapons, training, logistics, strategy, and mindset, that enable an army to create a greater outcome in battle.
- In weed strategy, force multipliers are unfair advantages, brought to bear in your market.
- Applying the weed mindset with a forceful execution of the W.E.E.D.S. model, replacing 1:1 leverage with collective scale, and dialing it all up to one hundred is how we scale like a weed.

CONCLUSION

GROW, EXPAND, DOMINATE, DEFEND

California poppy (*Eschscholzia californica*). California poppy is a mildly invasive species that is also the state flower of California. Native to the Western coastal states of the U.S., the California poppy is highly adaptive, switching from annual to perennial in response to competitive conditions for water and sunlight. When the plants bloom in springtime, they become a tourist attraction as they blanket foothills and valleys with brilliant splashes of color.[55,56,57] credit: © The Board of Trustees of the Royal Botanic Gardens, Kew

CALIFORNIA POPPIES ARE a very clever weed, indeed. Of all the plants featured in this book, they are the only invasive species ever to be named a state flower, anywhere. It isn't just named after California, *Eschscholzia californica is* the state's official flower.

Standing roughly fourteen inches tall with brilliant yellow to ochre blooms, California poppies are the quintessential picture of a wildflower. They spread easily, and when they bloom in springtime, they become a major tourist attraction, painting entire foothills and valleys bright yellow and orange. They are a much-beloved weed in their home state.

Considered "potentially invasive" by the U.S. Department of Agriculture, California poppies have a surprisingly adaptive process for their spread. If they sense abundant water and little competition for sunlight, they can spread quickly, and even convert from an annual to a perennial plant. If they like what they see, they're prepared to move in and stay a while.

With their obvious beauty and mildly aggressive spread, and their annual goodwill performances of brilliant roadside color, California poppies have managed something few weeds ever have: they have become darlings to their human hosts. It's hard to imagine anyone traveling an hour or two by car to marvel at hills and valleys blanketed with dandelions or poison ivy.

They have achieved a special status with humans and are rewarded for it. When they pop up wherever they do, they mostly receive our admiration. So they're free to colonize any bit of ground they want, with very little resistance from us. Their only concerns become water and competition for sunlight.

By cultivating our goodwill, California poppies teach us a valuable lesson. If businesses are weeds, California poppies are telling us it's much easier to thrive if we cultivate goodwill among the people around us. If they're on our side, life becomes much easier and fortunes grow.

Can you think of anyone who is a total weed in business, but also beloved by the public? How about the other way around: Can you think of anyone who is a voracious weed, and is hated for it by the general populace? Elon Musk immediately comes to mind as someone who is a total weed and deeply admired. I can also think of several billionaires, whose aggressive business tactics and outsized growth are inspiring calls for anti-trust action.

When Elon Musk dreams with us about colonizing Mars, creating a greener, more sustainable future, or hopping across the planet in a matter of minutes, we're fascinated and inspired. There are many calls to break up several of the large tech giants, but no one ever calls for the breakup of SpaceX.

Has Musk found a way to grow aggressively, dominate markets, and still have us rooting for his success? I would say he has. He and the California poppy have a lot in common.

A Look Back, a Look Forward

We've come a long way from the story I told at the beginning of this book, about the dandelion growing in the crack in the concrete freeway median. What a journey this has been.

We've all seen weeds at their worst, littering our lawns, clogging roadsides and vacant lots, growing where they're neither welcome nor wanted. We've noticed weeds growing from cracks and crevices, imposing their scruffy selves on our orderly world.

But when we take a closer look, we see order where there was chaos, and brilliance where we once saw waste. A whole new world of strategy, mindset, and scale, of tactics and unfair advantages and force multipliers, a whole new way of being in business has emerged.

We've seen the nature of weeds, how they disrupt not through dramatic inventions, but simple, brutal execution of process. And we've seen the true nature of an effective process, one that is honed over millions of years, but adaptable at a moment's notice to face new challenges. And we've seen how essential process is to recording and distributing expertise, and to building worth in our enterprises.

We've seen how, even though they don't have brains, weeds have a brilliant mindset that makes them consistent winners. They are optimistic, persistent, adaptive, aggressive, urgent, and resilient, which makes them naturally disruptive, but also nimbly fluid when they themselves are disrupted. Their aggressive mindset blends perfectly with defensive strategies to ferociously defend every shred of turf they claim.

We've examined how weeds don't do anything without unfair advantages. And we can see, through their unique variations and combinations of tools and attributes, how we can manufacture our own force multipliers through the W.E.E.D.S. model. We've examined the critical, interlocking relationship among mindset, strategy, and scale. We've even learned how to disrupt, negotiate, and scale like a weed.

We've seen the folly of expecting to scale through self-reliance and 1:1 leverage. But we've also seen how creating alliances can immediately add to our scale and how assembling a dedicated, talented, well-trained team can lead us to collective scale, the highest, most efficient architecture for building massive enterprises. And we've seen the sheer power of leveraging force multipliers against that collective scale.

We've come to understand the mechanisms and inevitability of the weeds' growth, expansion, and domination in their fields. And by extension, we've learned how to become total weeds ourselves. Just like Elon, Jeff, T. Boone, Sir Richard, and many others.

Our mission is to adopt the ferocious mindset of a weed, build our process from the W.E.E.D.S. model, and apply it against collective scale. That's how we grow our businesses like a weed. That's how we, too, become total weeds.

We've already covered how to use the W.E.E.D.S model to build a strategy that is uniquely suited to your business and challenges. You'll need to develop your own implementations of seed, seed pod, vine, segmentation, rosette, vine, root, and soil strategies. By nature, these will vary widely according to the size and structure of your enterprise and the intended velocity of ownership.

Solopreneurs

As you build out your weed strategy and consider how scaling relates to you, you've probably had more than a few forehead-slapping moments. Solopreneurs have many factors working against ever scaling up, in part because they have no idea they're working against it ever happening.

There is no velocity of ownership, because in most cases, there is no true business to sell. There is no recorded process; everything revolves around the owner for production, execution, and planning. There is no team to carry out a process. Any injury, hospital stay, or even vacation is an existential threat, because no one is there to keep things moving.

There are many good reasons to be a solopreneur: setting your own hours, multiple revenue streams, chasing your dreams. Building scale and succession are not on the list, but an aggressive application of weed strategy can change that outlook dramatically.

Several areas need your immediate attention. If you sell B2B, how can you become an irresistible force multiplier to your clients? Do you have a compelling story? Do you hold unique IP? Get your thorn strategy in order—including IP protection and spread elements—and then push an aggressive vine strategy to leap to multi-channel scale.

That will spark growth immediately, establishing a ring of referral and strategic partners providing a much bigger footprint in your market. Then comes the next critical issue. If you want to scale, you need people in your operation. Start by hiring virtual assistants if you must, but you desperately need to start building a team that can relieve you of the many tasks you handle now.

In building your team, start with training people who can cover for you and keep the business running when you're not present. Ultimately, you should be building toward a team that can operate fully without your presence, although certainly with your guidance.

Building an effective team requires the establishment of a recorded process. Remember: Process is how expertise is collected and leveraged across the team. It is also the key to clearing all vestiges of 1:1 leverage. As a solopreneur, your previous lack of leverage, and your ensnarement in the self-reliance paradox, will become more and more obvious as you remove your labor from day to day operations.

By working the W.E.E.D.S. model, you will accumulate force multipliers, which can be leveraged against your growing scale and sphere of influence. Eventually, you'll want to jump to collective scale. To do that, continue working the entire W.E.E.D.S. model, and look for ways to serve far more clients. That might require productizing what was once a highly specialized, hands-on process, and entering new sales channels to multiply sales.

Remember that building your process and making it easily shared are also keys to creating worth in your business. If an exit is part of your plan, you need to end up with an enterprise that has a base of loyal clients, an ongoing revenue stream, and a business that is easily transferrable. A recorded, well-honed, trainable process is essential.

SMBs

Small- to medium-sized businesses is a broad group. It can range from a mom-and-pop flower shop to a $50 million a year industrial powerhouse. The two businesses can both benefit from weed strategy, albeit with very different expressions.

Smaller businesses should start with the same advice given to solopreneurs. Your mission is still about being properly prepared and then jumping immediately to multi-channel scale. A retail business like the flower shop can produce explosive growth from referral partnerships with centers of influence in the community. Become the default choice for businesses that always need flowers to operate.

A small B2B business would do well to follow the steps in the preceding section. People, process, multi-level scale, and building transferrable worth are your biggest challenges. Extricating your labor from production, wherever possible, is essential as well. Like solopreneurs, you're likely fighting against 1:1 leverage and stifling self-reliance, which must be rooted out.

At the other end of the range are the $10–50 million businesses that have already achieved impressive scale. Still, the weeds would pose the same questions asked of solopreneurs and small business owners: Do you hold unique IP that remains unprotected? Is your company hyper-referrable? Is the company positioned to execute an aggressive vine strategy?

At this level, the opportunities for growth may lie in cultivating more business with existing clients, entering new markets, or doing more with less, enabled by technology. You get there with a cohesive team acting like a collective of weeds. You do that by adopting the weed mindset and using the W.E.E.D.S. model to produce overwhelming force multipliers at every level.

As weeds, we're always looking for unfair advantages, and for any sized business it's essential to become a force multiplier to our clients. It's what makes us irreplaceable and ensures continuity. For larger businesses, it's highly worthwhile to consider partnering down as well. Of course we want partnerships with the most impressive companies, but there may be smaller ones that can help you build an unmatched advantage over competitors.

And finally, consider hiring someone to take on a brand-new role: chief weed strategy officer. Their job description will be to ensure the entire staff are trained as weed operatives, cultivate a constant stream of unfair advantages, and create worth through process development and asset stewardship. Or appoint a committee, with members each holding responsibility for mindset, one of the eight W.E.E.D.S. model levels, or scaling up.

Startups

Of all the forms of business, startups are in a unique position for growth. Everything is fast-motion. The velocity of ownership is extreme, as are the pressures of burn rates, financing, launches, and scaling up. Everything has to happen at once, and the chances of failure are enormous.

Preparation is obviously a key factor before any startup launch. Every level of your weed strategy should be well thought out. I imagine startups are like some of the annuals among the weeds presented in this book. A water hemp would make a great startup in the weed world, putting out nearly five million seeds per plant, as would Canada fleabane, dispersing its breeze-surfing seeds over an area of a quarter-million square miles.

If seeds are generators of awareness and buying intent within the target market, a startup that produces that kind of impact during its short time in the hands of founders and angel investors has a great chance of raucous success. Perhaps on the order of an Airbnb, Uber, or Zoom.

And that's the point. Of all the forms of business, startups must literally grow, expand, dominate, and defend their turf *fast,* or they perish. Just like last year's annuals.

It would be wise to appoint a team member to be in charge of all weed strategy brainstorming and implementation. Given this is a startup, it's okay (and probably desirable) to shorten the title to just chief weed officer. You'll know the logic and everyone else will have fun with it, adding an entertaining element to your story.

The point is, you should have every element nailed down before you launch. If an investor asks, "What's your seed strategy?" you should have a ready answer. Ditto with seed pods, thorns, segmentation, rosettes, vines, roots, and soil. You should be able to describe a raft of unfair advantages and force multipliers you'll use to explode the scale of the enterprise.

Publicly Held Companies

Even titans have room for growth. Apple is one of the largest companies in the world, and it continues to grow through innovation, leading to the establishment of new product categories and markets. Elon Musk's SpaceX continues to push boundaries. Amazon continues to grow, as it expands into new markets with new products and services, always propelled by industry-leading innovations.

Publicly held companies have already achieved collective scale, but the same weed strategy applies: there should be a full rendition of each of the eight levels of the W.E.E.D.S. model, to constantly produce new force multipliers. The entire staff should be trained to operate under the weed mindset. There should be a constant push to find new advantages to wield over competitors.

Whether applying weed strategy to a competitive market or to establish new ones, it should be done with great urgency. Find ways to create new efficiencies, based on the way weeds do it in the field. Weeds spread. Does the impetus for a sale spread like a weed throughout each targeted account? Are the processes that drive the business honed to perfection and instilled in every employee? Is there newly disrupted ground to expand into? And are there potentially disruptive technologies that already exist in the enterprise?

While the company may have found collective scale, there is always room for growth and improvement. Remember, too, collective scale does not preclude multi-channel scale. Partnerships should be sought constantly to uncover new force multipliers and unfair advantages. Given the size of the company, it may not make sense to partner exclusively with other large companies.

Amazon very effectively partnered down, with its affiliate and storefront platforms, using thousands of new relationships to expand their reach and offer. You may find smaller companies holding perfect-fit technology or IP that, leveraged against your scale, can produce new force multipliers.

As with larger SMBs above, new C-Suite members should be hired or appointed, each to govern the role of weed mindset, the eight levels of strategy in the W.E.E.D.S. model, and achieving new scale. Thus, we might expect a chief weed strategy officer, or chief seed, seed pod, thorn, et cetera, strategy officers. Alternatively, appoint a weed strategy committee to steward the company from a weed growth perspective.

Franchises

I saved the best for last, because from a weed perspective, franchises may be the ultimate form of business. For the equivalent of a small business investment, an entrepreneur can step immediately into collective scale. There is already a well-honed, living process, already transferrable worth that can be sold at any time. It's already set up and continues to be steered by the top experts in the field.

There is already a network of peer entrepreneurs, at times sharing business, always ready to lend a hand, always adding new expertise to a process all members use to grow their businesses. There is also plenty of room to expand, by acquiring more franchise units.

If ever there was a business structure that looks and acts like the dandelions in our lawns, franchises are it. Like dandelions, franchisees never have to go it alone. They're always part of something bigger; someone always has their back. The structure, organization, and collective expertise assures success.

Still, franchises surely could benefit from an infusion of weed strategy. Adopted at the franchisor level, a committee should be formed among franchisees to produce and implement strategies from the W.E.E.D.S. model. Like earlier suggestions in the sections above, each member should be assigned one of the eight levels of strategy, weed mindset, or scaling the franchise like a weed as their area of responsibility.

Meeting regularly, the committee should be constantly cultivating new unfair advantages and force multipliers that benefit the entire membership. Weed mindset training should become a required element of onboarding any franchisee, and every employee within each franchise unit. The training will be vital as a cultural element of the franchise.

The franchisor should track with the committee, evaluating and implementing weed strategy recommendations. The work of the committee and franchisor should be shared with franchisees, reinforcing their weed-like execution and incorporating their suggestions.

Startups and franchises are most like the weeds we've examined in this book, but at different ends of a spectrum. With their quick turnaround to new investors, startups function like annuals, living a short lifecycle of ownership, while maximizing value for all stakeholders.

Franchises are more like perennials. They don't operate to change ownership per se, but they are in a rush to create value and worth. In both cases, the businesses are built with the objective of scaling like a weed.

Grow, Expand, Dominate, Defend

So there it is. Weeds win by leveraging their fierce mindset and unique force multipliers against collective scale. They win by distilling it all into a powerful process that's baked into their DNA. They don't require training, they simply act in unison and forcefully execute their process.

Each weed is different, and, through their variation, we see infinite possibilities for expressions within the W.E.E.D.S. model. Some are annuals, accelerating a lifetime's worth of living into a single season, while others are perennials, using the time to build lasting infrastructure that helps them thrive and spread.

Some are hyper-aggressive in their rates of growth, foraging of roots, and production and dispersal of seeds. And some, like the California poppy, are more laid back, almost seeming more concerned with creating art than aggressive growth. Yet they still conquer great swaths of territory.

The weeds have shown us that solopreneurs will never scale until they remove the word *solo* from their descriptor—and mindset. SMBs can scale rapidly through the use of weed strategy and the appointing of a weed strategy committee or chief weed strategy officer.

Startups, by definition, must grow like a weed. It's their one true mission. They can benefit greatly by incorporating weed strategy into their business plans, and hiring themselves a chief weed officer.

Publicly traded companies can benefit from the application of weed strategy, by becoming more weed-like and nimble, and using their scale to open new markets, while more fully infiltrating their current fields. Franchises are already perfectly patterned after weeds. Applying weed strategy can only reinforce their unfair advantages and strengthen their wins.

The business press and nearly everyone on social media are fond of dropping short lists of authoritative imperatives, as the "keys" to growth and success. They tell us, "Do these three things and double the size of your business!" And then they drop three random bits. *Be persistent. Build your team. Talk to your customers.*

But the weeds have now given us a framework that is cohesive and complete and utterly powerful. And we can immediately see where all the bits actually fit. Growth gurus and experts may tell us they have the key to making it all work, but I trust the weeds. They've been doing it for a long time and have it perfected.

Growth is not just about selling more. It's not just about being more persistent. It's about leveraging a fierce mindset and force multipliers against collective scale. And getting everyone on board.

Using the weed strategy framework—or any framework—might seem stifling, but it actually fosters creativity. We see that in the incredible expression of weeds in the world. They're all following the same basic plan, but they've taken such different paths. And every one of them is awesome.

Perhaps when you next see a weed, you'll take time to reflect, to watch what it's doing, to ponder how it got there. In fact, I'm counting on it. It's part of my seed strategy. From this point on, I'm counting on every weed that pops up anywhere in the world to serve as my meme, to remind people to buy this book.

Those weeds in your yard? They're working for me now. Let's get them working for you, too.

Points to Remember

- Solopreneurs have many challenges arrayed against them, simply by the nature of their being "solo" and relying on 1:1 leverage.
- In their application of weed strategy, solopreneurs should strive to involve others in their enterprises, create process, and remove their labor from production.
- SMBs should also root out 1:1 leverage and quickly replace it with multi-channel scale.
- The challenge for SMBs is to graduate fully to collective scale, by broadening their networks and channels, and removing friction from their offerings.
- Startups live in a world of high growth and velocity of ownership. They must grow quickly or fail.
- They would do well to hire chief weed officers to map out their growth and keep it on track.
- Publicly held companies still have much room for growth.
- They should appoint chief seed, seed pod, thorn, segmentation, rosette, vine, root, and soil officers—a whole suite of weed strategy officers to maximize growth, innovation, and disruption.
- Franchises are already the most weed-like of all business forms, because everyone starts at collective scale.
- They should appoint weed strategy committees to ensure growth through the weed growth formula in this book.

STUDY GUIDE

WEEDS WIN BY leveraging a fierce mindset and force multipliers against collective scale, then reducing it all to a fierce, living process with 100 percent buy-in. In the following exercises, we'll seek a deeper understanding of the weed mindset and W.E.E.D.S. model, and what it means to scale like a weed, by applying those to real-world situations.

These should not be treated as idle exercises, but as an exploration of a new field of study and a new branch of responsibility within organizations. Every enterprise is meant to grow, and chief weed strategy officers (or chief weed officers) will be uniquely equipped to make that happen.

As you complete each exercise, think about how you would organize the weed strategy mission, either in your own company, or as a new member of a company's C-Suite. Should there be one officer, or an entire cabinet of seed, seed pod, thorn, segmentation, rosette, vine, root, and soil strategy officers? Should the function be managed by C-Suite executives, by untenured committee members, or in some other fashion?

Alternatively, how can the four pillars of weed strategy—mindset, force multipliers, collective scale and process—be integrated into typical job functions in an organization? Is weed strategy additive or repetitive in typically organized businesses?

W.E.E.D.S. Analysis

Perform a W.E.E.D.S. analysis on Amazon, Tesla, SpaceX, Microsoft, and Uber. Consider their apparent weed strategies, and assign a ranking on a scale of one (worst) to ten (best) for the following ten categories: seed strategy, seed pod strategy, thorn strategy, segmentation strategy, rosette strategy, vine strategy, root strategy, soil strategy, scale, and commercial sustainability. Give a W.E.E.D.S. score based on cumulative rankings (with ten categories each worth ten points, scores will range from zero to one hundred points). Which companies fared best or worst and why? Compare results among the class.

Create a W.E.E.D.S. Plan

Invent a fictitious company and create a weed strategy plan for its growth. It should include separate strategies for each of the eight levels within the W.E.E.D.S. model. Classify the business type—solopreneur, SMB, startup, publicly traded, or franchise—and be prepared to discuss how your plan would change based on the different business types. If done as a team exercise, members should choose specific areas of responsibility (i.e., chief seed officer, chief rosette officer, etc.). Be prepared to discuss your choices and logic. Which business form is best suited to take advantage of weed strategy? How can each business type maximize growth through weed strategy?

Who Wins the Total Weed Award?

A new award has been established. The Total Weed Award will be granted annually to the businessperson who best exemplifies weed-like growth, strategy, and resilience. Who should win the first award and why?

How Will You Use Weed Strategy in Your Business Dealings?

Explain five favorite takeaways from weed strategy. How do you expect to use it in your own business or on behalf of an employer? Explain your rationale for being appointed chief weed officer at your next post.

How Will Weed Strategy Change the Business World?

Speculate on how weed strategy might change how the world does business and approaches growth strategy. Be prepared to present your thoughts and discuss your choices and logic.

You've Just Been Appointed Your Company's Chief Weed Officer. What's Next?

Describe your company, its market position, and your job description. What are your goals for the company as its chief weed officer? How will the company change as a result of your tenure?

If you're using this book as supplemental reading and would like to include the author in your program, you're welcome to book Mr. Heinecke for an author drop-by session on Zoom. For more information, visit *stuheinecke.com.*

Weeds have given us a new framework for understanding the nature of growth. Perhaps they have opened an entirely new wing in the C-Suite as well. Will you be part of a new generation of chief weed officers?

LET'S CONNECT

YOU'VE FINISHED THE book, but our story doesn't have to end here. Please visit my author page at *stuheinecke.com* to claim two bonus chapters that didn't fit into the book. You can also use the site to book me as a speaker or weed strategy consultant. If you're a member of the press, you'll also find a deep library of beauty shots of weeds, to accompany coverage of the book.

Weed strategy is a new area of study and expertise you can use in your own business. You can further hone your knowledge by taking my Weed Mindset Bootcamp, or becoming W.E.E.D.S. certified, to prepare for a chief weed officer role or to render officially authorized weed strategy consulting services. For more information or to enroll, visit *weedstrategy.com.*

Please note that "weed strategy," the "W.E.E.D.S." model, and "weed mindset" are trademarked and patented. They cannot be used without my involvement, participation, or permission. But if you become W.E.E.D.S. certified, you'll be eligible to join the Weed Strategy Network.

As part of an association of consultants, advisors, and specialists, you'll be able to step into collective scale, collaborating and sharing assignments as warranted with other members, under the aegis of weed strategy, and under proper, legal license. You'll be invited to join as part of the process of certification. More information is available at *weedstrategy.com* as well.

As I wrote this book, I kept thinking, "There ought to be a 'Total Weed Award' each year for the person who most personifies weed-like audacity and growth and resilience." And so there is. Visit *totalweed.org* for the latest info, to nominate a candidate, or to vote.

I also operate the How to Get a Meeting with Anyone online course, where you can learn how to use contact marketing to make the critical connections that can help you grow your business. Each student creates, produces, and tests their own contact campaigns during the six-week course, augmented with sponsored contact marketing test solutions. Visit *howtogetameeting.com* for more information or to enroll.

And finally, let's connect on social media. I'm active on LinkedIn, Facebook, and YouTube. Just look for me by name, and if you're reaching out to connect, mention you just finished this book. I'll be thrilled to hear from you.

Oh, and one last thing? If you enjoyed the book or if it had an effect on you or your business, would you consider leaving a nice review wherever you bought it?

See you out in the field sometime. I'll be the one hanging out with all the other total weeds.

ACKNOWLEDGMENTS

THE DESIRE TO write this book started long ago, driving on the Santa Monica freeway. But the project started in earnest with an interview with Facebook friend and gentleman gardener Bill Davin. Next was a flight to Dallas to meet with notorious billionaire oil man and corporate raider T. Boone Pickens.

The two couldn't have been more different, but mixed perfectly for this book. I was looking to stitch together perspectives from two very different fields—botany and business—to unearth insights hidden in plain view. How do weeds grow so fiercely and how can we use their methods to grow our businesses?

The answers came from a broad range of business experts and personalities, CIA officers, four-star generals, weed scientists, a supermodel, Olympic coaches, a Harlem Globetrotter, the Royal Botanic Garden at Kew in London, and more. It's been an amazing journey of discovery.

With profound gratitude, I acknowledge T. Boone Pickens, Kathy Ireland, General David Petraeus, General Barry McCaffrey, Henrik Fisker, Gareb Shamus, Giovanni Marsico, Esther Dyson, Christopher Lochhead, Carmen Medina, Jon Ferrara, Jon Ferrara, Jonna Mendez, and the Prince of Thorns, Dr. Nathan Myhrvold.

Thank you to my invaluable plant, weed science, and botanic guides, Antonio DiTommaso, Peter Sikkema, Clarence Swanton, Matt Mattus, Maureen Murphy, Bill Davin, and Pei Chu at the Royal Botanic Gardens at Kew in London for the historic botanical illustrations that head each chapter. And thank you to my super-connectors, Jeff Sheehan, Michael Roderick, Ken Rutkowski, and Brandon Adams, who made the book more broadly scoped and filled with character.

Thank you to my many business experts and sources, Alex Olley, Alexandra Watkins, Alice Heiman, Amy Walker, Andrew Breen, Angus Nelson, Anthony Iannarino, Bill Scott, Brandon Lee, Bruce Rogers, Cherie Ware, Chris Ortolano, Curt Cuscino, Dale Zwizinski, Dan Martell, Dan Monaughan, and Dan Waldschmidt.

Thank you also to Daniel West, David Brier, David Siegel, Douglas Burdett, Gregg Wallick, Heath Ritenour, Herb "Flight Time" Lang, Ian Palmer, Jack Kosakowski, Janine Warner, Jay Kim, Jeffrey Madoff, Jerry Timmermann, Jim Dickie, Jim Pack, Joe Galvin, Jonathan Schober, and Josh Steimle.

Thank you Judy Buchholz, Julie Pergola, Kare Anderson, Kate Sweetman, Leanne Hoagland-Smith, Marilyn Heiman, Mark Hunter, Mike Patey, Mike Weinberg, Nick Lowery, Nicholás Cedeira, Paul Harrison, Peter Horst, Pierre-R Wolff, Rick Bennett, Robert Wisneski, Ron Braley, Sam Watson, Sangram Vajre, and Dr. Sunnie Giles.

Thank you Scott Penick, Sid Kumar, Sonya Ruedlinger, Stephan Anema, Terry Steiner, and Tim Minert. Thank you Nicola Corzine for honoring this work with your kind and perceptive foreword. And a special thank you to my wife, Charlotte, who supported me in this project for the past five years. I couldn't have done this without all of you.

CHAPTER NOTES

1 Mabey, Richard. *Weeds: In Defense of Nature's Most Unloved Plants* (New York: HarperCollins Publishers, 2010).

2 Wohlleben, Peter. *The Hidden Life of Trees: What They Feel, How They Communicate* (Vancouver, BC: Greystone Books/David Suzuki Institute, 2015).

3 Cerdeira, Nicolás. *Failory.com.*

4 Mabey, *Weeds.*

5 Mabey, *Weeds.*

6 Cerdeira, *Failory.com.*

7 Pickens, T. Boone. *The First Billion Is the Hardest: Reflections on a Life of Comebacks and America's Energy Future* (New York: Crown Publishing Group, a division of Random House, 2008).

8 Holm, Leroy, et al. *The World's Worst Weeds: Distribution and Biology* (Krieger Publishing Company, 1991).

9 Hagy, Jessica. *The Art of War Visualized: The Sun Tzu Classic in Charts and Graphs* (New York: Workman Publishing), pp. 25, 31.

10 Christensen, Clayton. *The Innovator's Dilemma* (Harvard Business Review Press, 1997, 2000, 2016).

11 Merriam-Webster Dictionary online. *merriam-webster.com.*

12 Powell, Colin. "Perpetual Optimism Is a Force Multiplier." BrainyQuote .com. *brainyquote.com.*

13 Seligman, Martin. *Learned Optimism: How to Change Your Mind and Your Life* (Vintage Books, a division of Random House).

14 Holm, et al., *The World's Worst Weeds.*

15 "Velvetleaf Identification and Control." King County, WA, Noxious Weed Control Program. *kingcounty.gov.*

16 "Zoom Rides Pandemic to Another Quarter of Explosive Growth." KLTV News. *kltv.com.*

17 *sciencedirect.com.*

18 *nyis.info.*

19 Mabey, *Weeds.*

20 "Russia's Space Chief Just Took Yet Another Swing at SpaceX." Futurism, December 20, 2020. *futurism.com.*

21 Conradt, Stacy. "15 Companies That Changed Their Names." Mental Floss, September 5, 2017. *mentalfloss.com.*

22 "The 10 Greatest Car Designers in Automotive History." *Goliath.com.*

23 "17 Quotes on Design Philosophy from Apple's Sir Jony Ive." *jacobtyler.com.*

24 "*Cardamine Hirsuta* L., Hairy Bittercress." USDA Natural Resources Conservation Service. *plants.usda.gov.*

25 "*Urtica Dioica,* Stinging Nettle." Wikipedia. *en.wikipedia.org.*

26 Francis, Ejiofor. "What to Do If an Employee Sues You or Your Company." *Entrepreneur,* May 22, 2020. *entrepreneur.com.*

27 "*Equisetum Hyemale.*" Wikipedia. *en.wikipedia.org.*

28 "*Equisetum Hyemale.*" USDA Natural Resources Conservation Service. *plants.usda.gov.*

29 Bergeson, Dave. "Strategic Planning: Moltke the Eleer, Dwight Eisenhower, Winston Churchill and Just a Little Mike Tyson." American Management Center. *connect2amc.com.*

30 Holm, et al., *The World's Worst Weeds. Cirisium arvense* (L.) Scop., pp. 217–224.

31 Archer, Seth. "A Key to Warren Buffett's Investing Strategy Is Incredibly Easy to Replicate (MOAT)." Markets Insider, February 13, 2018. *markets.businessinsider.com.*

32 Archer, "Warren Buffett's Investing Strategy."

33 "Wistaria Festival." Sierra Madre News. *sierramadrenews.net.*

34 "Wisteria." Wikipedia. *en.wikipedia.org.*

35 Holm, et al. *The World's Worst Weeds.* (Malabar, Fla.: University of Hawaii Press, Krieger Publishing Company), p. 269.

36 "Leafy Spurge, *Euphorbia Esula* L." Invasive Plant Atlas of the United States. *invasiveplantatlas.org.*

37 "*Euphorbia Esula.*" Fire Effects information System (FEIS), USDA, US Forest Service. *fs.fed.us.*

38 Murphy, Jr., Bill. "Warren Buffet Says This Is When the Best Leaders Should Retire (There's Just 1 Little Catch)." *Inc. Magazine,* February 7, 2021.

39 "Purple Loosestrife (*Lythruym Salicaria*)." Minnesota Department of Natural Resources. *dnr.state.mn.us.*

40 Jaffee, Eric. "The Case for Letting Employees Choose Their Own Job Titles." *Fast Company,* September 15, 2014. *fastcompany.com.*

41 Holm, *The World's Worst Weeds* (1991), pp. 450–55.

42 Panoff, MPH, RD, Lauren. "Chickweed: Benefits, Side Effect, Precautions, and Dosage." *healthline.com.*

43 Mann, Harold H., and T.W. Barnes. "The Competition between Barley and Certain Weeds under Controlled Conditions." *Annals of Applied Biology. onlinelibrary.wiley.com.*

44 "Chickweed, Common." Alberta Agriculture and Forestry. *agric.gov .ab.ca.*

45 "Plant of the Week, Scarlet Beebalm." USDA, U.S. Forest Service. *fs.fed.us/.*

46 "Bee Balm—Garden Pest or Protected Species?" *Adirondack Almanack. adirondackalmanack.com.*

47 "*Ambrosia Trifida,* L. Great Ragweed." USDA Natural Resources Conservation Service. *plants.usda.gov.*

48 "Giant Ragweed." Illinois Wildflowers. *illinoiswildflowers.info.*

49 "*Ambrosia Trifida.*" Lady Bird Johnson Wildflower Center, University of Texas at Austin. *wildflower.org.*

50 "*Ambrosia Trifida*" (Wikipedia).

51 "*Ambrosia Trifida.*" Invasive Species Compendium, CABI. *cabi.org.*

52 Dowaliby, Meg. "Just How Big Is the Amazon Associates Program?" Geniuslink blog. *geniuslink.com.*

53 D'Angelo, Matt. "What Is Amazon Storefronts?" *Business News Daily. businessnewsdaily.com.*

54 "74 Amazon Statistics You Must Know: 2020/2021 Market Share Analysis & Data." Finances Online. *financesonline.com.*

55 "California Poppy." WebMD. *webmd.com.*

56 "California Poppy (*Eschsholzia California*)." Plant Guide, USDA. *plants. usda.gov.*

57 "*Eschsholzia California* Cham. California Poppy." USDA Natural Resources Conservation Service. *plants.usda.gov.*

INDEX

C

D

E

F

K

L

M

N

O

P

Q

R

T

Y

Z

ABOUT THE AUTHOR

© Jim Carroll jshuimages.com

STU HEINECKE is a bestselling author, twice-nominated hall of fame marketer, and *Wall Street Journal* cartoonist. *How to Get a Meeting with Anyone,* which introduced the concept of contact marketing, spawned an industry, launched businesses and careers worldwide, and was named one of the top sixty-four sales books of all time. The American Marketing Association named him the "father of contact marketing."

Mr. Heinecke is also a Nasdaq Entrepreneurial Center Author-in-Residence and mentor, and founder of Cartoonists.org, a group of cartoonists from *The Wall Street Journal* and *New Yorker,* who donate art to help charities raise funds. He lives on a beautiful island in the Pacific Northwest with his wife, Charlotte.